5 YEARS

L'École VALRHONA BROOKLYN

PROFE[illegible]SE SCHEDULE 2020

2020 marks the fifth anniversary of L'École Valrhona Brooklyn! To celebrate this exciting milestone, Valrhona is thrilled to extend our chefs' expertise to the West Coast for the first time with **FOUR classes in California**!

Discover the entire class schedule, which is full of new and innovative classes, including a special class taught in France by one of the godfathers of L'École Valrhona, **Pierre Hermé**!

To learn more, visit *https://us.valrhona.com/by-your-side/classes-catalog*

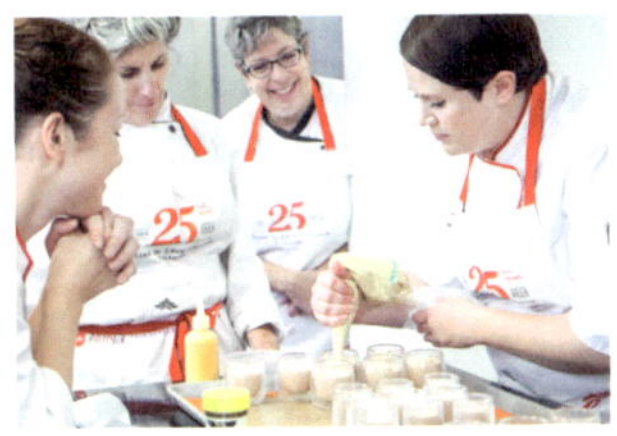
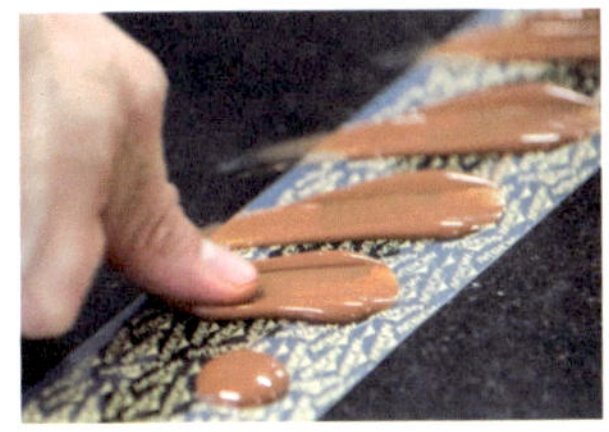
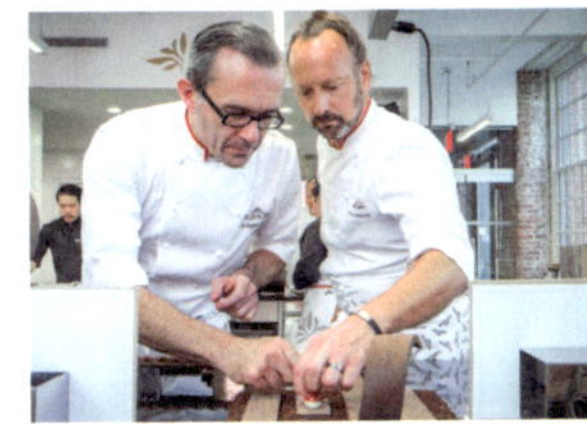

FEBRUARY

24-26 Panning & Chocolate Snacks
Chef Derek Poirier

MARCH

2-4 (OFFSITE) Sugar Flowers & Valrhona Chocolate
Chef Ron Ben-Israel
Chef Guillaume Roesz

9-10 (NEW) Pastry According to Claire Heitzler
Chef Claire Heitzler

17-18 Seasonal Buffet Flavors & Design
Chef Sarah Tibbetts

23-25 Gelato, Ice Cream & Frozen Desserts
Chef Christophe Domange

23-25 (5 YEAR ANNIVERSARY CLASS) (CLASS IN CALIFORNIA OFFSITE) Artistic Chocolate Showpieces
Chef Stéphane Tréand

APRIL

14-15 Introduction to Chocolate & Pastry
Chef Paul Saiphet

27-29 (NEW) The Business of Bonbons
Chef Christopher Elbow
Chef Derek Poirier

MAY

11-13 (5 YEAR ANNIVERSARY CLASS) (NEW) (CLASS IN CALIFORNIA OFFSITE) 'One Spoon': Flavor & Functionality in Plated Desserts & Petits Gâteaux
Chef Philippe Givre
Chef Derek Poirier

12-13 (NEW) Travel Cakes
Chef Guillaume Roesz

JUNE

1-3 Framed Chocolate Bonbons & Snacking Bars
Chef Philippe Givre

9-10 (5 YEAR ANNIVERSARY CLASS) (CLASS IN CALIFORNIA OFFSITE) Rethinking Ingredients & Pastry Trends
Chef Sarah Tibbetts

16-17 Tastes & Variations on Viennoiserie
Chef Greg Mindel

JULY

7-8 Entremets & Petits Gâteaux
Chef Nathaniel Reid

13-15 (NEW) Signature Petits Gâteaux & Entremets by KB
Chef Karim Bourgi

14-15 (5 YEAR ANNIVERSARY CLASS) (CLASS IN CALIFORNIA OFFSITE) Pastry by Lincoln Carson
Chef Lincoln Carson

AUGUST

10-12 Plated Desserts & Petits Gâteaux
Chef Patrice Demers

18-19 Seasonal Buffet Flavors & Design
Chef Sarah Tibbetts

SEPTEMBER

1-2 Molded Chocolate Bonbons
Chef Paul Saiphet

14-16 (NEW) Chocolate, Sugars & Flavors by Miro
Chef Miro Uskokovic

22-23 Rethinking Ingredients & Pastry Trends
Chef Sarah Tibbetts

OCTOBER

SEPTEMBER 29-1 (OFFSITE) ONE-SHOT Machine Bonbon Production (NEW)
Chef Romain Grzelczyk

5-7 Panning & Chocolate Snacks
Chef Guillaume Roesz

12-15 (5 YEAR ANNIVERSARY CLASS) (NEW) (CLASS IN FRANCE) Creative Pâtisserie with Pierre Hermé
Chef Pierre Hermé

19-21 Viennoiserie, Panettone & Tea Time
Chef Oriol Balaguer

27-28 (NEW) Luxury High Volume Pastries & Amenities
Chef Adam Thomas

NOVEMBER

2-4 Mindful & Modern Desserts
Chef William Werner

16-18 Petits Gâteaux by Antonio Bachour
Chef Antonio Bachour

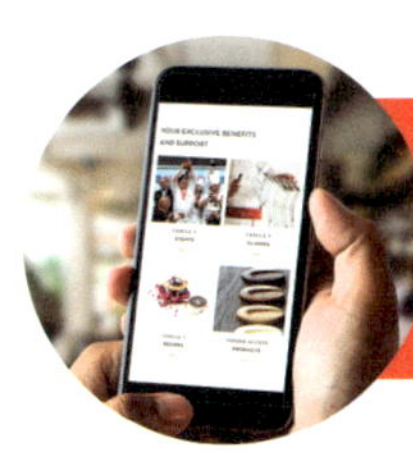

REGISTRATION:
Use the VALRHONA APP or visit us.valrhona.com and click OUR CLASSES

VALRHONA

222 Water Street, Brooklyn, NY 11201 • 718-522-7001 • ecolebrooklyn@valrhona.com @valrhonausa #EcoleValrhonaBK #ValrhonaUSA

Nick Muncy LLC
San Francisco, CA

WEB
www.toothachemagazine.com

CONTACT
For inquires about advertising, distribution, or collaborations:
nickm@toothachemagazine.com

Printed in Canada

First Printing, 2019

ISBN: 978-0-9988640-5-1

FSC
www.fsc.org
MIX
Paper from responsible sources
FSC® C014956

zero 100% carbon neutral
by Hemlock Printers www.hemlock.com/zero

editor & creator:

nick muncy

contributers:

mei lin
george mendes
laurent gras
alex stupak
justin binnie
elianne padlan
lincoln carson
sam mason
isabel coss
mark welker
alexander r. terrazas

publisher:

nick muncy llc

printer:

Hemlock Printers Ltd.
7050 Buller Ave.
Burnaby BC Canada VSJ 454

instagram & twitter:

@toothache_mag

thank you:

jenny kondrasky
austin muncy
michelle matvey

photography:

all photography by nick muncy unless otherwise specified by photo credit.

"An aching tooth is better out than in.

To lose a rotting member is a gain."

- Richard Baxter

ISSUE NUMBER SIX:

Ironically, I have a horrible toothache as I'm trying to finish this. I'm going to keep this short and sweet before my aspirin wears off and my molar decides the pulsate pain up the side of my face.

For this issue, I went to New York and Los Angeles and met some of my culinary heroes. Chefs that I looked up to as a young cook and who still inspire me today. Honestly, I've been neglecting the East Coast and relying on the group of amazing chefs in California, but it hasn't been for malicious reasons. Instead, it's been because of a lack of resources. Although I started the magazine with the idea that I would travel the world, I'm stricken with the realities of running an independent magazine and the fact that it's not going to pay the bills.

I hope this magazine sparks some creativity within you. I created this issue of Toothache, for the most part alone, sitting in my tiny efficiency studio in San Francisco after working a full day in the restaurant. From my desk, I can see out my ninth-floor window to a strip club, a shitty pizza spot, and a tent city below lofting the smell of pot, the sound of glass breaking, and people howling. Creating amazing things doesn't require as much as we all think. Instead, it takes a bit of hard work, effort, and perseverance. More importantly, it needs the support of you, the restaurant industry, so thank you for continuing to embrace Toothache Magazine. I feel like I'm creating a unique magazine that a cook or chef would want to read. I hope to continue to empower chefs to share whatever they'd like, and I hope this magazine continues to evolve into an even better platform for chefs to inspire one another.

Toothache Magazine is for chefs, by chefs. I hope you enjoy issue 6.

Nick Muncy - *editor and creator*

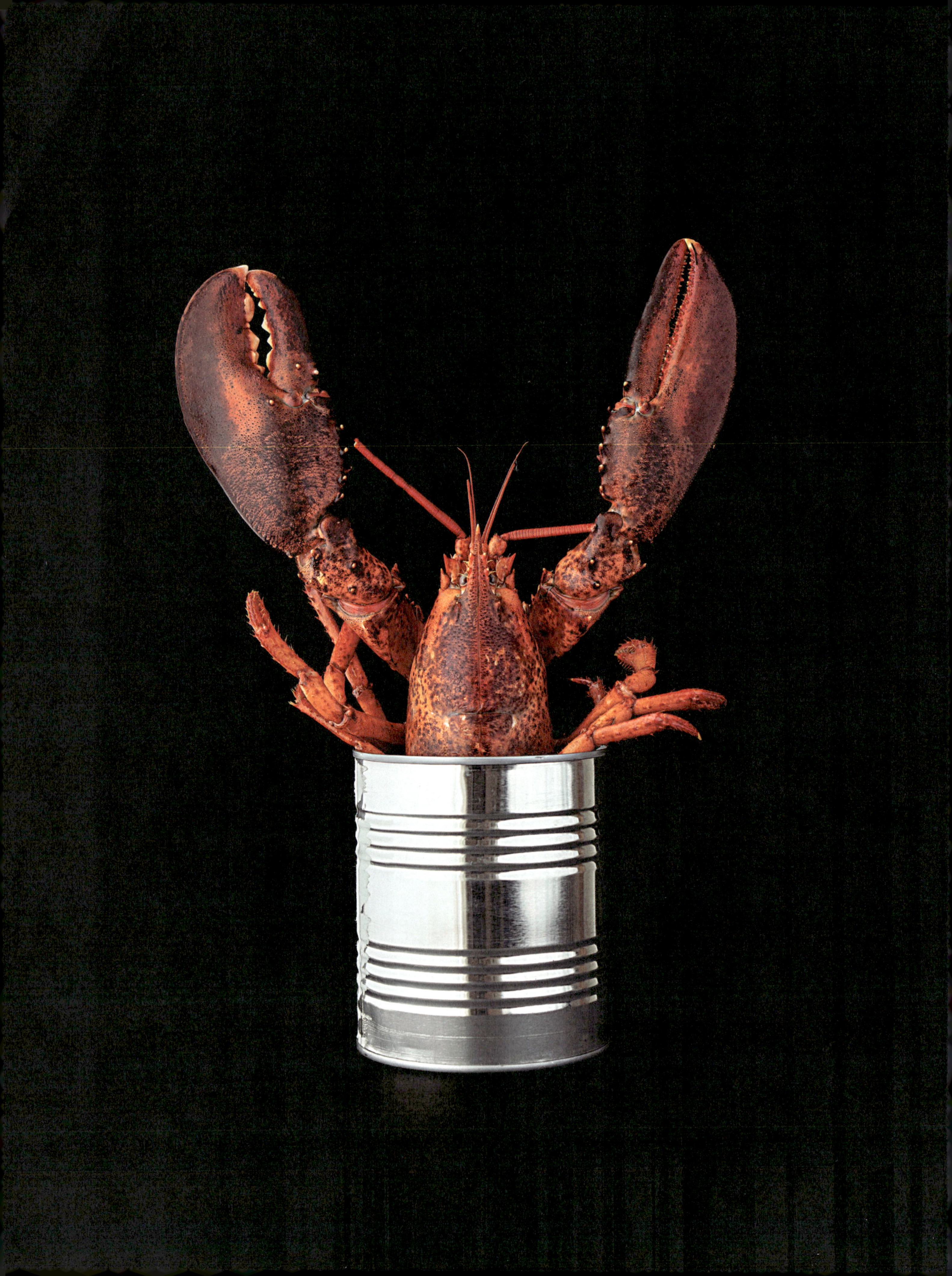

table of contents

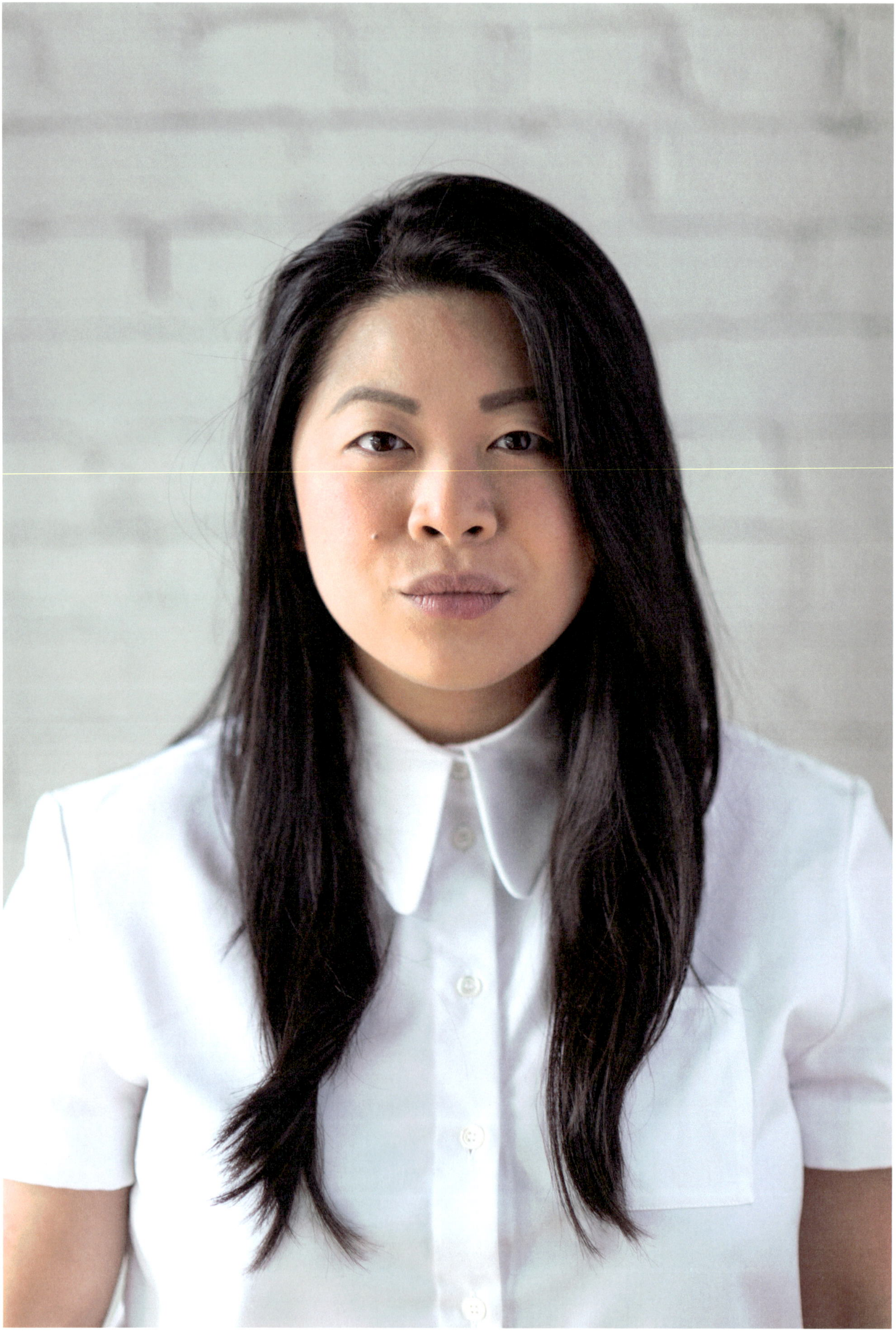

Portrait by Wonho Frank Lee

RETURNING TO YOUR ROOTS

mei lin

nightshade

los angeles, ca

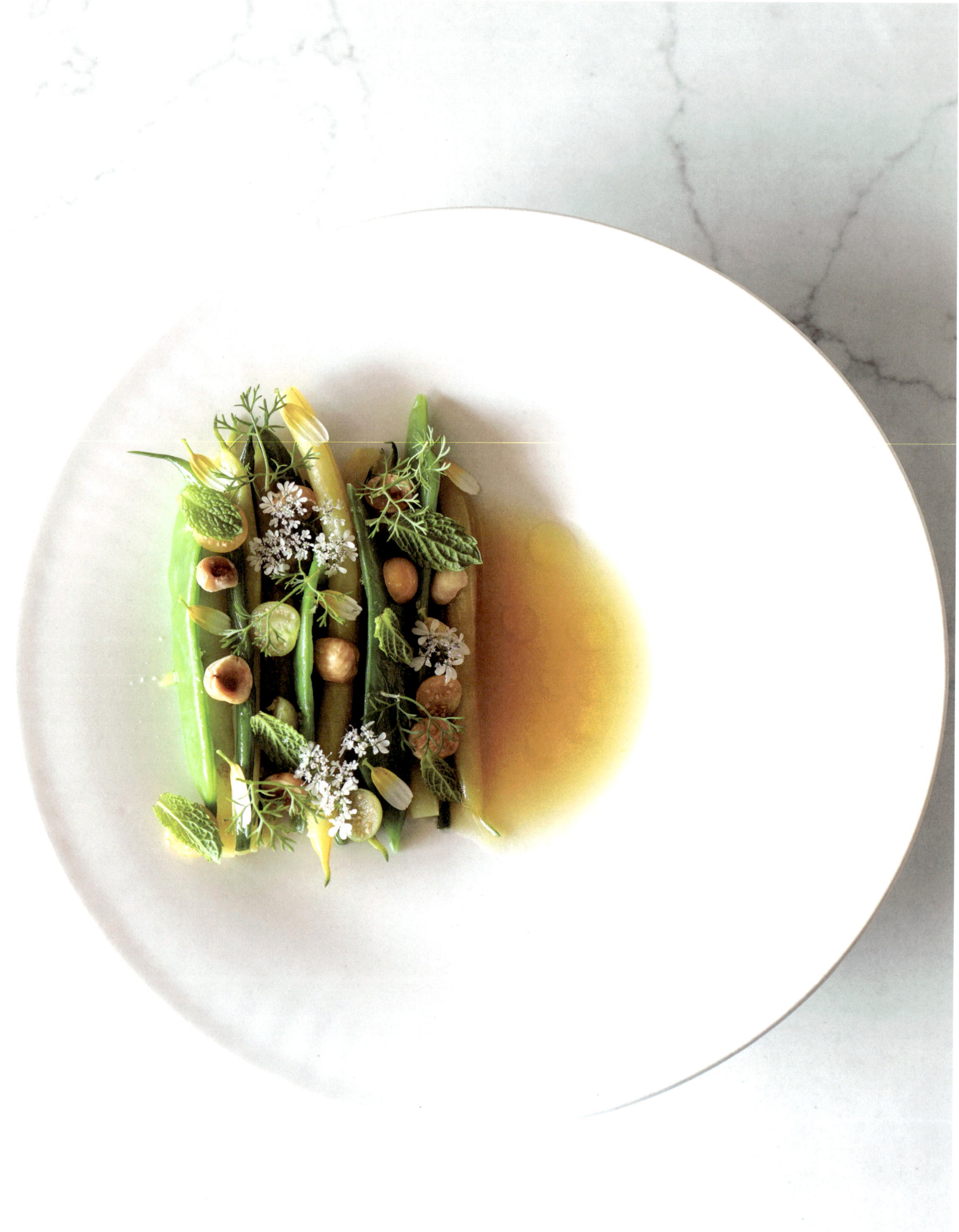

Tell us about your background. How did you get started cooking?

I'm from Dearborn, Michigan, and I grew up in my aunts and uncles restaurants. When I was eight, I started going to work with my dad, who was a cook in my aunt's restaurant. I would work a full 12-hour shift every Saturday helping out with all the side work like peeling potatoes, picking pea pods, and filling up ramekins with sauces. Later on, my parents decided to open up their own Chinese-American restaurant, and I started working there. In high school, I went through that phase, where I didn't want to work in restaurants and just wanted to hang out with friends. I didn't know what I wanted to do with my life, and I wasn't the best at school. I slacked off a lot, and I wasn't passionate about anything else but food and cooking, so I decided to go to culinary school. After graduating, I started working at Michael Symond's Roast Steakhouse in downtown Detroit. Then I moved to Chicago and worked a few months at the now-closed Marcus Samuelson Seafood restaurant, Seahouse. There I realized I particularly enjoyed working with seafood and moved to San Diego, where I worked at a place called Truluck's. I then went to Las Vegas to work at Spago for two years and then moved to Los Angeles to work with Michael Voltaggio at Ink. I worked for Michael for about three years, did Top Chef, went to work for Bryan Voltaggio at Volt in Maryland, and then took a break to work on myself and the restaurant that I wanted to open.

Is this a restaurant concept that you had been thinking of for a long time?

After Top Chef, there was a lot of pressure from people about my next steps. They would always ask, "What are you going to do? When are you going to open a restaurant?" That was something I had to think about for a long time before finally making a move to do it.

It's probably hard at that point to go back to working for someone after winning a big show like that.

Yeah, well, I briefly thought about working for someone and being their chef. But I think at the end of the day I didn't want to cook someone else's food anymore. I have a lot more to show about who I am, and so I just started doing pop-ups and cooking dinners with friends around the country — doing those helped me figure out what I wanted to do and the type of food that I wanted to cook.

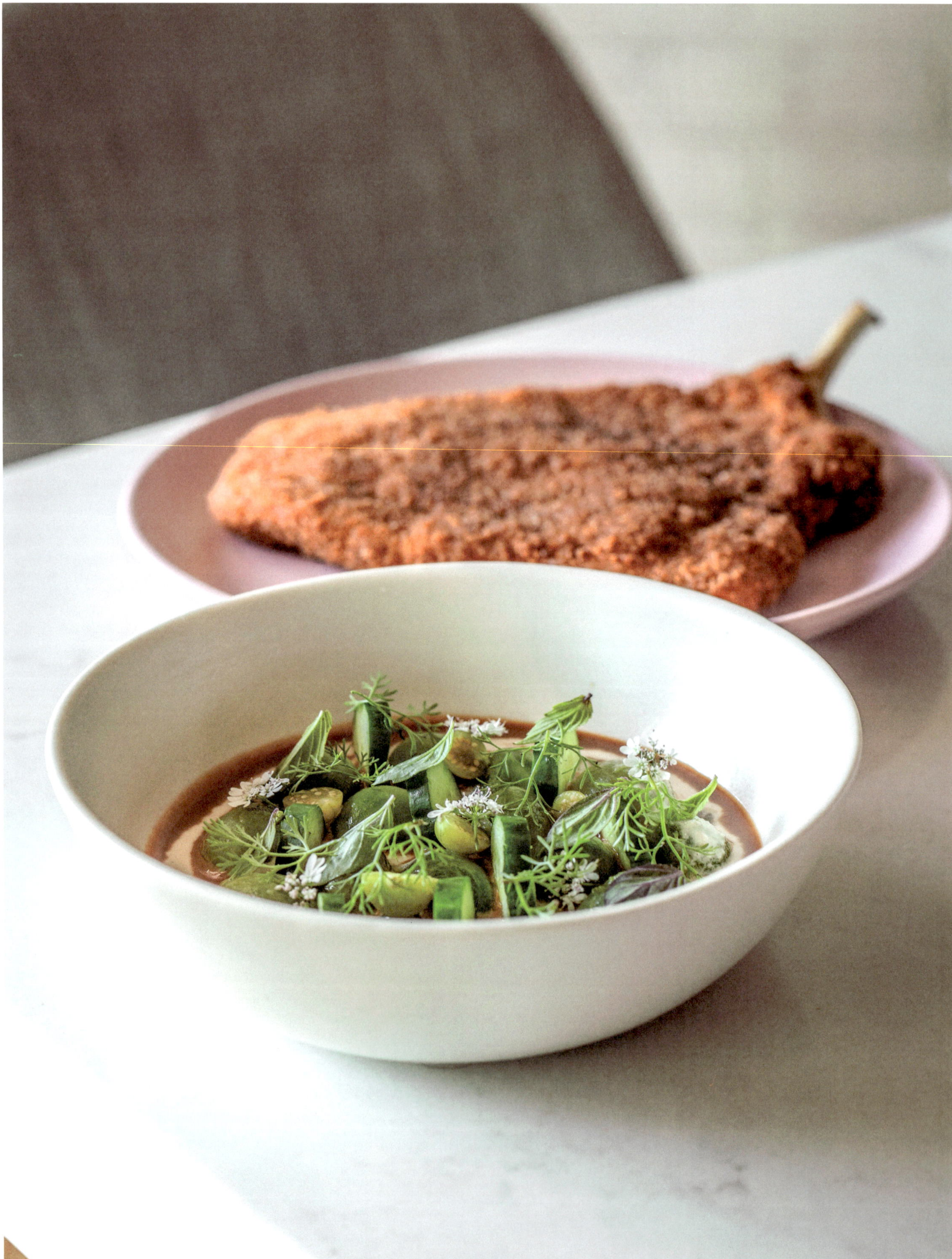

Your food at Nightshade has some Chinese going on, but it also seems to pull from a lot of other cuisines and incorporates it into American Cuisine. Does that sound correct?

Yeah. The schnitzel alone is essentially me pulling from my time working for Wolfgang Puck. It's a dish he's known for, but I wanted to remake it utilizing the flavors that I grew up eating. I want to bring that nostalgic factor to my guests. We have a lot of Asian diners here, and they take these flavors very seriously. They can be judgemental, but if it lives up to their standards, then they love it.

Your customers might give you a hard time for calling a dish a specific name if it isn't close to the traditional dish?

Yeah, for example, we have lasagna on the menu, but it's a ma-po tofu lasagna. A lot of diners say, "This is not lasagna." But it is lasagna, just not the way they were thinking. We make a pork ragu with those ma-po tofu flavors and do 17 layers of thin noodles. To the Asian diners, it's familiar and is simply noodles with ma-po tofu. I'm not trying to do anything really difficult. I want to do simple food that tastes good.

Have you changed the menu much since you opened? Did these dishes take a lot of r&d before the opening?

Before opening, I had a rough draft of 25 menu items. Some of them made it, and some of them didn't, but for the most part, the menu has pretty much been the same since we opened. It's been about eight months now, and I would say 75 percent of the menu is the same.

I feel like chefs have this romantic idea about changing the menu every day. But when you have a killer dish, and you flip it that quickly, not that many people get to experience it. Maybe it doesn't get the recognition it might deserve.

The shrimp toast, scallops, and the OG congee are probably never going to leave the menu because they have become staples to what this restaurant is.

What inspires your food?

Going out to eat and traveling. I just got back from New York, and I came into the restaurant with tons of ideas and changes. Anywhere you travel, you're going to draw inspiration, and that's the beauty of it.

Is there a specific process to your creativity. Do you throw things together, or do you entirely think a dish through and draw pictures?

Typically, I'll see an ingredient and work around it. For example, when I go to the market in Santa Monica, and a new ingredient comes into season, I start working with it and see where it goes. I then pick other elements that might work together with it and play around.

You worked with Voltaggio when all the molecular stuff was trendy. Do you feel the need to keep with the trends? Like fermenting and aging everything?

When I was working with Voltaggio, I learned those techniques, but I don't utilize them here. I don't find a need. I mean, we use liquid nitrogen, but that's as far as we go. We do some aging and fermenting though.

Are there any food trends you see on the horizon?

I think right now; everyone is going back to their roots. Going back to their heritage and cooking easy and simple food.

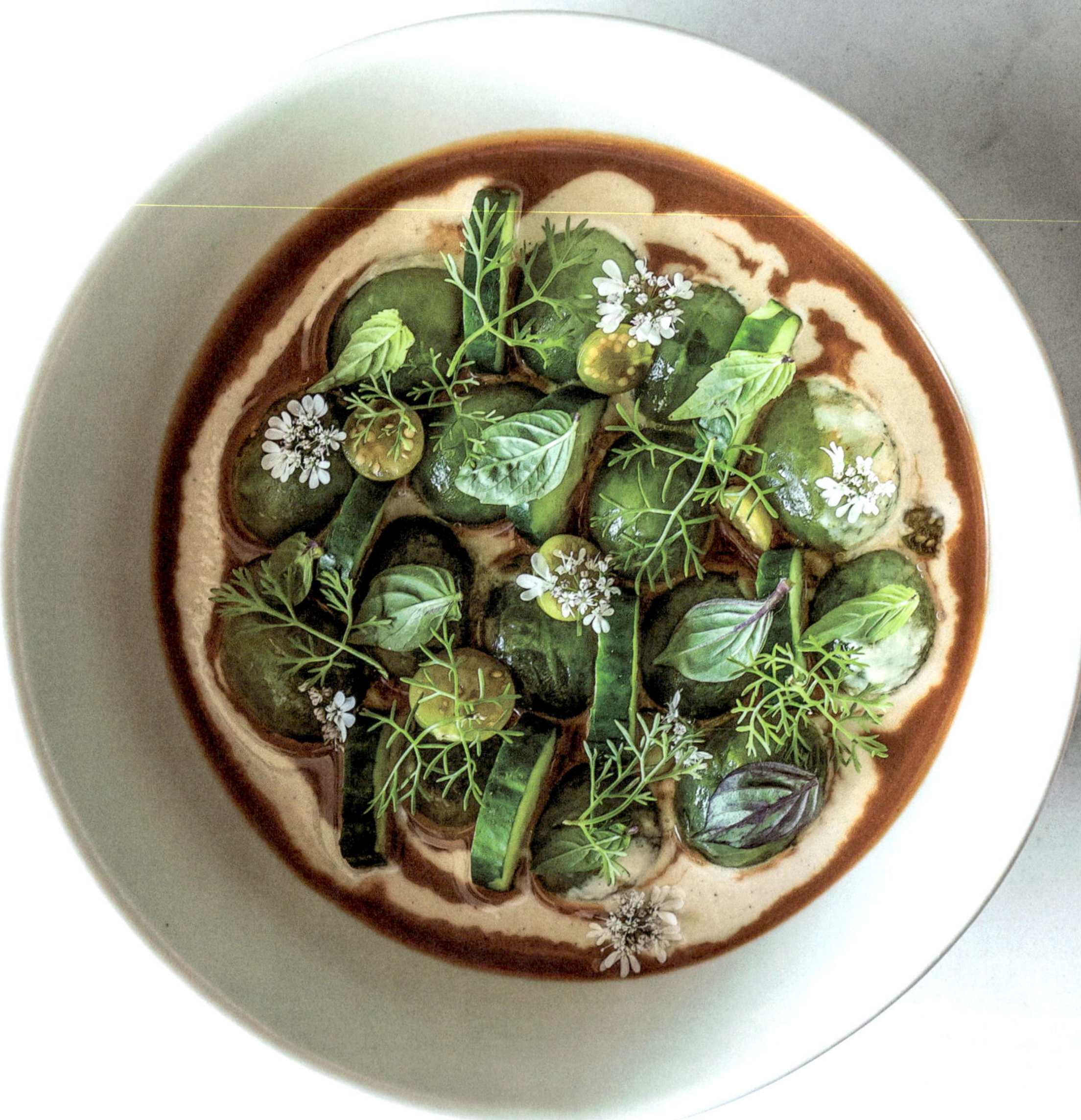

green jade tomatoes, Persian cucumbers, gwaimei dressing

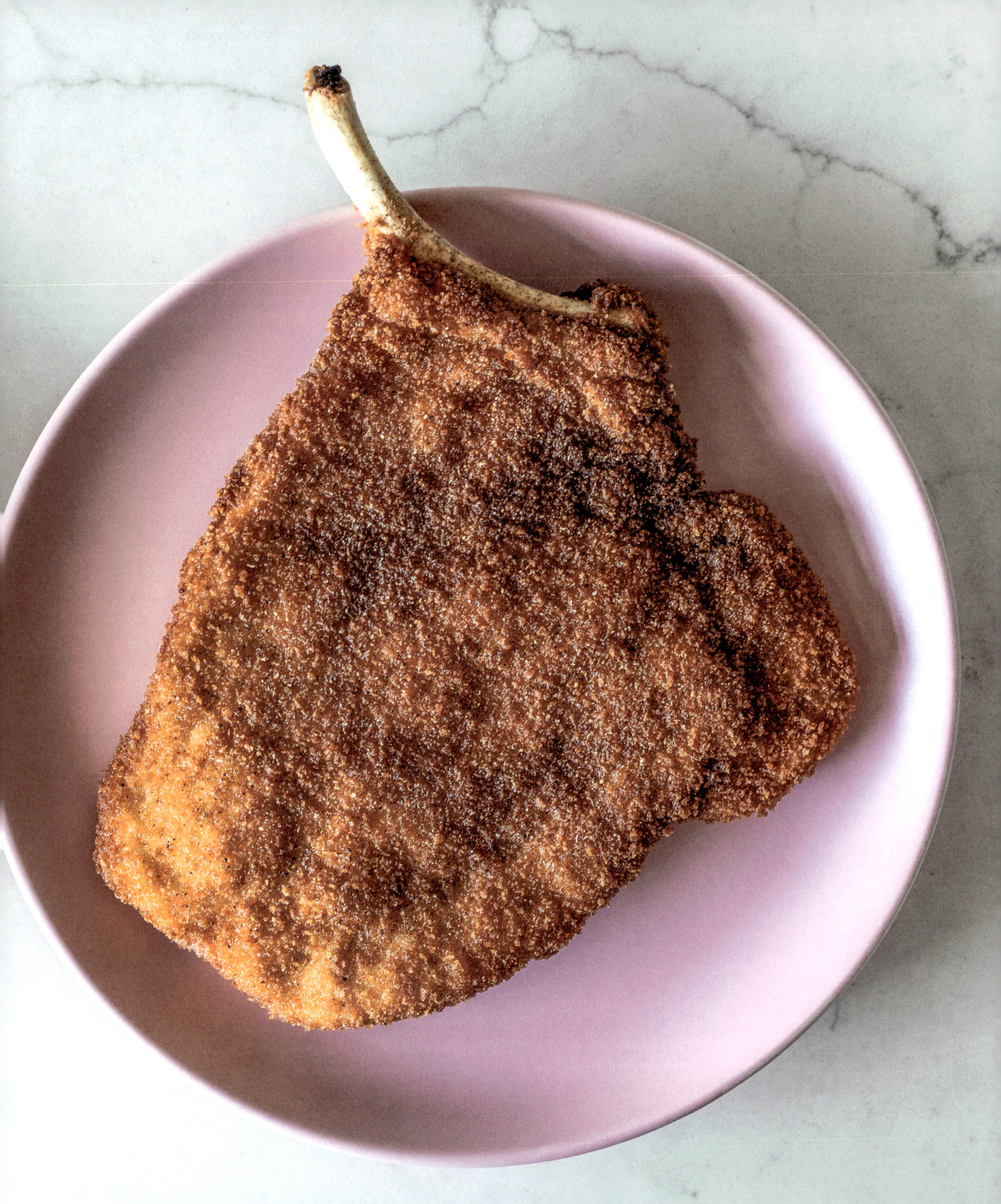

pork schnitzel

Koshihikari Rice Congee, Pork Floss, Fried Shallots, XO Sauce

Congee

Ingredients:

1 tbsp	grapeseed oil
½ cup	small yellow onion, small dice
2 tbsp	ginger, minced
1 cup	Koshihikari short grain rice (sushi)
10 cups	water

Method:

Heat a four-quart pot to medium-high heat, add oil and sweat onions and ginger until aromatic. Add the rice and slightly toast. Add half of the liquid and add the rest gradually throughout the cooking process until it resembles porridge consistency.

Pork Floss

Ingredients:

500 g	lean pork shoulder
2 L	water
75 g	tamari
1 stick	lemongrass, smashed
3 ea	scallion, cut in 2 in pieces
5 ea	Szechuan peppercorns
2 ea	star anise

Method:

Cut the pork into big cubes and blanch to remove any scum. Pressure cook for 30 minutes on medium heat. Cool the pork down and shred with a fork. Dry out the pork in a nonstick pan, low and slow, and transfer to a kitchen aid heating bowl set at 200*F. With the whisk attachment, start whisking the bowl on medium-high and then add the seasoning mix. Stop the mixer and switch out the whisk for a paddle.

Seasoning Mix

Ingredients:

15 g	oyster sauce
15 g	tamari
5 g	sugar
½ tsp	five spice

XO Sauce

Ingredients:

1/4 cup	ground prosciutto
1/4 cup	dried anchovies
1/4 cup	dried shrimp, ground in a high-speed blender
1/2 cup	shallot, sliced thin
1/2 cup	garlic, minced
3 tbsp	oyster sauce
3 tbsp	fish sauce
½ cup	xiaoshing wine
2 tbsp	sugar
1 tsp	Szechuan peppercorn (ground)
4 tsp	chili de arbol chilies (ground)

Method:

In a deep saucepot, heat 1 qt of grapeseed oil over medium heat and start to fry the shallots until golden. Strain into another pot and start to fry the garlic until golden and strain into another pot. Reserve the fried shallots and garlic until the end. Once the XO has cooled you will need to add them in. Fry the ground prosciutto until crispy, and add the dried anchovies and shrimp. Stir in the Szechuan pepper and chili de arbol and cook for about 3 minutes until toasted. Add the xiaoshing slowly. It will bubble really hard and steam. Your pot is still at medium heat at this point, and now you're going to add the rest seasonings and fish sauce. Once the XO has cooled, add the shallots and garlic.

To Finish

Onsen egg, cooked 63*C for 1 hour (immersion circulator).
Shaved scallions
Fried shallots/garlic
Fried fuielle de brick

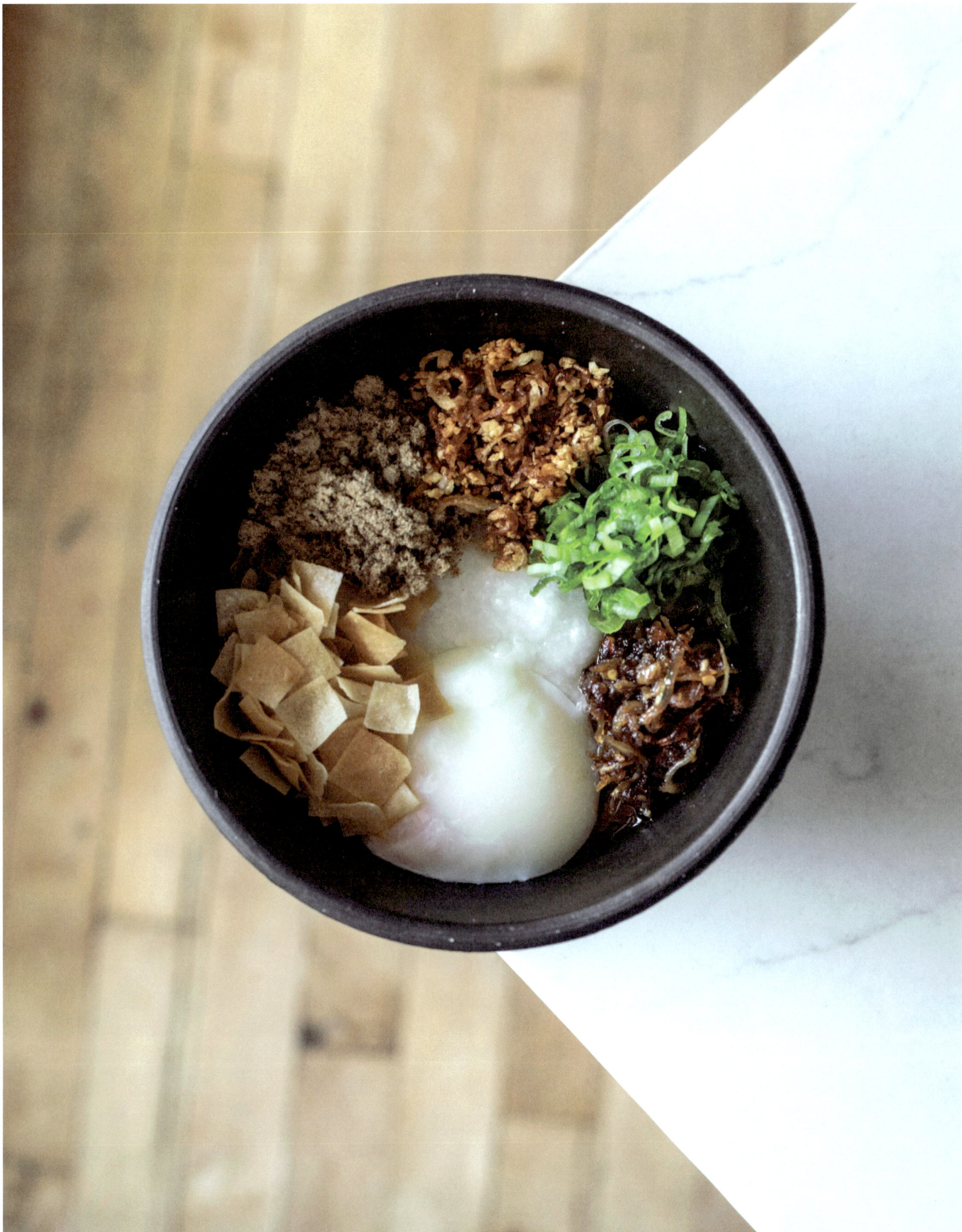

koshihikari rice congee, xo, pork floss, onsen egg

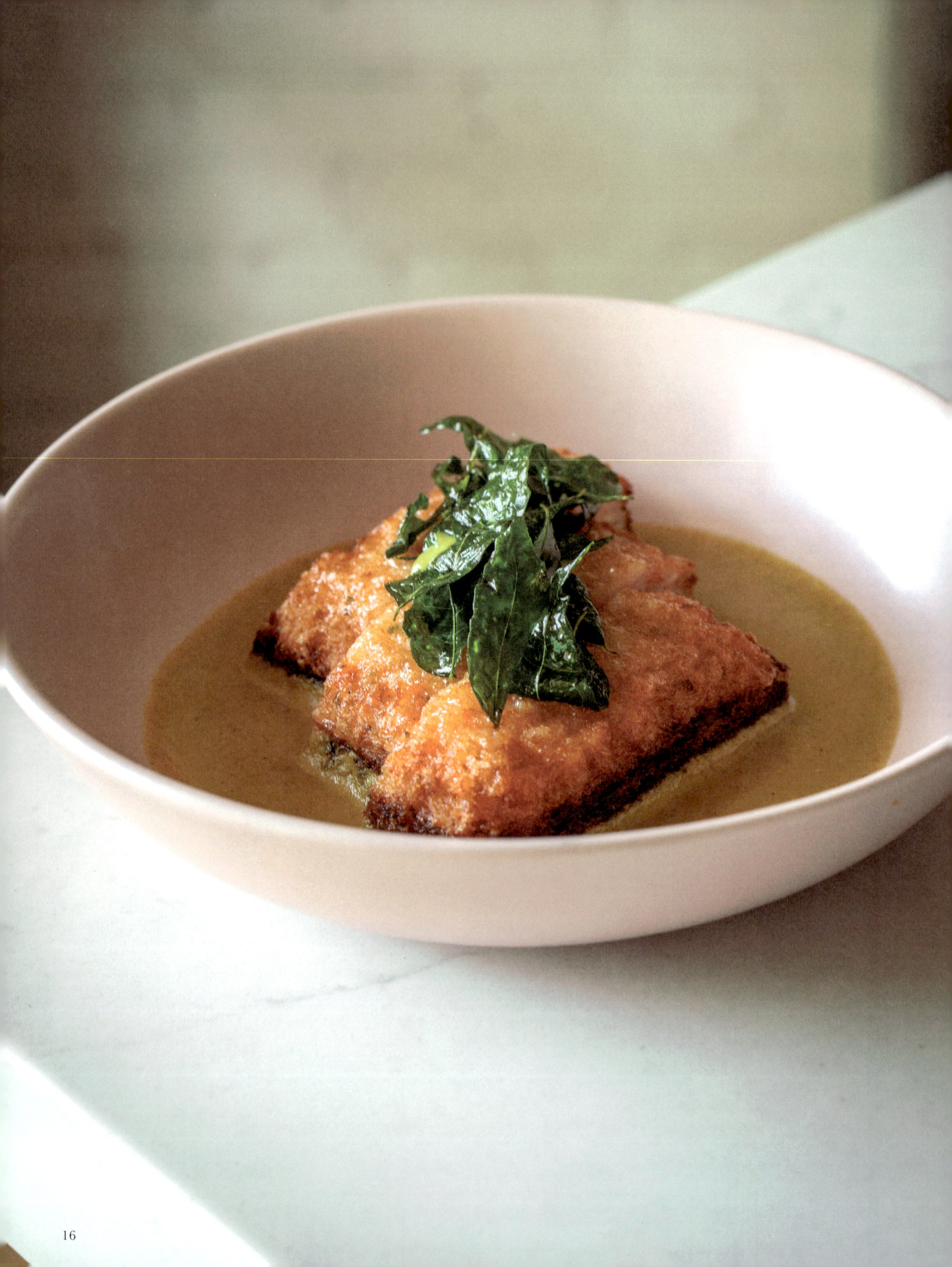

Shrimp Toast

Ingredients:

1135 g	shrimp, peeled and deveined 21/25
55 g	pork fat, cold
85 g	shmaltz, cold
8 g	sesame oil
50 g	ginger, brunoise
50 g	garlic, minced
50 g	cilantro stems
20 g	fish sauce
20 g	xiaoshing
65 g	egg whites
15 g	corn starch
15 g	salt
55 g	sugar
20 g	white pepper

Method:

In a meat grinder or food processor, grind or pulse the shrimp until it becomes pureed. Add all the ingredients to make the mousse. Cut pain de mie to ¼ in thick with crusts off and let it dehydrate semi-dry. If it dries out too much, it will become brittle and will break.

Cantonese Curry

Ingredients:

50 g	garlic
130 g	shallots
50 g	ginger
215 g	onion
45 g	lemongrass
20 g	fresno chilies
15 g	serrano chilies
14 g	madras curry powder
50 g	palm sugar or rock sugar
5 g	salt
1000 ml	Kara coconut milk
35 g	fish sauce
390 g	chicken stock

Method:

In a food processor, blitz the garlic, shallots, ginger, onion, lemongrass, and chilies until it forms a paste. Transfer to a mixing bowl and add the madras curry powder. In a stockpot, add the curry paste and toast until fragrant. Add the palm sugar, chicken stock, and coconut milk and reduce until it's nappe. Strain through a chinois. Add fish sauce at the end.

To Finish

Garnish with fried curry leaves.

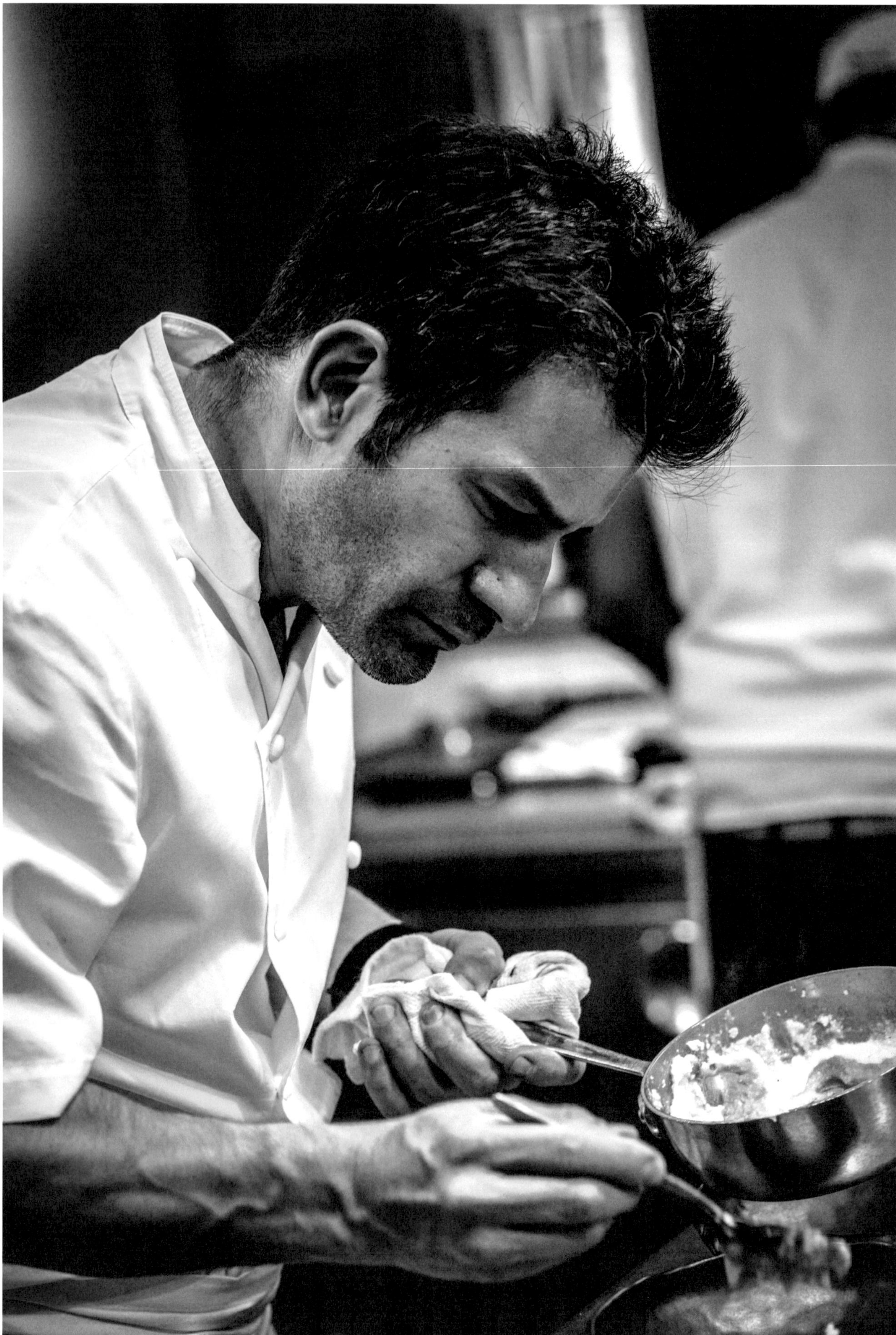

A DEEP CONNECTION TO MY PAST

george mendes

aldea

new york, ny

Pickled Portuguese Sardine

on brioche toast, smoked steelhead trout caviar and black garlic

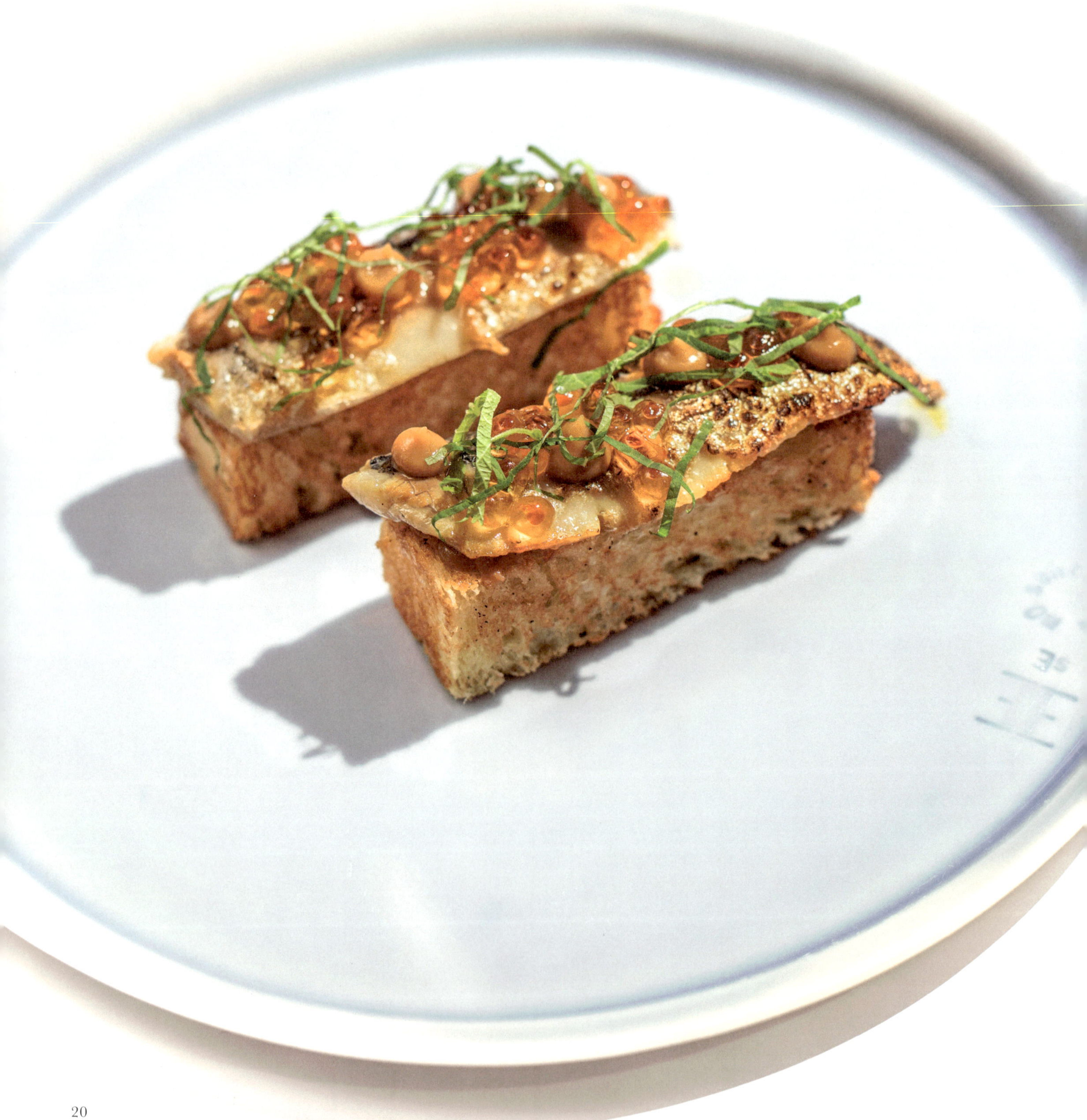

Tell us about your background.

When I think about my background, it brings me to my childhood and my introduction to good food. My family showed me what it was like to grow vegetables, and I would often go outside to pick parsley or collard greens for dinner. The most significant impact on me was coming home every night to a Portuguese family and having a home-cooked meal.

Your parents were immigrants from Portugal, so you were eating some real Portuguese food growing up.

My mother immigrated in 1969. My aunt had come around a year prior and was working at a bakery with my uncle. They eventually opened a restaurant together, which is still there today in Danbury, Connecticut. So, my mother would spend time with her in the kitchen, and they would interchange different traditional Portuguese recipes. Although my mom had Portuguese cooking knowledge, my aunt was also teaching her.

So, that's how I grew up. I grew up around food and eating these traditional Portuguese dishes all the time. During the holidays, especially Thanksgiving, it was not only a turkey feast, but it was a buffet table of roast suckling pig, rabbit rice, baby goats, and all kinds of salt cod preparations.

A lot of that isn't the typical foods that American kids eat. I don't think I would have touched salt cod when I was young.

Oh, I hated it. It was a big pot of boiled salt cod with potatoes and hard-boiled eggs. My favorite part of the dish was cracking open the eggs and eating only the whites. But just the smell of the salt cod was so off-putting.

So let's get into your cooking career. I read that you went to the Culinary Institute of America, and then you worked at the original Bouley for a few years. How was that experience?

Intense. Working at Bouley was a complete immersion in French gastronomy but in a very light way. I came from the CIA learning all the traditional French fundamentals, but the cooking at Bouley was herbaceous, light, brothy, and used all of these infused oils. It was a launching pad and made me fall in love with the industry more. At that time, I was a little bit on the fence, and I wasn't sure if I really wanted to cook. But I had one chat with Bouley where he said, "Everything I've got in life, I got from being in a restaurant. If you put your head down and cook, everything else will eventually fall into place."

Bouley was also my liaison to go to Paris for the first time.

You staged quite a bit in France, right?

My first stage in Paris was in 1994 at L'Arpège before Alain Passard received his third Michelin star. I mostly cleaned a shit ton of chanterelle mushrooms and broomed the floor. I did meet some great people there, though. Pascal Barbot of Astrance and Ludo Lefebvre were in the kitchen then, and it was a great time. When Bouley closed, I went back to L'Arpège for the second time in 1997, and at that point, it had its third Michelin star.

Is there a reason you went to France to stage rather than Spain or Portugal?

At that time, we were taught that's where you needed to go to learn. The Spanish avant-garde revolution wasn't happening yet. There was nothing else compared to France, and it was the place to stage.

You worked and staged in a whole bunch of kitchens between Bouley and opening Aldea. Are there any restaurants, in particular, that had a significant influence on you?

The years I was the chef de cuisine at Tocqueville was a hugely formative time for me. There I was trying to find my voice and develop my own style.

Then, when I staged at Restaurante Martin Berasategui, I saw the chef interpret and refine a lot of his grandmother's recipes. He was taking rustic Basque cooking and translating it through the avant-garde lens, and that's when I had a light bulb go off. I realized I wanted to do something similar with Portuguese food, and that's how the seed got planted for Aldea.

So you had a trip to Portugal recently. How was that? What do you take away from those trips?

It's a revisit and tasting the rustic recipes again. I was able to cook with this lady named Rolanda in the Douro region. She made this amazing octopus-rice dish, for example. She cut everything in her hands over a pot of sizzling olive oil. This one-pot dish of garlic, tomato, parsley, and octopus just screamed tradition and authenticity. That type of dish brings me back to honest and soulful cooking. Every time I go to Portugal and taste the traditional dishes, it's grounding, it's a deep connection I feel with my past, and it reminds me of being in the kitchen with my mother.

Do those trips inspire you to cook more rustically? Or is it just about recreating those flavors in your dishes?

Yes and no. I try to look at traditional recipes and add some refinement in the technique or plating. I get inspired by the flavor and authenticity, but then try to encapsulate it into something new that fits our fine-dining creative lens. It's not always as simple as slicing white truffles over the top, but instead taking a part of the dish and translating it or refining it while still having some restraint. Some recipes are easier than others to do that with. It's like eating really good guacamole with chips. What else could you ever want to do with that?

It's awesome when people come in and say, "I understand what you're doing. It's not traditional Portuguese, but I can taste Portuguese influence." That's when I know I've succeeded in getting its essence onto the plate.

How are you sourcing these Portuguese ingredients in New York?

I have some great relationships with olive oil producers in Portugal, and we're able to bring these fantastic oils into the restaurant. One of them being Casa Migmag and another being Bare. We also have some great distributors in New Jersey and Massachusetts that bring us great Portuguese products, such as tin items, varieties of rice, spices, and salt cod.

One of my favorites is a charcuterie master in Newark that is breeding Iberian pork and making some amazing rustic charcuterie like Jamon Iberico and chorizo. There's another Iberian pig breeder in Georgia that's shipping meat to us, and we have a farm in upstate New York growing us Portuguese kale. The products are out there, and it's cool to see people growing varieties of products that haven't been here before.

Does your mom enjoy your food at Aldea?

She's probably my biggest critic. By all means, she enjoys it, but she's always pushing me to go back to more simple cooking. She's all about flavor and rusticity.

Hokkaido Sea Urchin Toast

cauliflower purée, mustard seed and shiso

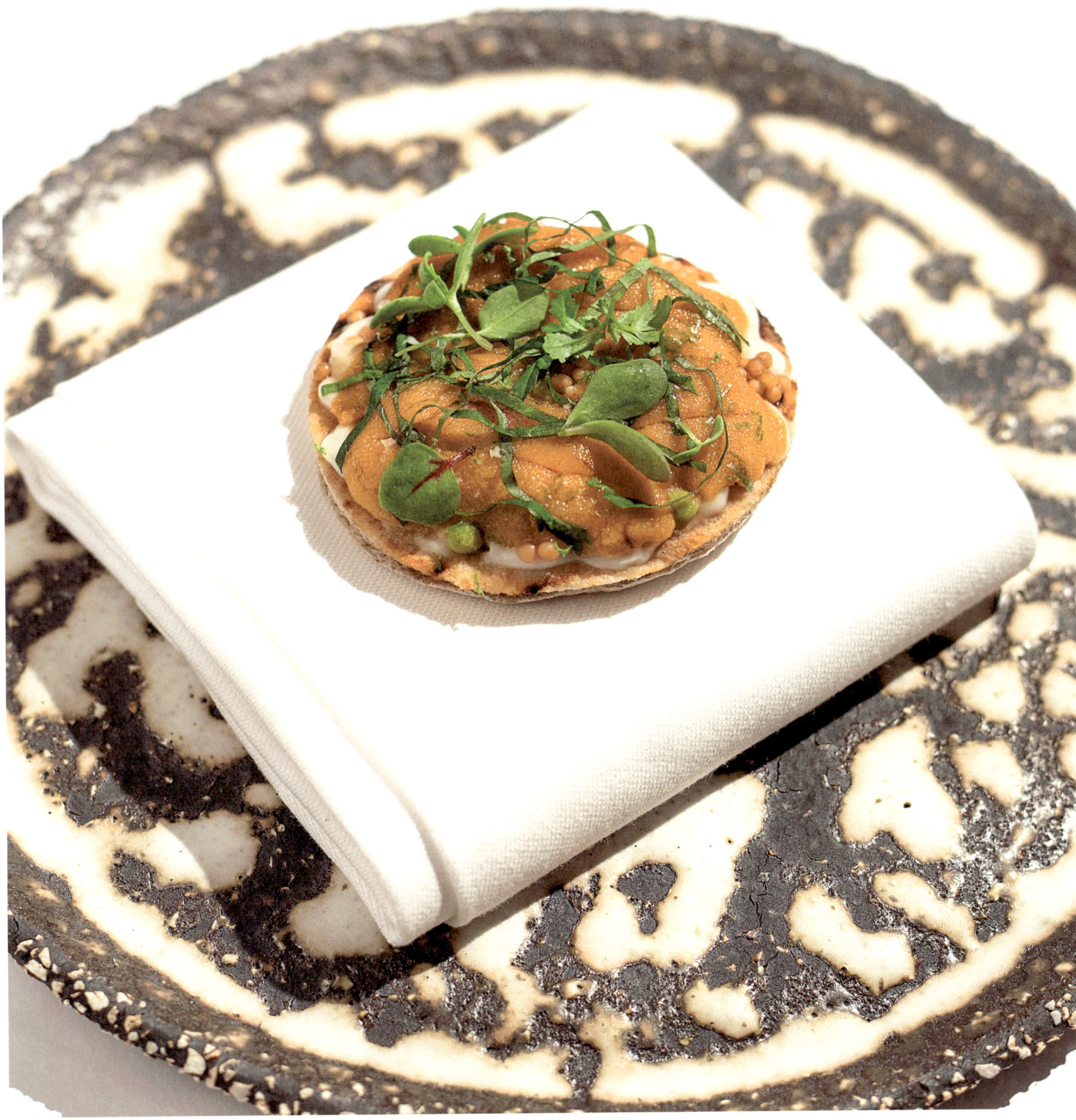

Shrimp Alhinho

Portuguese corn porridge, mussels and clams

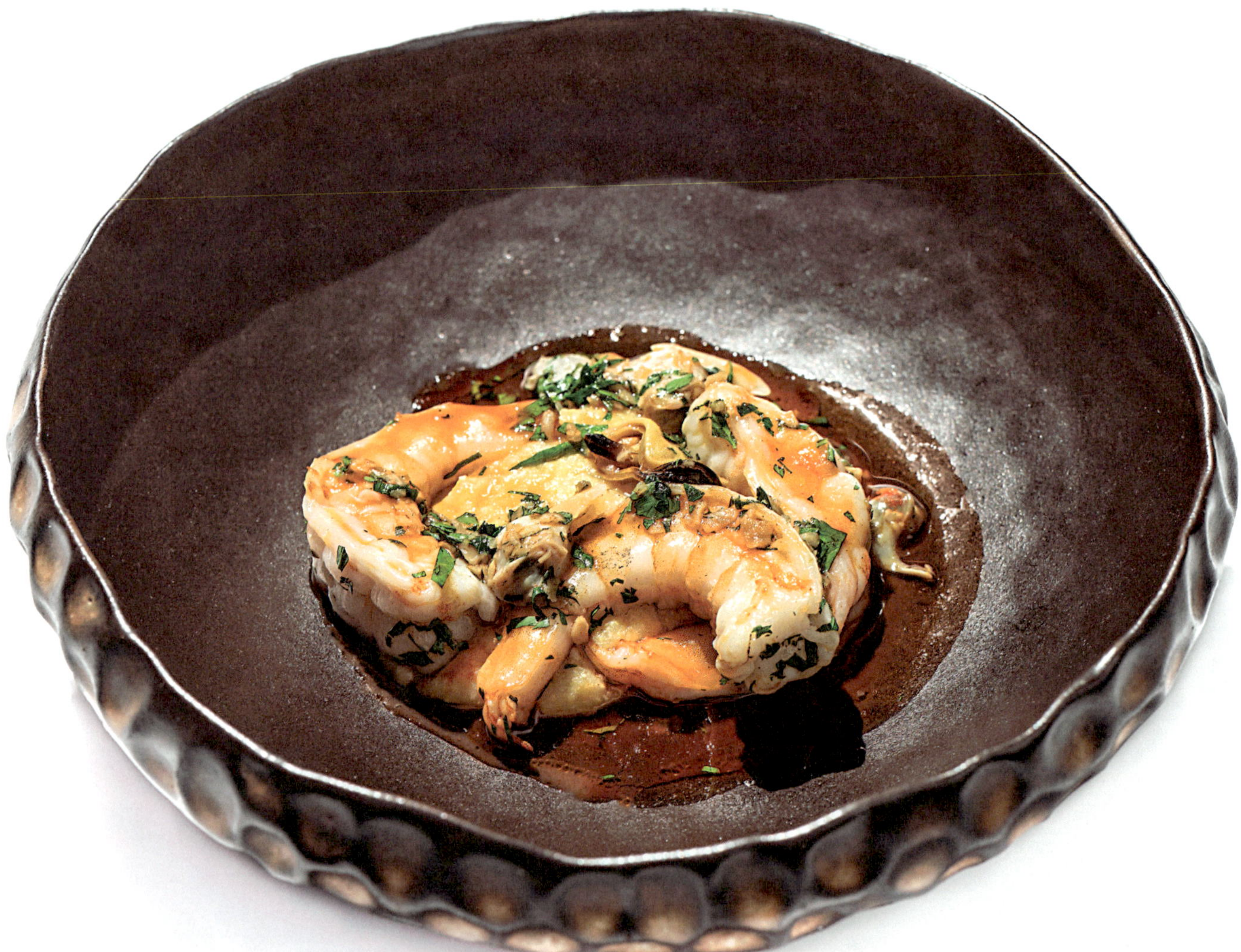

How did the sardine toast dish come about?

My childhood inspired that. When I was eight or nine, I was in the countryside in Tondela, Portugal, celebrating Saints' Day Festival. I had my first really fresh grilled sardine served on a Portuguese roll, and it was the first time I devoured sardines. That memory is what inspired the sardine on toast dishes that we've done throughout the years.

It's such a simple dish that everything has to be perfect.

I think, as chefs, we have a tendency to overcomplicate things, and we always want to add more. It feels like the more simple we make the food, the less clothing we have on and feel naked. For me, it's a very fine line.

The trend right now is everyone embracing their roots. What do you think about that when you've been doing it for years?

I think it's important. I think it brings truth, honesty, and identity to the plate that you're sharing with customers. When I'm mentoring a cook that's forming their career and taking on a chef position for the first time, I always ask, "Where did you grow up? What did you eat? Where are your parents from?" I try to get that story out because I think it's important to connect with your roots.

I've seen from your social media that you're into running and marathons. How did that start, and how do you feel motivated to run after working in the restaurant all day?

Back in 2013, I hit a wall mentally and physically. I was trashing my body and my mind, I wasn't a happy person, and I hit a point of burnout. After talking with loved ones, I realized that something needed to change in my lifestyle.

It began with a straightforward run in Central Park. I was running for leisure and hadn't trained, and a mile in, I was gasping for air and thinking I was going to have a heart attack. But I just kept going. Then I took a trip to Aspen, Colorado, did a 5K race, and that added on to the thrill and adrenaline. I started to pay attention to how I was feeling after finishing the run. My endorphins were kicking in. There was an overall clarity of mind and strength and a sense of accomplishment. That's what began to shift my thoughts to take care of myself. Instead of going out after work for beers, I started going to bed earlier and waking up to go on runs.

Ten years is a huge landmark for a restaurant. How has the industry changed in that time? Is the situation with staffing different?

The restaurant scene in New York remains highly competitive. There will always be cooks that want to learn and work at new places to add to their resume. I think we have a responsibility as chefs to create an environment to keep nurturing and mentoring. I firmly believe that fine dining isn't ever going to go away. People love the ritual of getting dressed up and experiencing a restaurant.

I thought it was great to see you still in the kitchen with the cooks. Usually, chefs tend to check out at a certain point or focus on building an empire. I love that you're still cooking and in the trenches.

You know, it's a craft that I've fallen in love with. I've always been a very hands-on chef, and at the end of the day, I still like being in the kitchen. I enjoy cooking, creating, and teaching the team in the kitchen. I thrive in that environment.

Do you think at this point in your career you've found an ideal work-life balance?

It ebbs and flows. There are times I want to be submersed in the kitchen and do the 75-80 hour work-weeks, and there are also days where I need a break. I love the European model of closing for August and spending time with your family. But, I think right now, having two days off a week, I have a balance.

Is there anything else that you want to say?

My philosophy about food is that it's a gift to provide nourishment for our customers, and I'm grateful to have a platform and restaurant to do that. The opportunity to express myself on a plate is extraordinary, and I thrive on that. Whether you're putting food in a box, a paper plate, or expensive china, it's a gift.

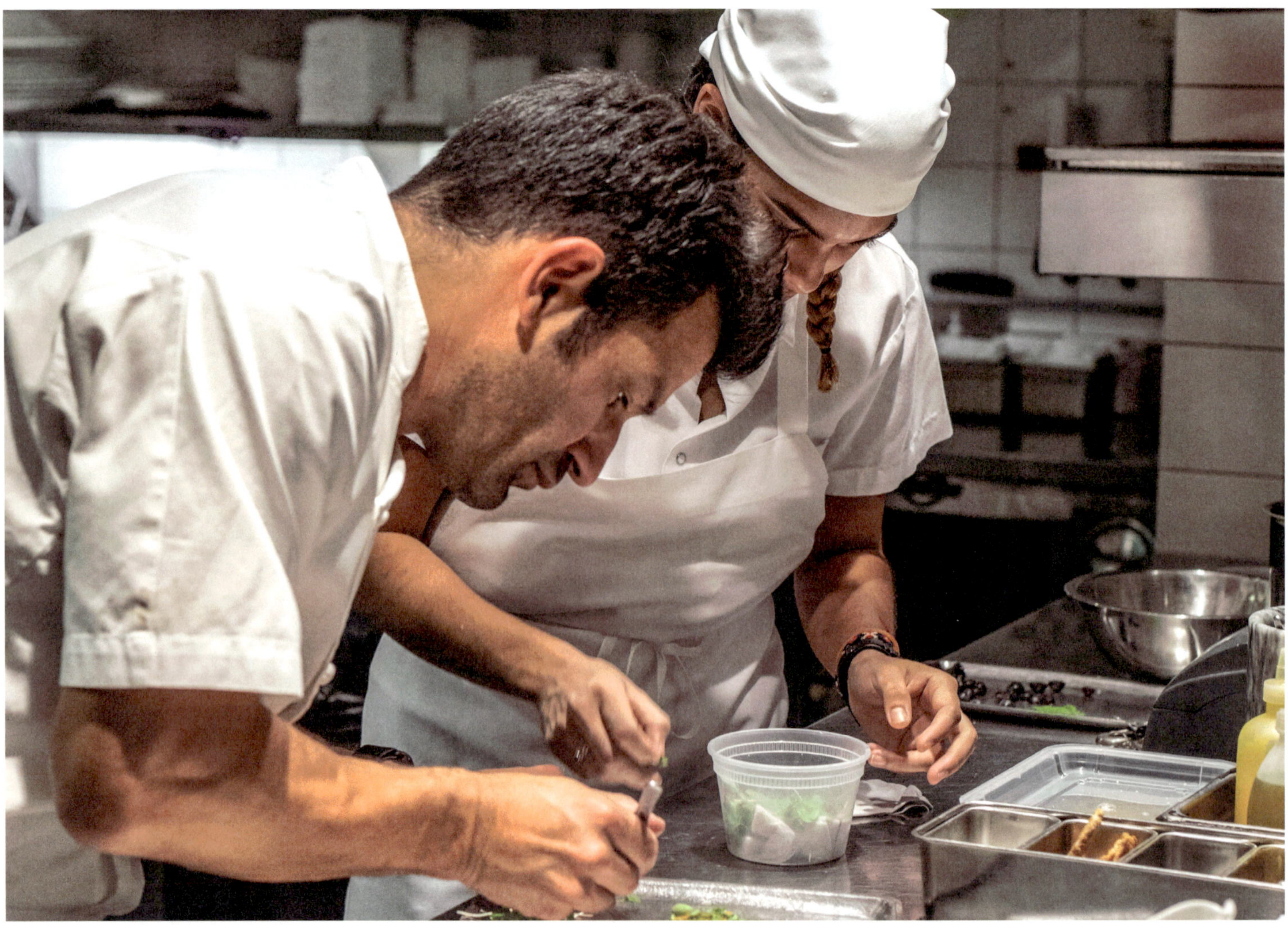

Day-Boat Salted Cod

zucchini and summer squash roulade, preserved tomatoes and smoked olive oil broth

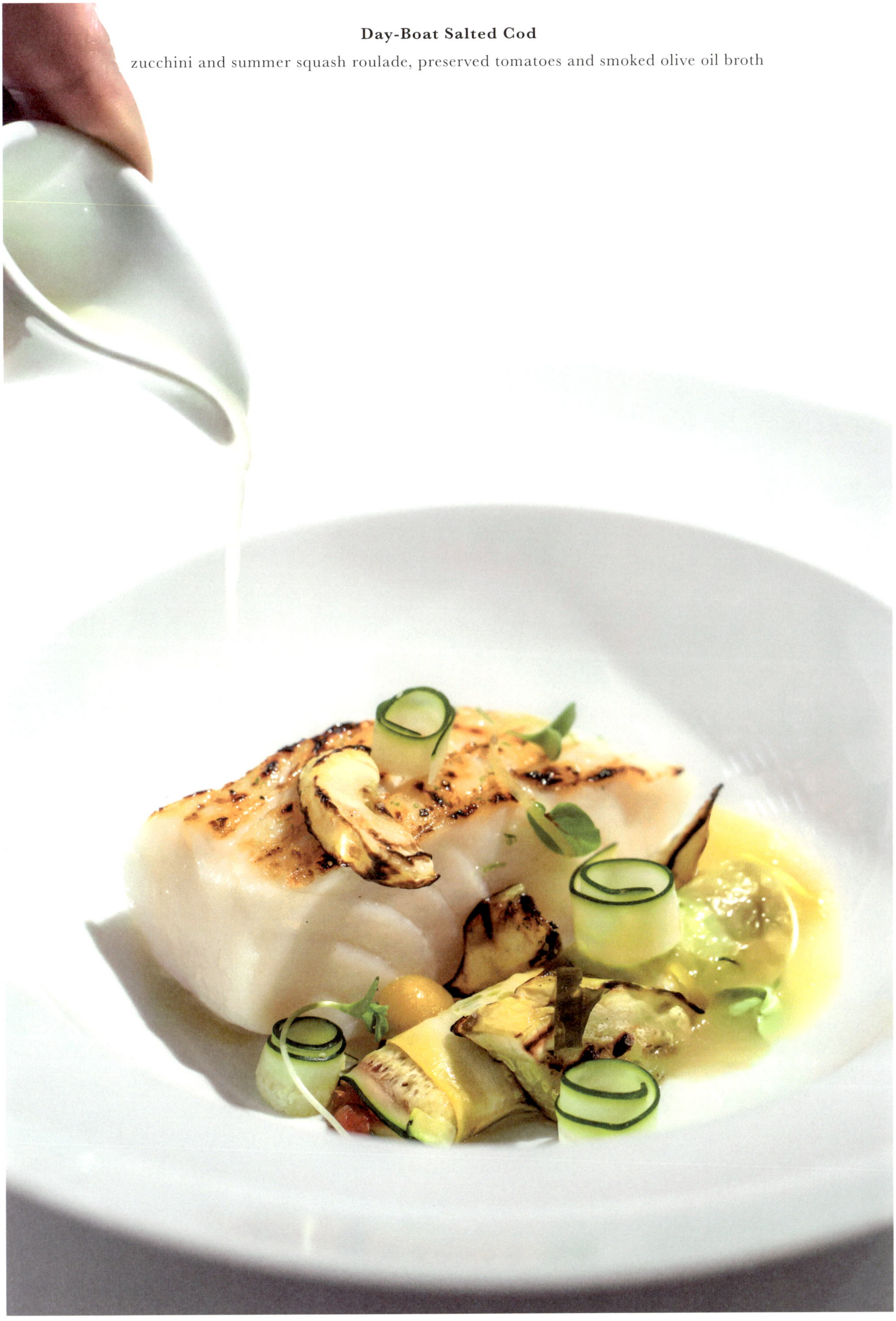

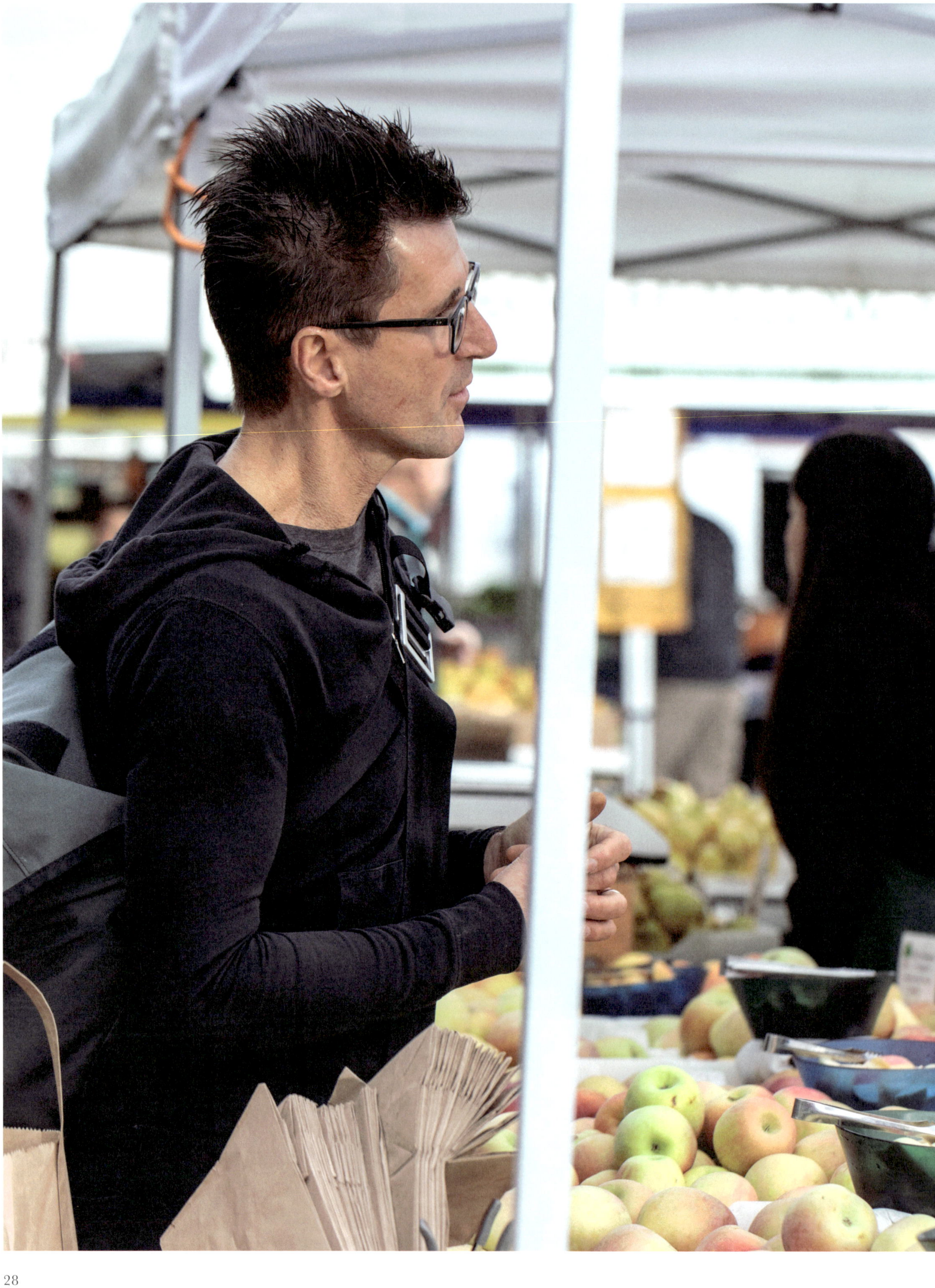

a day with laurent gras

saison

san francisco, ca

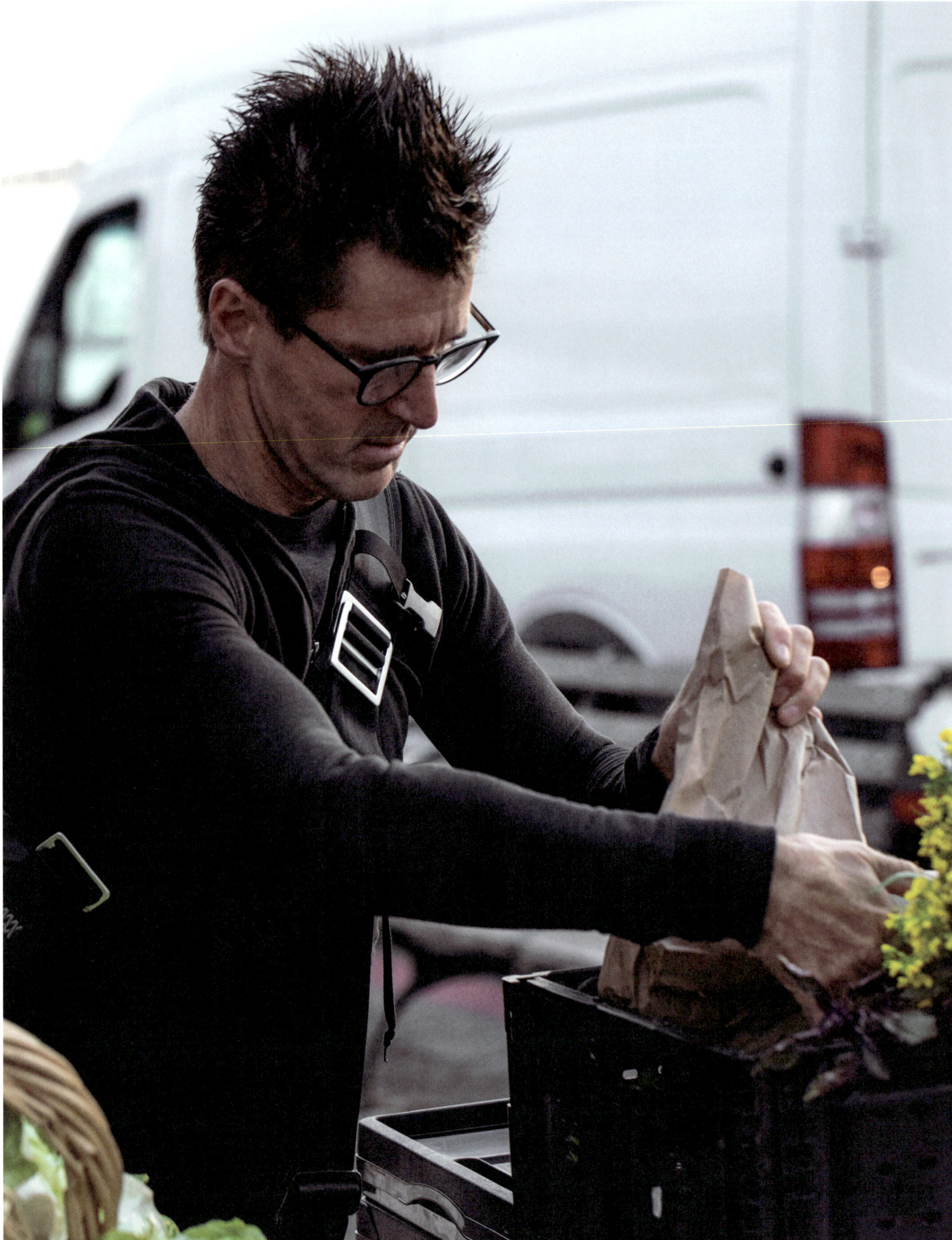

You like to go to the farmer's market before everyone else, huh?

I hate it when the market is crowded. Especially when it's a nice day, there's a lot of people, and you lose a lot of time. Efficiency is a term I love, and when you come to the market early, you get everything. This is also the only time that I'm out of the restaurant. I'm at Saison at 6:30 in the morning, and I stay until 10 PM. Usually, when I open the doors to the restaurant, I run until I'm done with my production, which is around 3 PM. Some days are lighter, and those days I'll work on r&d or doing staff training.

Do you need to be in the restaurant that long, or do you like to be there that long?

I think both. When you're working at such a high level, you need to put yourself fully into it. The morning team comes in around 7 AM, the sous chefs come at 10 AM, and the cooks come at noon. The sous chefs take care of all of the ordering, receiving, and logistics so that my day is just cooking. I think it's the best situation for me that I can imagine. We all work hard, we work as a team, and it's really a peaceful kitchen.

Tell me about your background, your first influences of food, and some of the highlights of your career.

I had a very natural path. I was born and grew up in Antibes, in the southeast of France, and I went to culinary school in Nice, which is just ten miles away from there.

I enjoyed cooking and school, and after graduating, I started cooking right away in restaurants. One of my first jobs out of school was at a small restaurant in Cannes, and the chef knew Jacques Maximin. He was one of the best chefs at the time at Hotel Nogresco in Nice, and so I went there and worked for a couple of years. Then I started with Alain Ducasse, and I spent twelve years with him on and off at various restaurants, including opening Le Louis XV in Monte-Carlo.

I went to Paris for seven years and worked twice with Guy Savoy, and at Maison Blanche. Then I went back to Louis XV to be the executive chef and spent a few years there. After that, I opened Restaurant Alain Ducasse in Paris, and that was an amazing and intense experience. The expectations were very high, and we were pushing hard.

How was the kitchen different back then? Is there a big difference between a three-star Michelin restaurant in France when you were becoming a chef versus a three-star Michelin restaurant now in the USA?

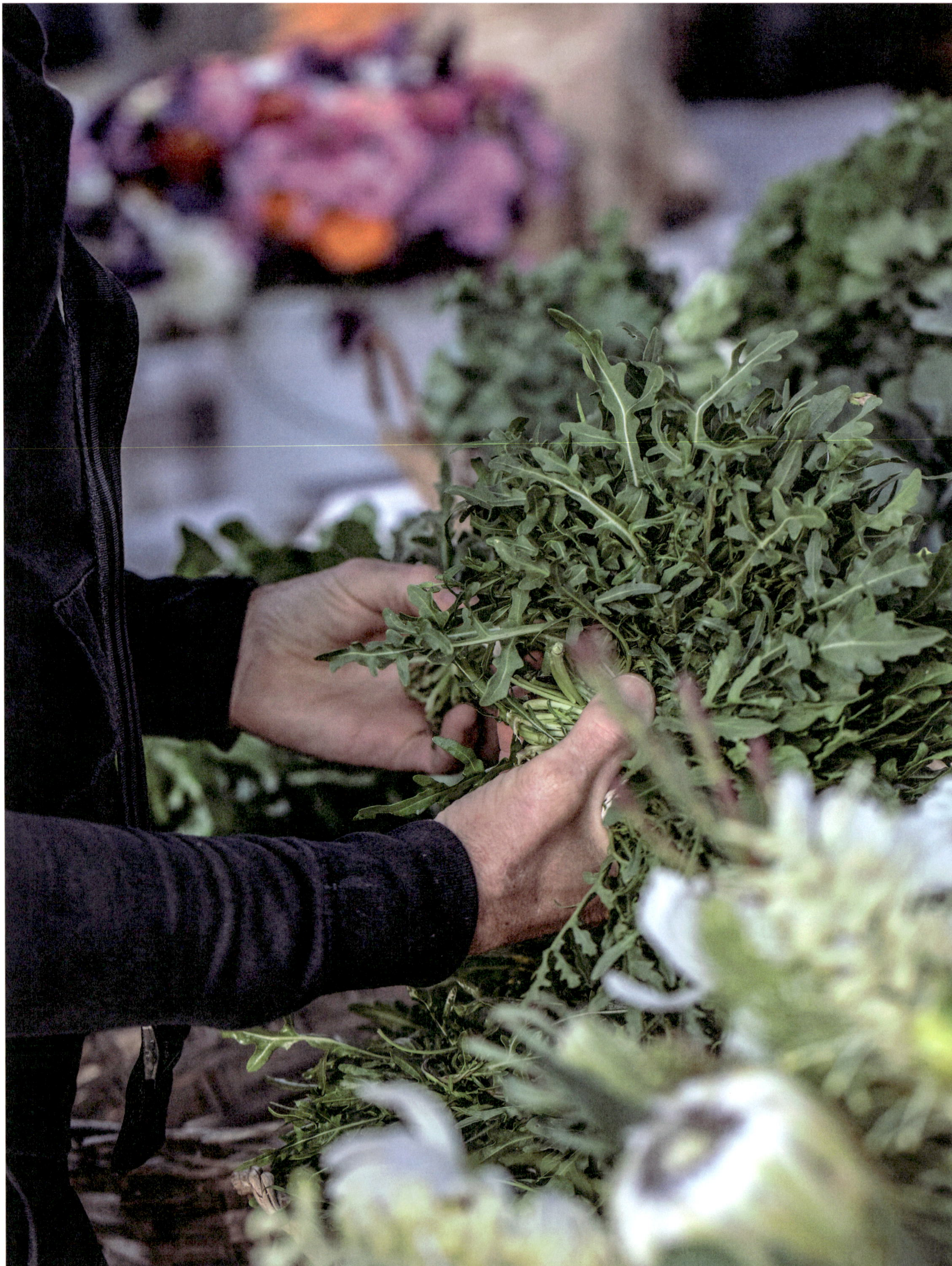

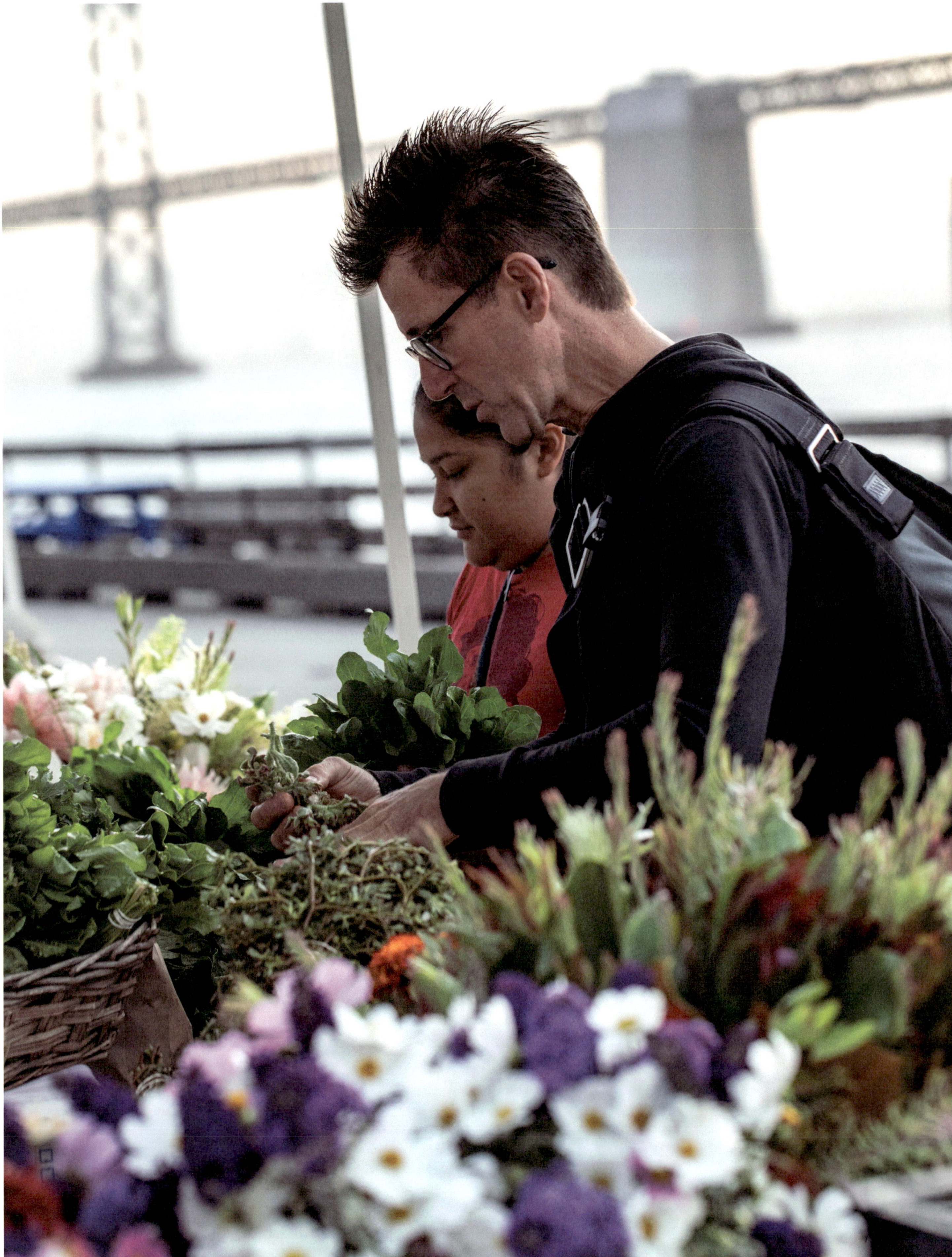

It is difficult to explain, but it was a different generation. People had a different mindset as a young professional. People were more narrowly driven, in the sense that there wasn't as much opportunity as today. The internet and cellphones didn't exist. In France, the mentality was that you pick a job, and you stick with a single place for your whole life. So as a young teenager, a cook would go to a famous restaurant, spend a year or two, go to another one, and another. It was a very straight path that was intense and strict. It would require strong focus and learning, and it was probably more difficult to become a great cook or chef at that time. Today it is easier, and as a teenager, people have a lot more opportunities, and they don't need to work so long to become a chef. You know, someone can become a chef after being in a kitchen for 2 or 3 years, which before in France they had to be in the kitchen for 10-15 years before they could even start thinking about it.

Yes, things have changed, and I'm grateful to have the two spectrums. I can almost say that I learned the hard way, but now I can come into a situation where the kitchen is a lot more relaxed, the relationship between everyone is much better, and there is a lot more cohesiveness in the kitchen today. At Saison, there is a lot of collaboration and sharing of ideas. When I was coming up in France, that didn't exist. Cooks just followed the rules.

It seems like a lot of chefs that came up in the older generation complain about cooks nowadays being weak. Do you think the level of cooks has changed?

I disagree with that. I think, as a chef, you need to build a team, get them interested, and give them knowledge. That's where you create a balance. The cooks at Saison work hard, but they are also learning, and they have my support. It's important as a leader to be a part of the team and work alongside everybody else. Cooks learn from watching how the chef works and how the chef conducts themselves.

So, after working in France, what brought you to the USA?

When I was younger, I traveled a lot. Since I was working so hard, every chance I had during restaurant closures or time between jobs, I needed to go somewhere. The longest trip that I did was a year in South America, and that was so valuable for me. After a lot of traveling for leisure, I realized that I wasn't getting a real interaction with the country, people, or life. I wanted to taste what it meant to live and work in another country. I was very interested in New York, and my initial idea was to spend a couple of years there and then go back to France, but I never left.

So that's when you went to Peacock Alley?

Yeah, it was a very abrupt change of kitchen culture. In France, cooks sometimes get trained in kitchens that are very abusive, and after a while, they believe that's how it's supposed to be. That idea is totally untrue and looking back at that job, that lesson was probably one of the great things that happened to me. It's where I learned to communicate better and learned how to manage a kitchen in a way that is valuable for everyone.

In 2001 after 9/11, Waldorf-Astoria closed most of its restaurants for economic reasons, and so I moved to San Francisco to be the chef at the Fifth Floor and spent four years there. San Francisco is great because it feels very similar to where I grew up. The climate, the resources, the way of living, the air, and so it was an effortless move. I almost felt like I was back home.

After the Fifth Floor, I moved back to New York to get married. My wife never left New York, so it was a good idea to be there with her, and then I started consulting, and one of the projects was for the Lettuce Entertain You group. I spent a year at Tru when Rick Tramonto left to re-concept, and I built a good relationship with the company. They said they had a wonderful place that had been open for 25 years and that they wanted me to make it one of the best seafood restaurants in the country. That's how L2o was born.

How did you make your way back to San Francisco as the chef at Saison?

I never meant to stay here. Joshua Skenes reached out asking if I'd like to do a residency at Saison while he was opening Angler and things progressed from there. When the opportunity presented itself for me to become a partner and the executive chef, I decided to stay.

Is there a reason you stayed in the USA and didn't go back to Europe.

I love it here, and it's an open field. There are so many things you can do. In between L2o and Saison, I didn't work for five years other than consulting and pop-ups. Instead, I raced my bike three times a week, six months a year.

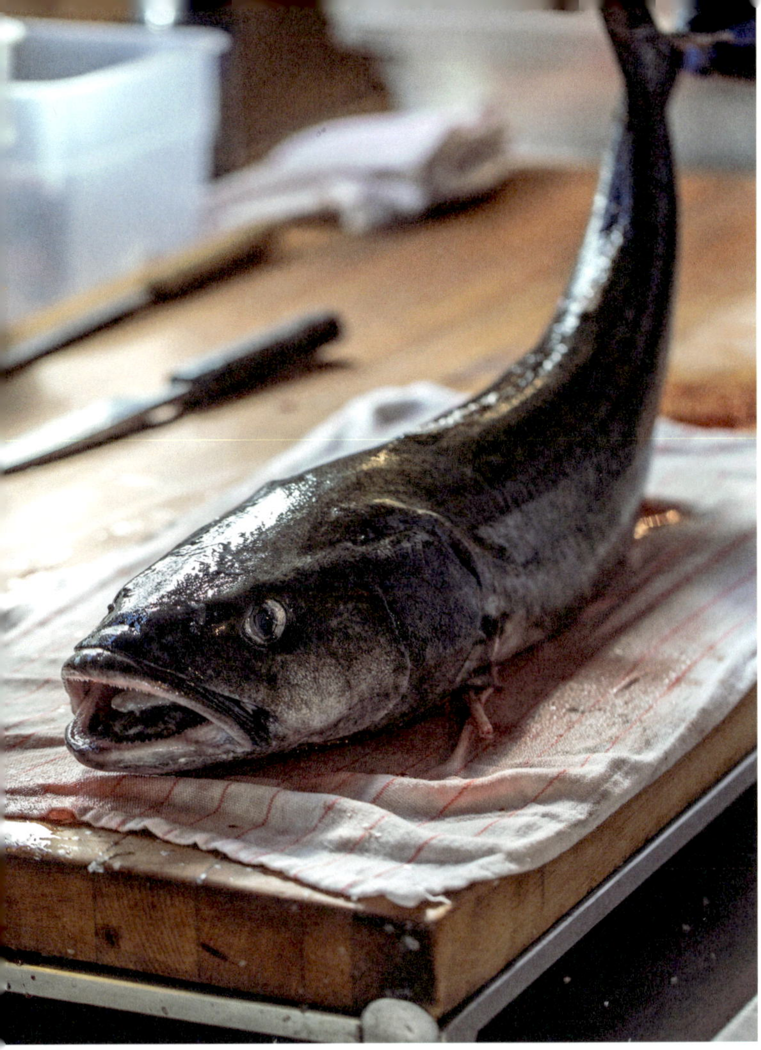
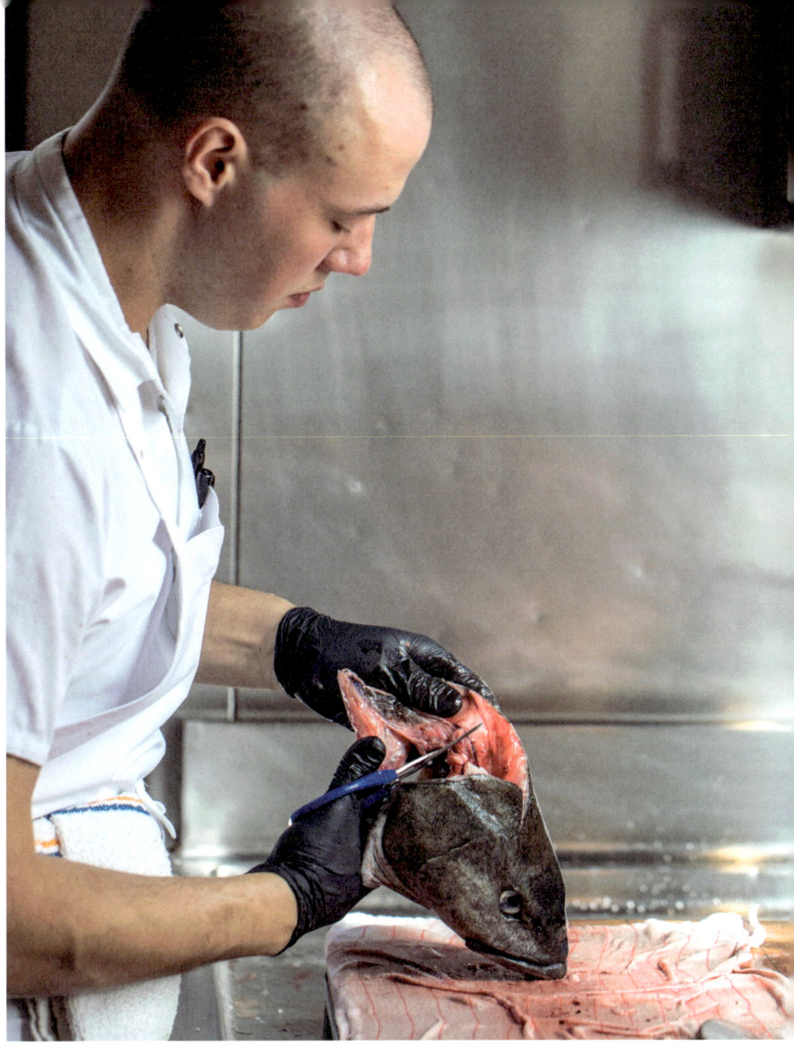
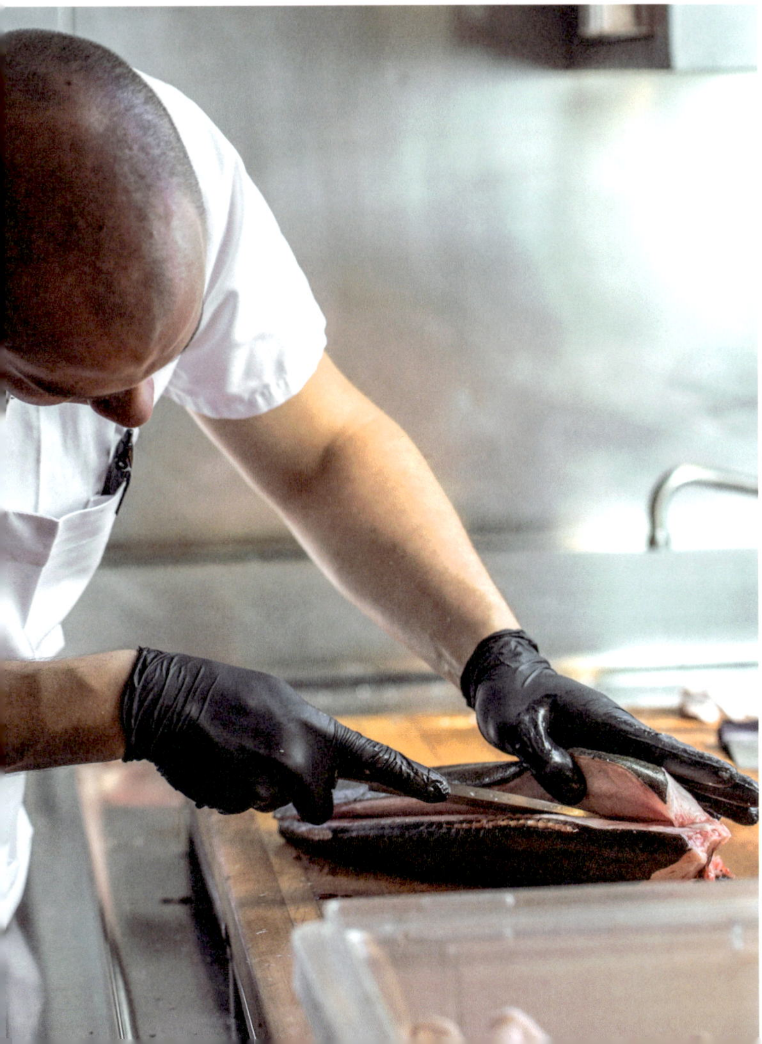
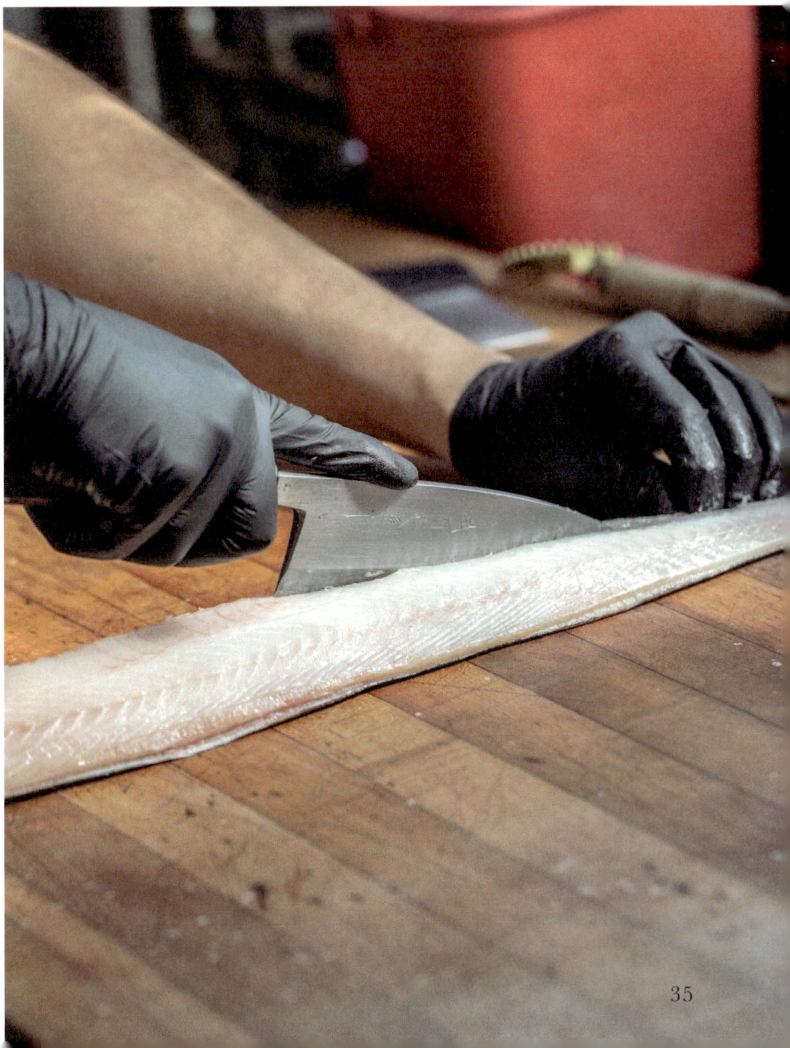

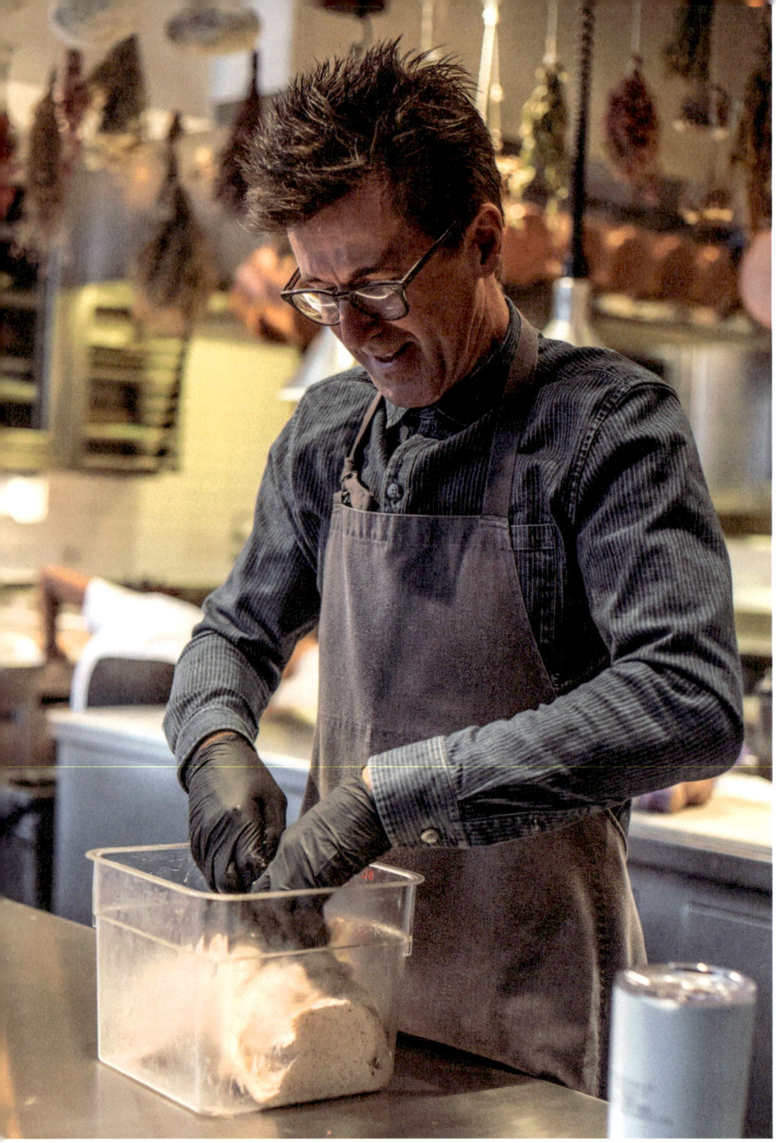

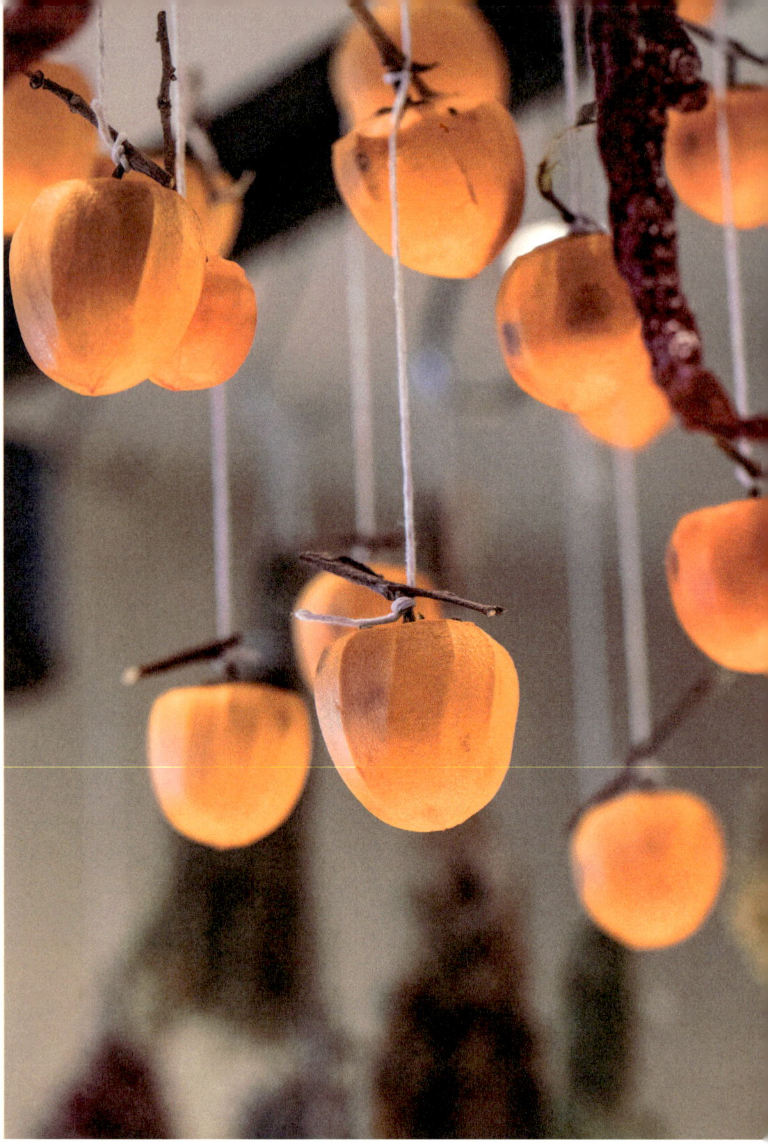

Are you still cycling?

Yeah. I ride Sundays and Mondays. When I was in New York, I was fit and would ride 200 miles a week. I was 10 pounds lighter than I am now. I was really skinny but very strong. I put 12,000-15,000 miles a year on my bike, and 40 races a year.

Is it hard to cycle now that you're cooking?

I can't do both. When I race, it involves high-intensity training, recovery, and sleeping ten hours a night. To race, I need to put myself in a position where I'm in my top condition because there is no way you can win a race without it.

I have a hard time thinking about exercising after working in the kitchen all week.

Yeah, but it's good for so many different reasons. I started cycling in Chicago to relieve stress. When you're tired, and you exercise and push yourself, the fatigue goes away. You're tired from the exercise, but it is like you've washed the body.

Your state of mind is the most crucial thing in your work. I think the state of mind translates to how your body functions and the life you give to yourself. Rest is crucial so that you have the low to balance the high. When I raced, I trained hard, rested hard, ate well, and didn't drink. I think the kitchen is the same. You need to push at work, you have to rest, and you have to eat well. Use your time off to create a balance within yourself. Cooks need to make themselves a strong car. It is a very physical job, so if you have weak legs, then you're going to be tired. If your legs are strong, then you can run every day and be fine. Core strength gives you stability within your body and allows you to perform at the highest level. If you have proper nutrition, and good rest, then you can have more focus and increase your performance.

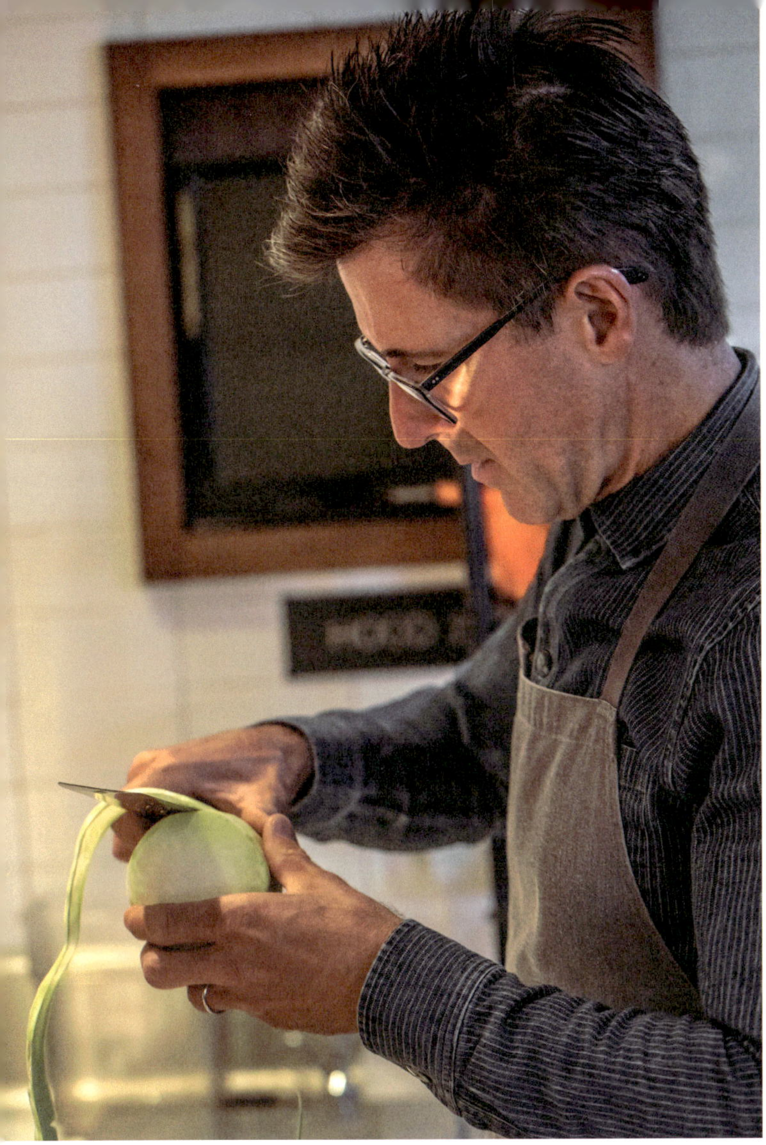

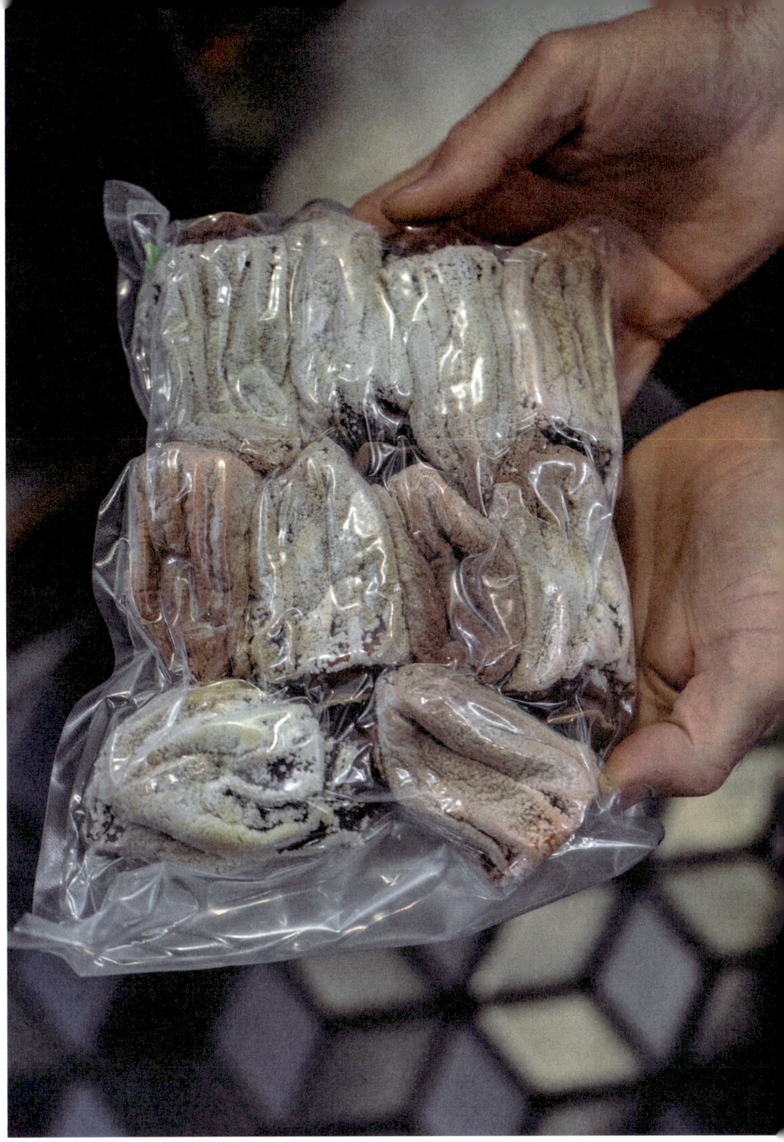

You seem like the type of person that is 100% dedicated to anything you do.

When I'm cycling, I'm 100% into it. When I'm cooking, I'm 100% into cooking, and when I rest, I'm 100% into resting.

How did you get involved with using equipment like a Gastrovac machine? I feel like you were one of the first chefs I heard of using them.

I'm very interested in technology, and I believe it can give you an edge. I love Formula One racing, for example, and I follow not only the calendar and the races but also the way those companies work. The number one factor is who has the best technology and resources. So, If I can take the old techniques of cooking, which are the foundations of flavor, and incorporate new technology, then I can do something new with a better result. I have a totally open mind for things like that.

What are your immediate plans for the future?

I try not to force anything, and I want to let things happen in a very natural way. I like to say that I'm just going with the flow. Whatever happens today will shape the restaurant tomorrow. The long term plan is the people here, the relationships we build, and the opportunities we can create. I want our values, our interests, and our work to evolve the restaurant organically.

Are you at all chasing the accolades like Michelin or Pellegrino's World's 50 Best Restaurants List?

I've never chased that. Even when I was 20 years old, I was more focused on the work. Instead of pursuing something you can't control, I want to create a team around me and an amazing space for us to enjoy ourselves. It's great to get recognition for what you have done, but it is not where a chef's focus should be.

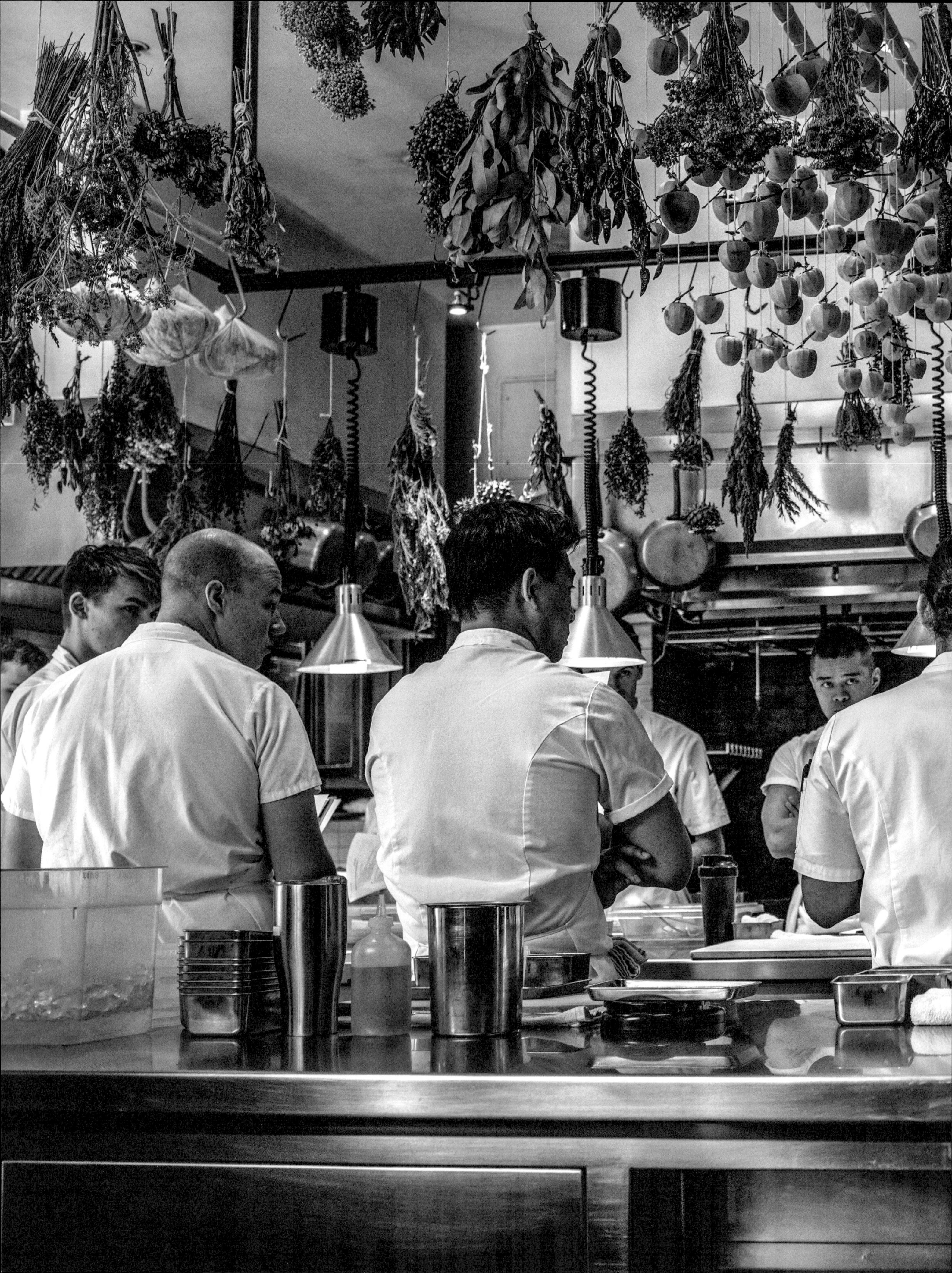

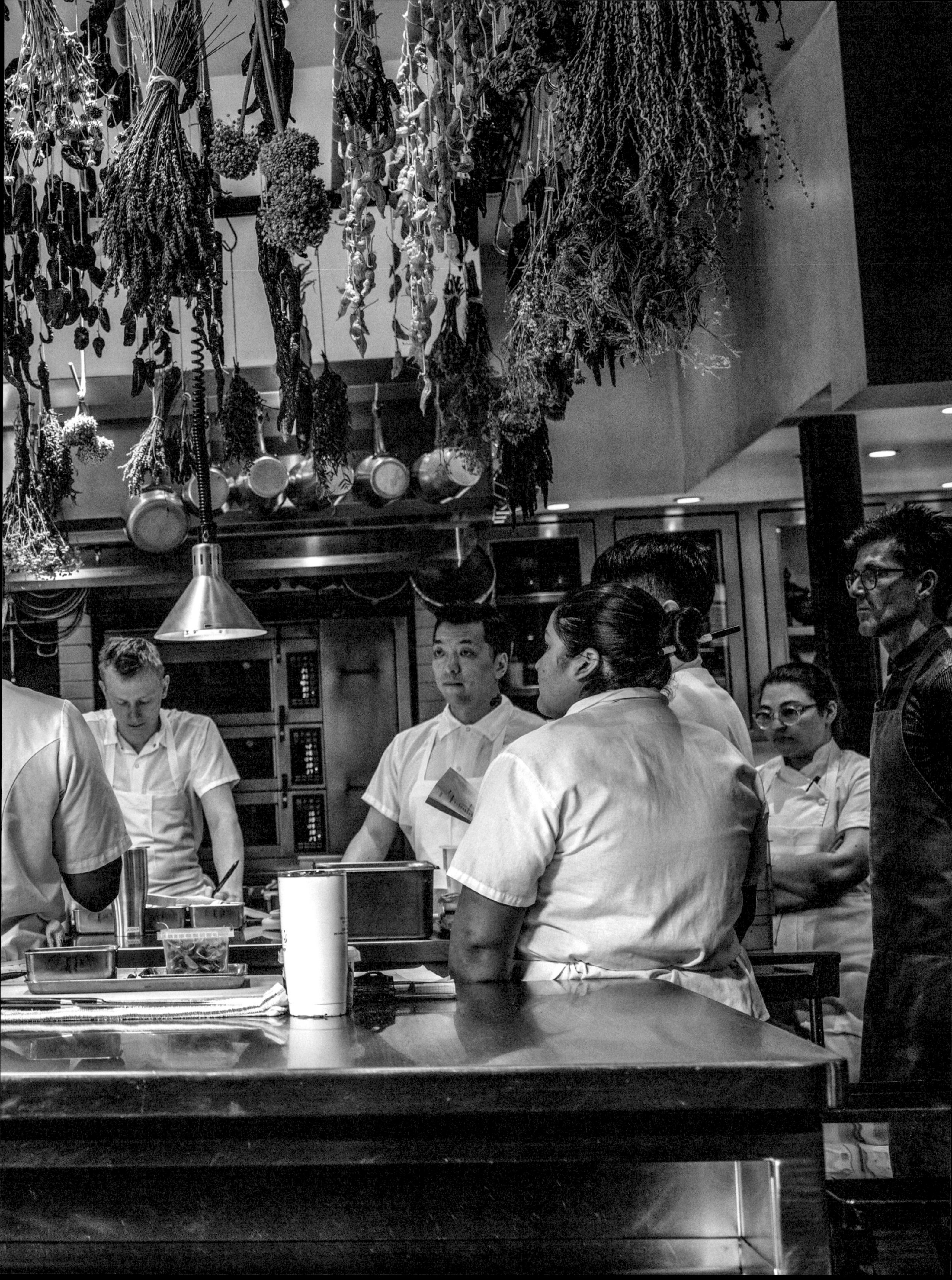

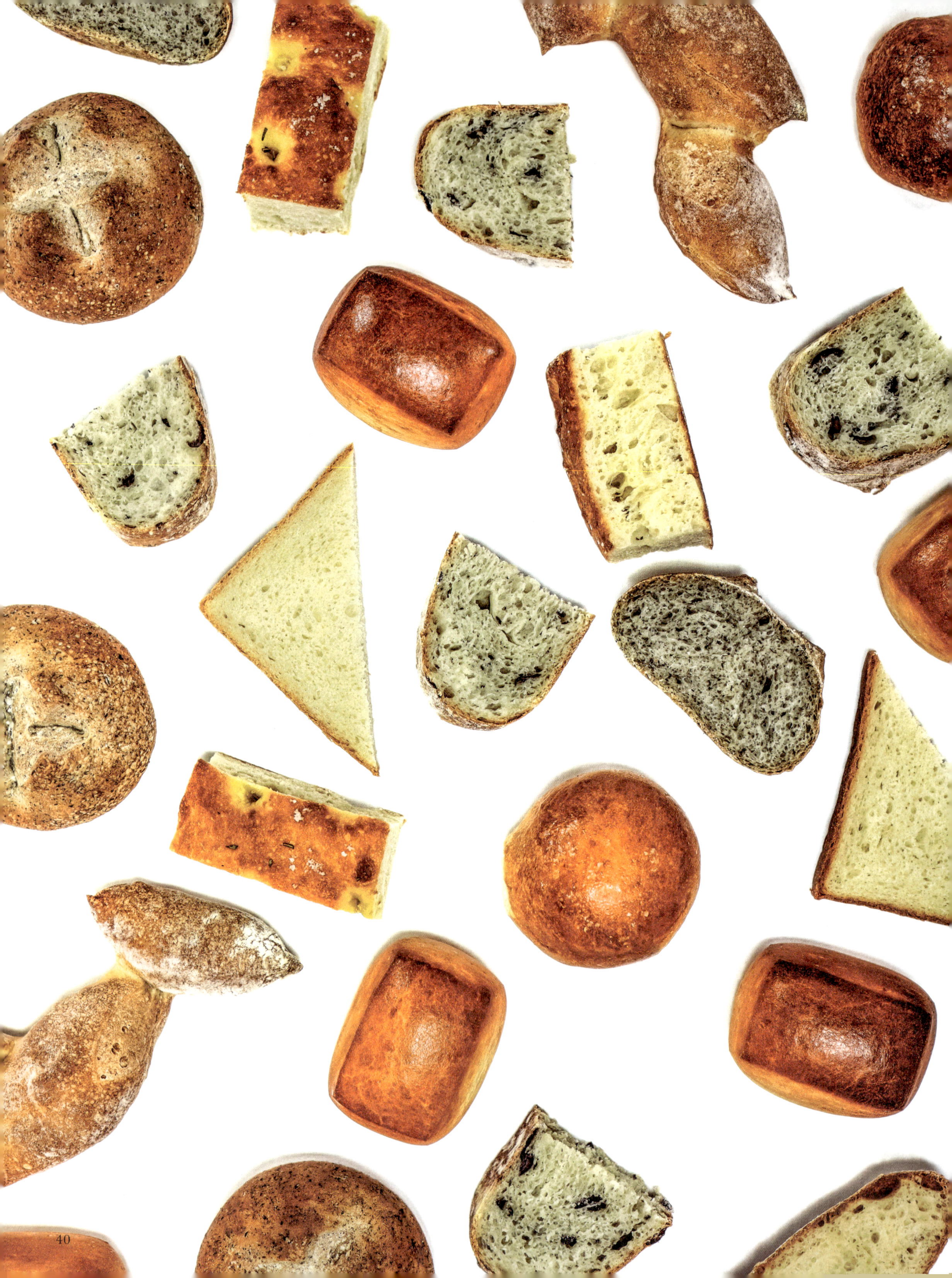

BAKING BREAD

WITHIN A RESTAURANT

by nick muncy

toothache magazine
michael mina
san francisco, ca

Being a pastry chef, I need to be a jack of all trades. Even though my main job is creating plated desserts, I need to know chocolate work, bread, cakes, and even some savory cooking. With this feature, I wanted to show some great breads to execute in the restaurant environment.

The first big thing to remember is: a restaurant is not a bakery. The majority of restaurants don't have a deck oven or other necessary equipment to create amazing bread. The problem is, everyone wants to make these large dark loaves of crusty, high-hydration, open crumb levain bread. And I get it; those breads are delicious. But why attempt to make a bread that a bakery can produce at a higher level? Are you giving people a better experience by offering a flawed bread just because it's unique to the restaurant? A truly great bread baker needs years and years of mastery and is continually learning. Interestingly enough, many times restaurants, we believe the 22-year-old savory cook who read some cookbooks, is the one who is going to make our bread.

I believe enriched bread, meaning doughs with other things added to it other than flour, water, salt, and yeast, is what a restaurant should focus on creating. Will a guest see buttery parker house rolls or flavorful focaccia as less of a bread service in comparison to a deeply baked sourdough? Baking these breads remove

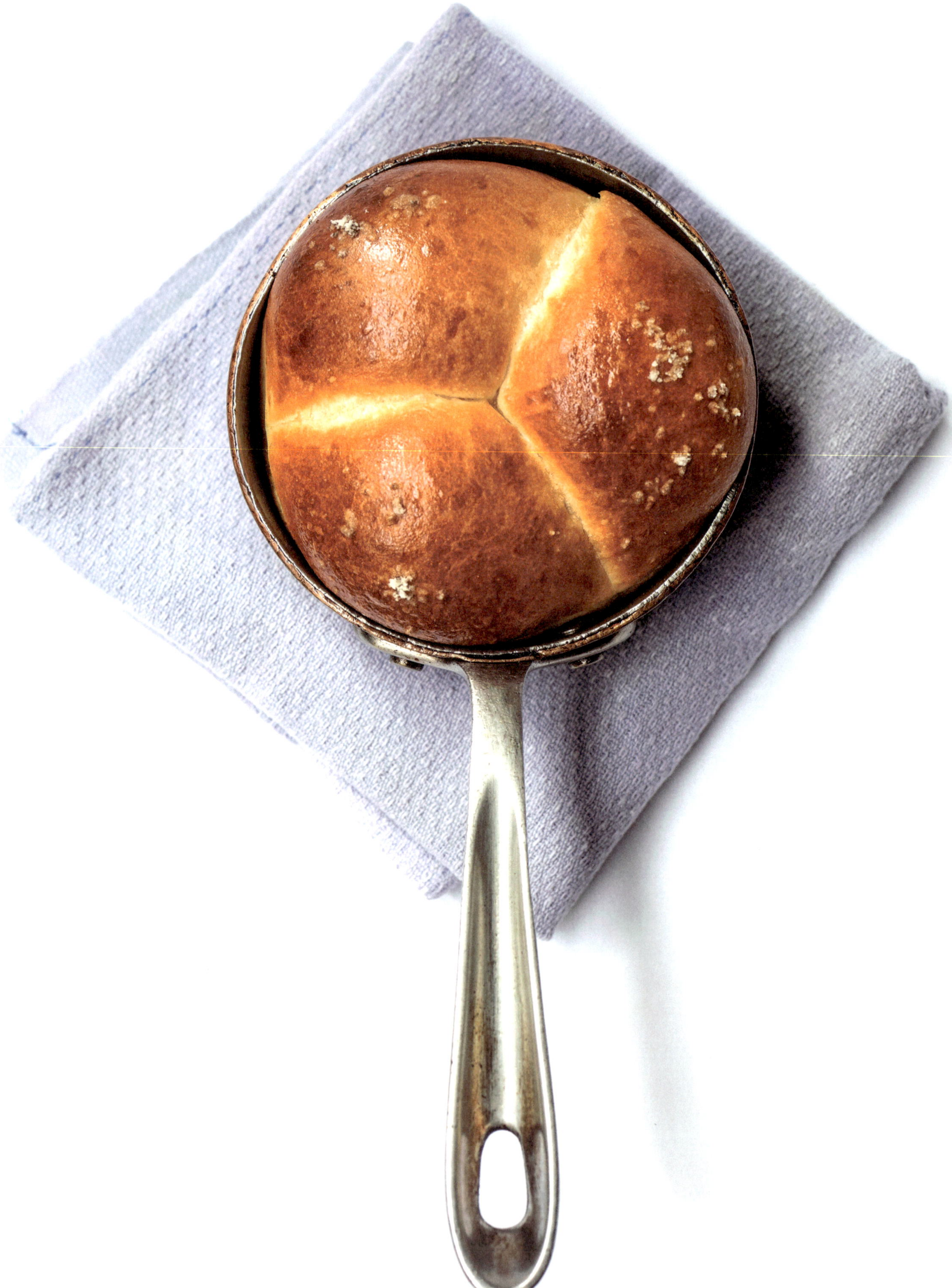

many of the biggest baking obstacles. I purposefully picked recipes that do not include sourdough starter (because most people don't understand them well), and instead use commercial yeast for day to day consistency. All of these recipes were made using a convection oven and without a proof box. I wanted this to be a way for all cooks to create delicious bread for the equipment found in a typical restaurant.

To be honest, some bread knowledge and kitchen common sense are necessary for these recipes. These recipes were tested in a California kitchen in the fall. If you live in New Orleans and you're baking in the summer, your proofing times will need to be adjusted.

A good rule that I use to tell if the bread is properly proofed is: The bread should rise, but when you press firmly with a finger, the indentation shouldn't spring back. If you press the dough with your finger, and it starts to deflate, you're on the verge of it over proofing, and you need to quickly and gently get it in the oven. It the bread has risen and is now fallen saggy and sad looking, it's dead and should be tossed in the bin.

Good luck, and I hope this inspires a few cooks out there to start baking bread.

Parker House Rolls

Dough:

Ingredients:

1500 g	bread flour
1500 g	all-purpose flour
120 g	sugar
60 g	salt
36 g	dry yeast
2100 g	milk, cold
700 g	butter, softened

Mix:
In a large mixer bowl, hydrate the yeast and milk together. Place the flours, sugar, and salt into the bowl and mix on speed 1 for 3 minutes. Turn the mixer to speed 2 for 3 minutes, then add the butter. Mix the butter in on speed 2 for 4 minutes. After the mixing, remove from the bowl and place it on a lightly floured table. Divide the dough into four equal portions and wrap in plastic wrap. Place on a sheet tray and freeze.

Fermentation and Shaping:
Remove the dough from the freezer the night before and let defrost in the refrigerator. The next day, place the dough at room temperature for 1 hour. Portion the tempered dough into 54-60g pieces using a lightly floured surface to keep the dough from sticking. Shape the dough into small boules and place 5x7 on a half sheet tray with sprayed parchement. Loosely cover the top of the dough with plastic wrap and let proof for 1 hour and 15 minutes in a warm(but not hot!) area. Before baking, carefully brush with egg wash and sprinkle finishing salt.

Bake:
Preheat a convection oven to 400F. Bake for 14 minutes with high fan until nicely browned. Let cool on a rack before serving.

Notes:
This dough can also be proofed and baked in a small copper pot or any other baking vessels you want. You want to make sure that the dough is close enough in whatever vessel you bake so that they proof and bake together into a pull-apart bread. You could also think about replacing portions of the milk with other liquids to flavor the bread, such as buttermilk, squid ink, and vegetable juices. Other fun variations could be replacing half of the all-purpose flour with whole wheat flour, buckwheat flour, or rye flour.

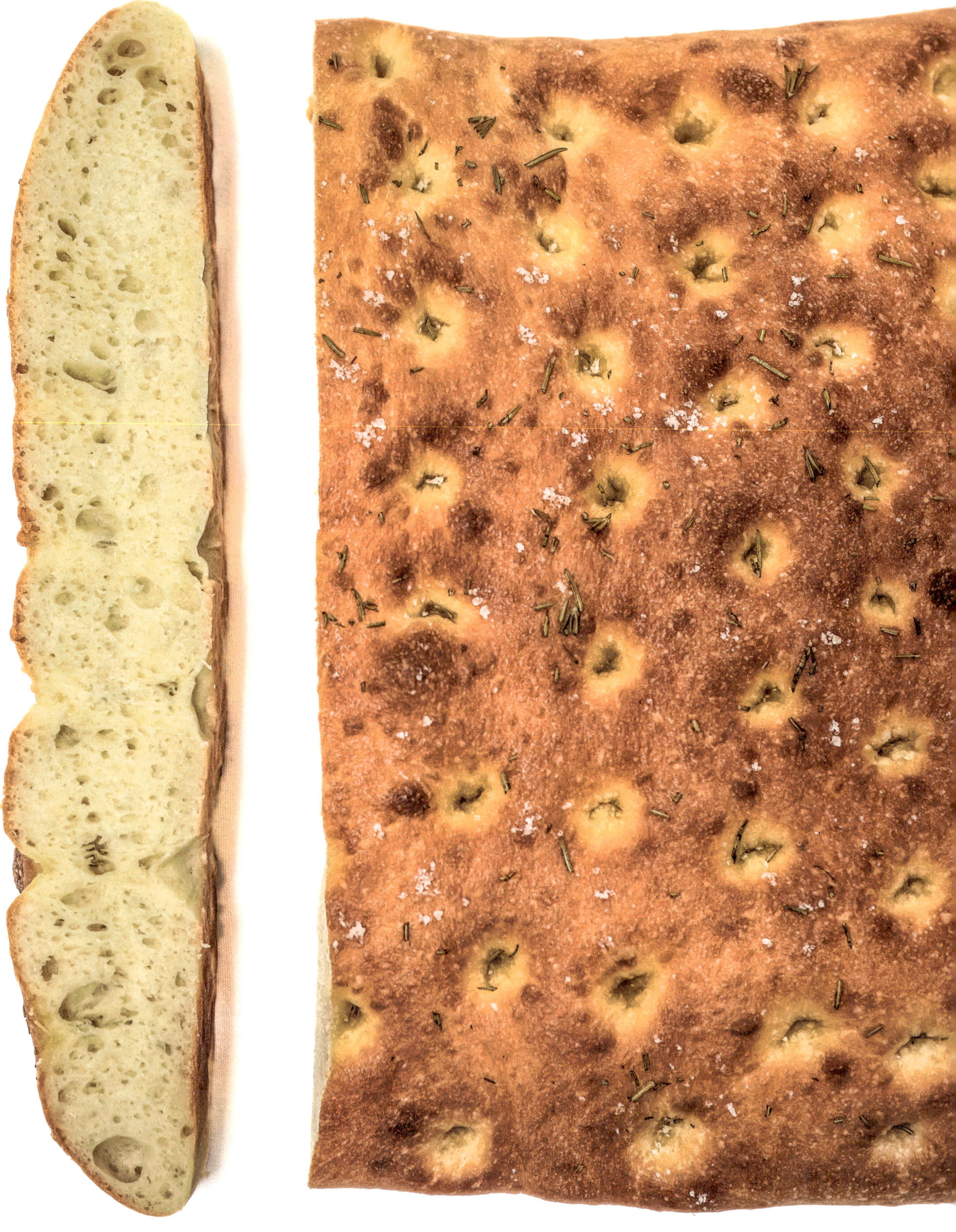

Focaccia

Dough:

Ingredients:

poolish:

500 g	all-purpose flour
500 g	water, room temperature
6 g	dry yeast

dough:

1000 g	all-purpose flour
60 g	sugar
34 g	salt
6 g	barley malt
60 g	olive oil
8 g	dry yeast
400 g	water, room temperature

Preferment:

For the poolish, combine all of the ingredients and place them in a container overnight in the refrigerator.

Mix:

Remove the poolish from the refrigerator. In a mixer bowl, combine the water, poolish, yeast, and olive oil. In a separate bowl, combine the flour, sugar, salt and malt. Place the dry ingredient mix on top of the wet ingredients and mix with the dough hook on speed 1 for 2 mintues. Turn the mixer to speed 2 and mix for an additional 6 minutes. Place the bowl in a greased container and cover.

Fermentation and Shaping:

Place the container of dough in a warm, but not hot, area. Let proof for 40 minutes. Fold the dough in from each side as if to make the dough into a square. Return the dough to a warm spot and proof for another 30 minutes. Flour a table and carefully invert the dough, making sure to keep it in its square shape. With a rolling pin, lightly roll the dough out to half an inch thickness. Transfer the dough to a sheet tray that has been lined with parchment paper and sprayed with grease. Lightly over the top of the dough and let the dough final proof for 1 hour.

Bake:

Preheat a convection oven to 400F. Liberally coat the surface of the bread with olive oil and press dimples into the dough. I like to use a wine cork to do this. Drizzle additional olive oil over the top and sprinkle sea salt and whatever flavors you'd like. Bake for 12-14 minutes with high fan until nicely browned. Let cool on a rack before serving.

Pain au Lait

Dough:

Ingredients:

2000 g	bread flour
2000 g	all-purpose flour
160 g	sugar
80 g	salt
144 g	fresh yeast
2800 g	milk, cold
800 g	butter, softened

Mix:

In a large mixer bowl, place the yeast and milk together. Top with the flours, sugar, and salt and mix on speed 1 for 6 minutes. Turn the mixer to speed 2 for 6 minutes, then add the butter. Mix the butter in on speed 2 for 6 minutes. After the mixing, remove from the bowl and place it on a lightly floured table. Divide the dough into 6 equal portions and wrap in plastic wrap. Place on a sheet tray and freeze.

Fermentation and Shaping:

Remove the dough from the freezer the night before and let defrost in the refrigerator. The next day, pull one dough at a time from the refrigerator to roll out. Using a rolling pin (or a sheeter if you're lucky), roll the dough out into a large rectangle approximatley 1/3 inch thick. Fold the dough as if to make a simple book fold. Roll out again into a longer rectangle and book fold again to form an even square of dough. When rolling the dough, avoid using too much flour or brush the flour off between folding so that the dough adheres to itself. Wrap the square of folded dough in sprayed plastic and place back in the freezer for 1 hour. Repeat the process until all the blocks of dough have been folded. Once the dough is firm and cold, but not frozen, place onto a floured table and roll out to approximatley 2/3 inch thickness. Cut into squares, making sure that the cut is straight vertically. If cut on an angle, the dough will rise and bake slanted. Place the squares of cut dough on a sheet tray with sprayed parchment and proof at room temperature for around 1 hour 20 minutes. Once proofed, lightly brush the top of the dough with egg wash, making sure to avoid getting egg on the sides of the dough.

Bake:

Preheat a convection oven to 400F. Bake for 12 minutes with high fan until nicely browned. Depending on your oven, this may take a few minutes longer. The key is that the top and sides are all evenly browned. Let cool before serving.

Notes:

This bread seems labor-intensive because of the book folding. The reason we book fold the dough is so that it pulls apart in layers. Oftentimes, you can see the layers in the final baked bread.

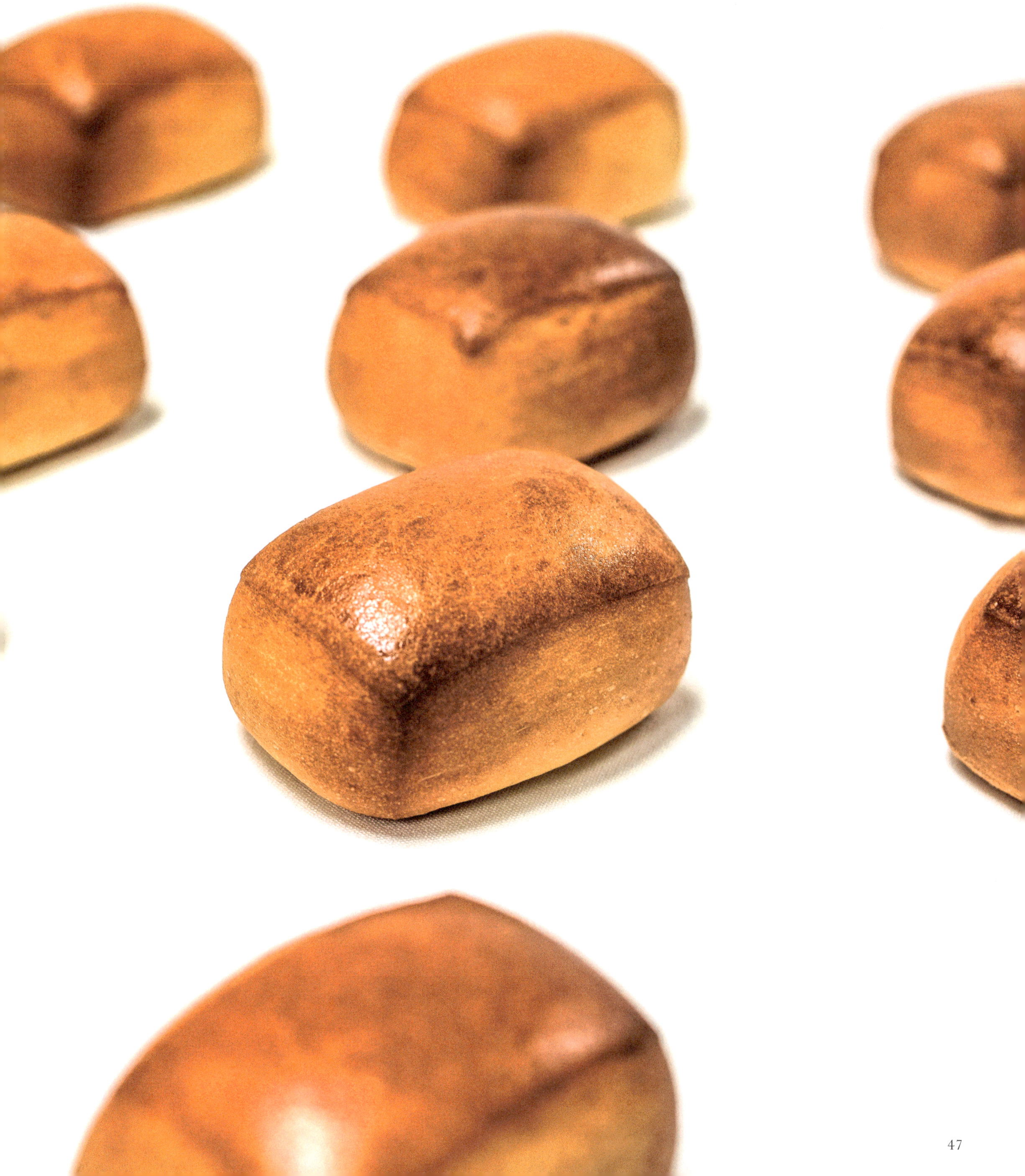

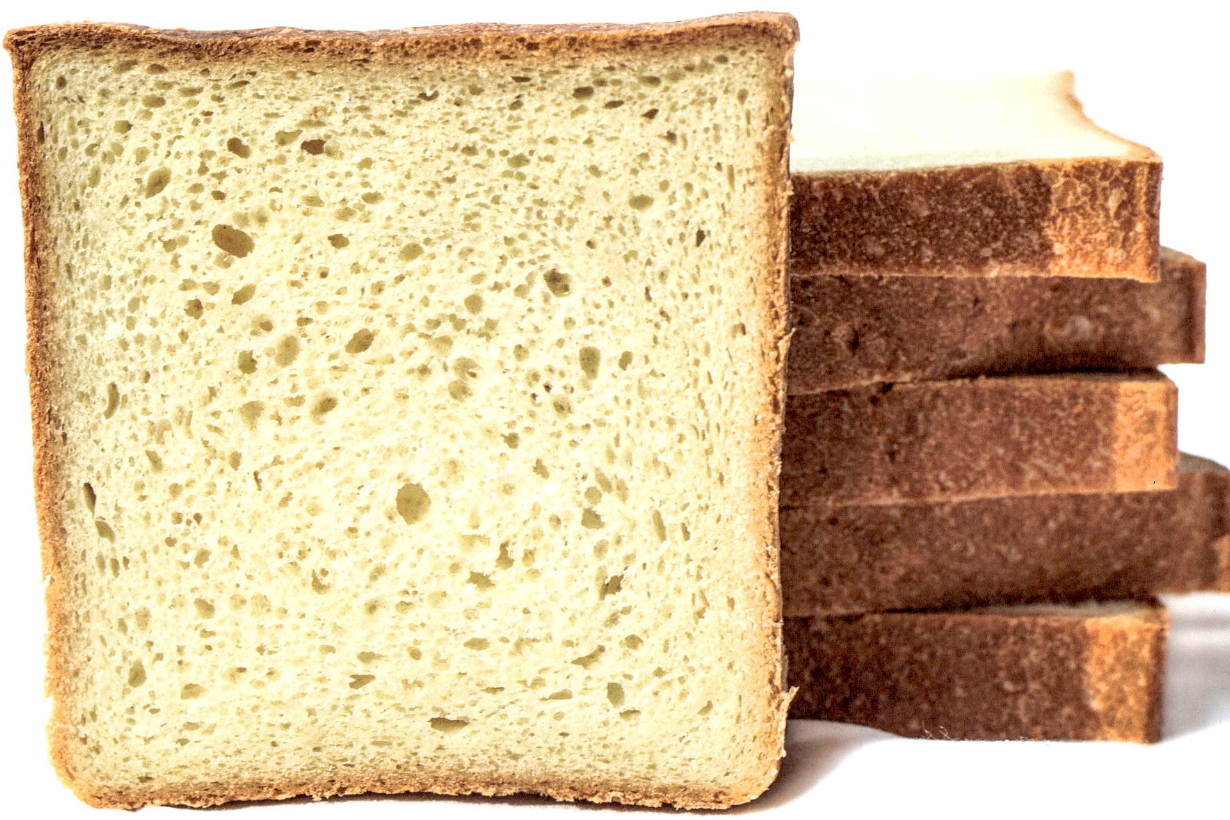

Pain de Mie (White Bread)

Dough:

Ingredients:

1000 g	bread flour
40 g	sugar
20 g	salt
60 g	butter, softened
5 g	malt
100 g	milk
8 g	dry yeast
5 g	glucose syrup
600 g	water, room temperature

Mix:

In a large mixer bowl, place the wet ingredients, followed by the dry ingredients on top. With the hook attachment, mix on speed 1 for 2 minutes. Turn the speed up to 2, and mix for an additional 6 minutes. The dough should pull away from the sides of the bowl and look homogenous and smooth. Remove from the bowl and place it in a greased container.

Fermentation and Shaping:

Bulk proof the dough for 10 minutes, and then fold from each side of the dough. Proof for an hour, and then invert onto a lightly floured table. Shape the dough to fit into a greased pullman loaf pan. Make sure to grease the lid of the pullman loaf pan as well so that it doesn't stick. Proof in the pan for 1:30-2 hours, or until the dough is just about to reach the top of the pan.

Bake:

Preheat a convection oven to 375F. Bake for 40 minutes with high fan until nicely browned. Remove the dough from the pan and let cool on a rack fully before slicing or serving.

Notes:

I have incorporated squid ink into this recipe before to make a very stark black dough for savory use. This dough is very easy to work with, and you could incorporate many different flavors into it.

Seaweed Bread

Dough:

Ingredients:

1400 g	bread flour
100 g	rye flour
1065 g	water, room temperature
22 g	dry yeast
30 g	olive oil
4 g	malt
30 g	salt
30 g	sea lettuce, ground

Mix:

In a large mixing bowl, combine the water, yeast, and olive oil. Add the flours and malt to the top and mix by hand until a shaggy dough forms. Let sit for 15 minutes. Add the sea lettuce and salt and mix on speed 1 for 6 minutes. Scrape the bowl and then mix on speed 2 for 2 minutes. Remove from the mixer and place it in a greased bin.

Fermentation and Shaping:

Let sit at room temperature for 15 minutes, and then fold the dough. Let proof for an hour and then fold again. Put the dough in the walk-in refrigerator and let retard overnight.

The next day, remove the bread from the refrigerator and let sit at room temperature for 30 minutes. Invert the dough onto a lightly floured table and portion the dough into your desired size. I portion mine for individual rolls to 60g. After all the dough is portioned, immediately pre-shape the dough. Cover loosely with plastic and let sit for 40 minutes. Final shape the dough into boules and place on sheet trays lined with sprayed parchment. Once the dough is all shaped and on sheet trays, loosely cover with plastic wrap and proof for 1 hour 30 minutes.

Bake:

Preheat a convection oven to 475F with a small sheet tray on the bottom of the oven. Score the tops of the dough in the shape of an "X" and lightly spray the boules with water by using a spray bottle. Place the trays of bread in the oven and pour a cup of water on the hot pan at the bottom of the oven. This will add steam to your convection oven. Once you've added the water and closed the door, drop the temperature to 450, and bake for 4 minutes with high fan. Quickly rotate the bread trays so that they bake evenly and close the oven immediately so that they do not deflate. Drop the oven fan to low and bake for 12 more minutes. Let cool at room temperature.

Since we are not using a deck oven, these breads will have a very thin crust that gets soft once cooled. To remedy this, a la minute during dinner service, I will place the bread in the oven at 350F for 5-7 minutes to re-crisp the outside crust as well as warm the inside through. That way, the guest receives warm bread with a nice crunchy crust.

Notes:

Adding the steam to the oven is what will give your bread a nice color. If there isn't enough steam and your bread comes out dull, a cheating hack is to grease a towel with oil lightly and gently brush the outside of the bread. This will help show the color of the bread.

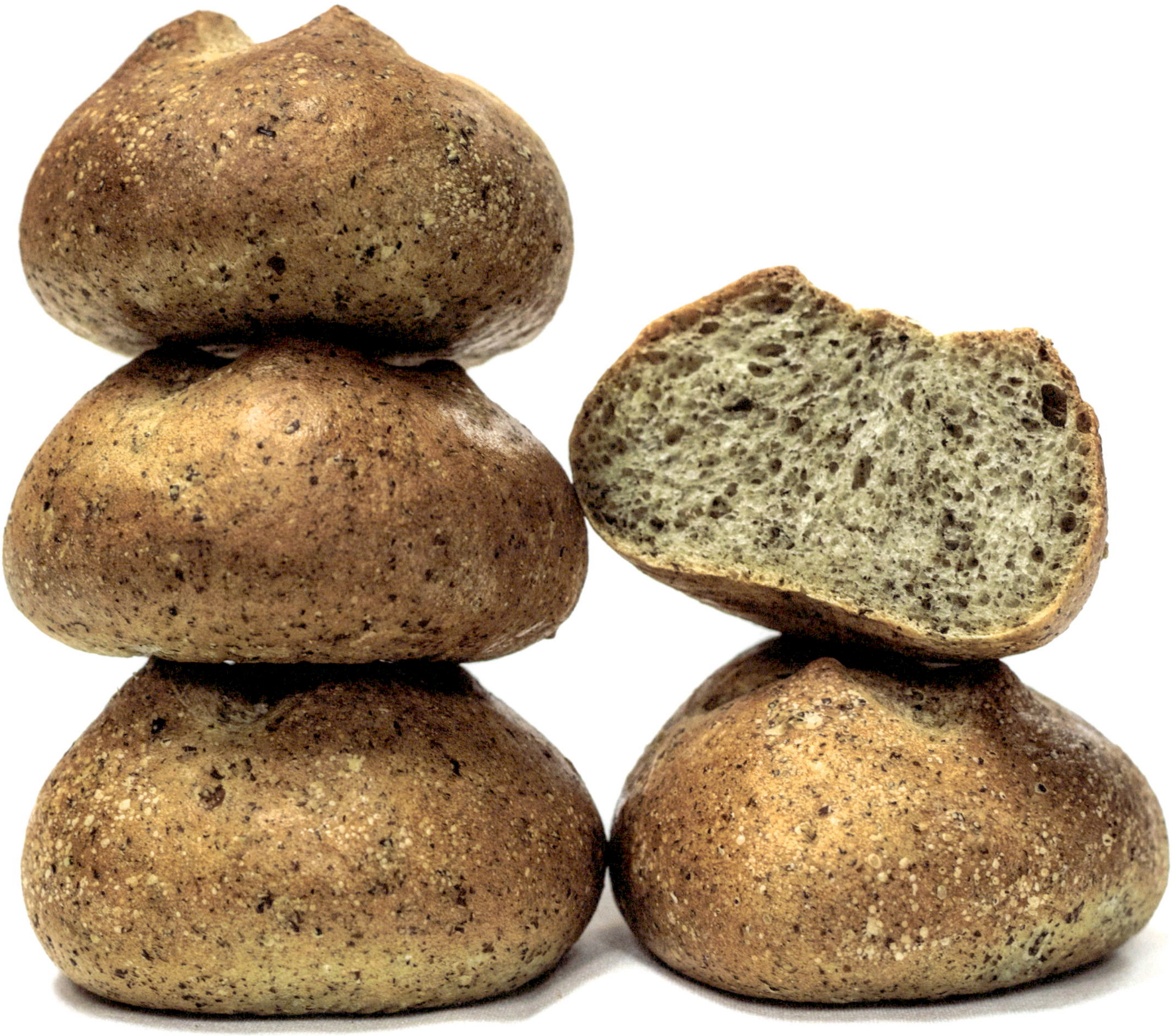

Olive Bread

Dough:

Ingredients:

poolish:

1500 g	all-purpose flour
1500 g	water, room temperature
8 g	dry yeast

final dough:

630 g	water, room temperature
36 g	fresh yeast
60 g	olive oil
3000 g	poolish
1500 g	bread flour
9 g	malt
660 g	olives, pitted, chopped
63 g	salt

Preferment:

For the poolish, combine all of the ingredients together and place it in a container overnight in the refrigerator.

Mix:

In a large mixing bowl, combine the water, yeast, poolish, and olive oil. Add the flours and malt to the top and mix by hand until a shaggy dough forms. Let sit for 15 minutes. Add the salt and mix on speed 1 for 5 minutes. Scrape the bowl and then mix on speed 2 for 6 minutes. Add the olives and mix on speed 2 for 6 minutes. Remove from the mixer and place in a greased bin.

Fermentation and Shaping:

Let sit at room temperature for 10 minutes, and then fold the dough. Let proof for an hour and then fold again. Let the dough proof for 30 minutes and then invert the dough onto a lightly floured table and portion the dough into your desired size. After all the dough is portioned, immediately preshape the dough. Cover loosely with plastic and let sit for 30 minutes. Final shape the dough into boules and place in floured baskets. Cover with plastic and proof for 45 minutes.

Bake:

Preheat a convection oven to 500F with a small sheet tray on the bottom of the oven. Invert the dough out of the baskets onto a silpat lined sheet tray. Score the tops of the dough and lightly spray the dough with water using a spray bottle. Place the trays of bread in the oven and pour a cup of water on the hot pan at the bottom of the oven. This will add steam to your convection oven. Once you've added the water and closed the door, bake for 10 minutes with high fan. Quickly rotate the bread trays so that they bake evenly and close the oven immediately so that they do not deflate. Drop the oven fan to low and bake for 10 more minutes. Rotate the bread again and bake for 5 more minutes. Let cool at room temperature.

Since we are not using a deck oven, these breads will have a very thin crust that gets soft once cooled. To remedy this, a la minute during dinner service, I will place the bread in the oven at 350F for 5-7 minutes to re-crisp the oustide crust as well as warm the inside through. I then cut the bread lengthwise down the center and then slice the bread into thick slices. That way the guest receives warm bread with a nice crunchy crust.

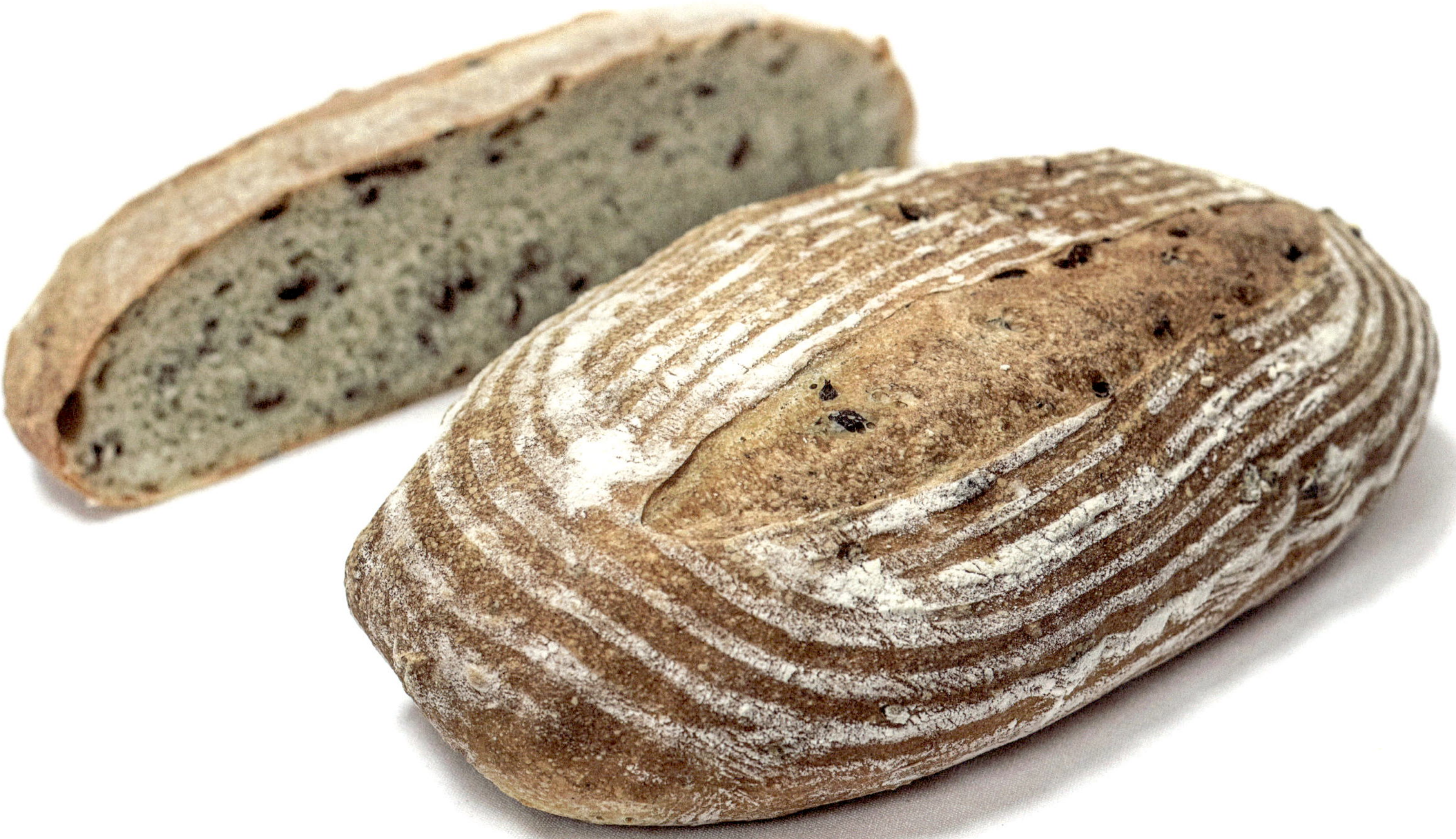

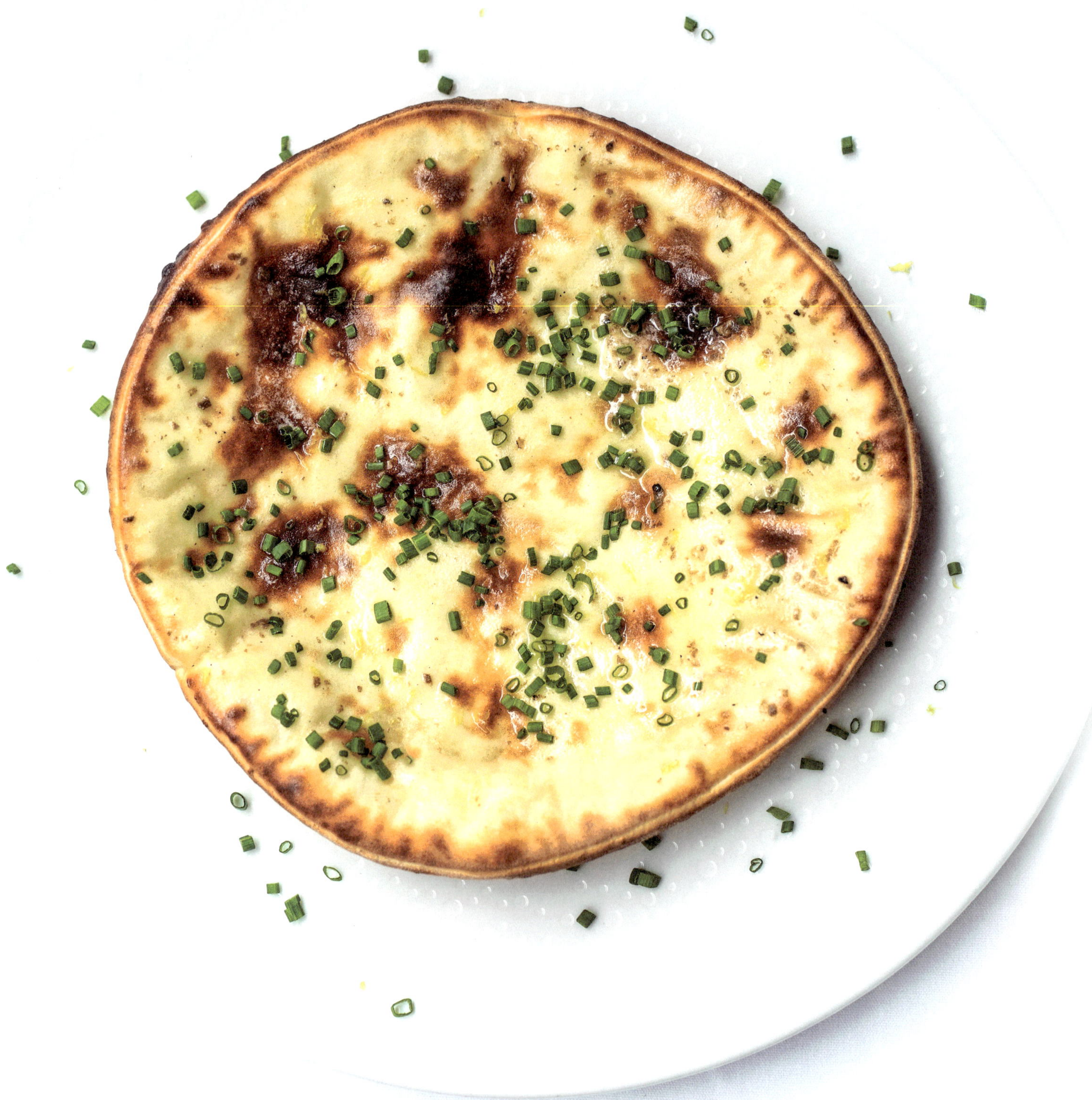

Dough:

Ingredients:

500 g	milk
900 g	water, cold
100 g	whole egg
200 g	heavy cream
65 g	olive oil
64 g	baking powder
60 g	salt
2825 g	all-purpose flour

Mix:

In a large mixer bowl, place all of the wet ingredients in the bottom followed by the dry ingredients. Mix with the hook attachment on speed 1 for 12 minutes. Transfer to a greased container and cover with plastic wrap and a lid. Retard overnight in the refrigerator.

Shaping:

Remove the dough from the refrigerator. Using a sheeter, sheet down to 1. If using a rolling pin, roll out thin on a floured surface, but not to the point that the dough is seethrough. Punch into circles or desired shape.

Bake:

Preheat a convection oven to 500F with an inverted sheet tray or pizza stone. Bake on high fan until brown blisters appear and the dough has souffled. Around 1-2 minutes.

Brush the dough with butter and sprinkle the top with whatever flavorings you would like. The version pictured is brushed with truffle butter, and seasoned with salt, lemon zest, and chives.

Baguette / Epi

Dough:

Ingredients:

1000 g	all-purpose flour
21 g	salt
3.3 g	dry yeast
1 g	malt
680 g	water

Mix:

Place all the ingredients except the salt in a large mixing bowl. Mix with the hook attachment on speed 1 for 3 minutes. Let the dough sit for 20 minutes. Add the salt, and then mix the dough on speed 1 for 4 minutes. Turn the mixer up to speed 2 and mix for 1 minute. Remove the dough from the mixer and place in a greased bin. Check the temperature of the dough; it should be around (24C).

Fermentation and Shaping:

Bulk ferment the dough at room temperature for 2 hours. Fold the dough, and then proof another hour. For baguettes and epi, portion the dough to 350g. Preshape the dough and proof 30 minutes. Final shape the dough and proof another hour.

Bake:

Preheat a convection oven to 450F with a small sheet tray on the bottom of the oven. Score the tops of the dough or cut the epi with scissors and lightly spray with water by using a spray bottle. Place the trays of bread in the oven and pour a cup of water on the hot pan at the bottom of the oven. This will add steam to your convection oven. Once you've added the water and closed the door, drop the temperature to 425, and bake for 10 minutes with high fan. Quickly rotate the bread trays so that they bake evenly and close the oven immediately so that they do not deflate. Drop the oven fan to low and bake for 12-14 more minutes. Let cool at room temperature.

Since we are not using a deck oven, these breads will have a very thin crust that gets soft once cooled. To remedy this, a la minute during dinner service, I will place the bread in the oven at 350F for 5-7 minutes to re-crisp the outside crust as well as warm the inside through. That way, the guest receives warm bread with a nice crunchy crust.

Notes:

This is a good base dough to add other flavors. You could add roasted garlic, olive and feta, or other flavors into it. This dough can also be used to make petit breads.

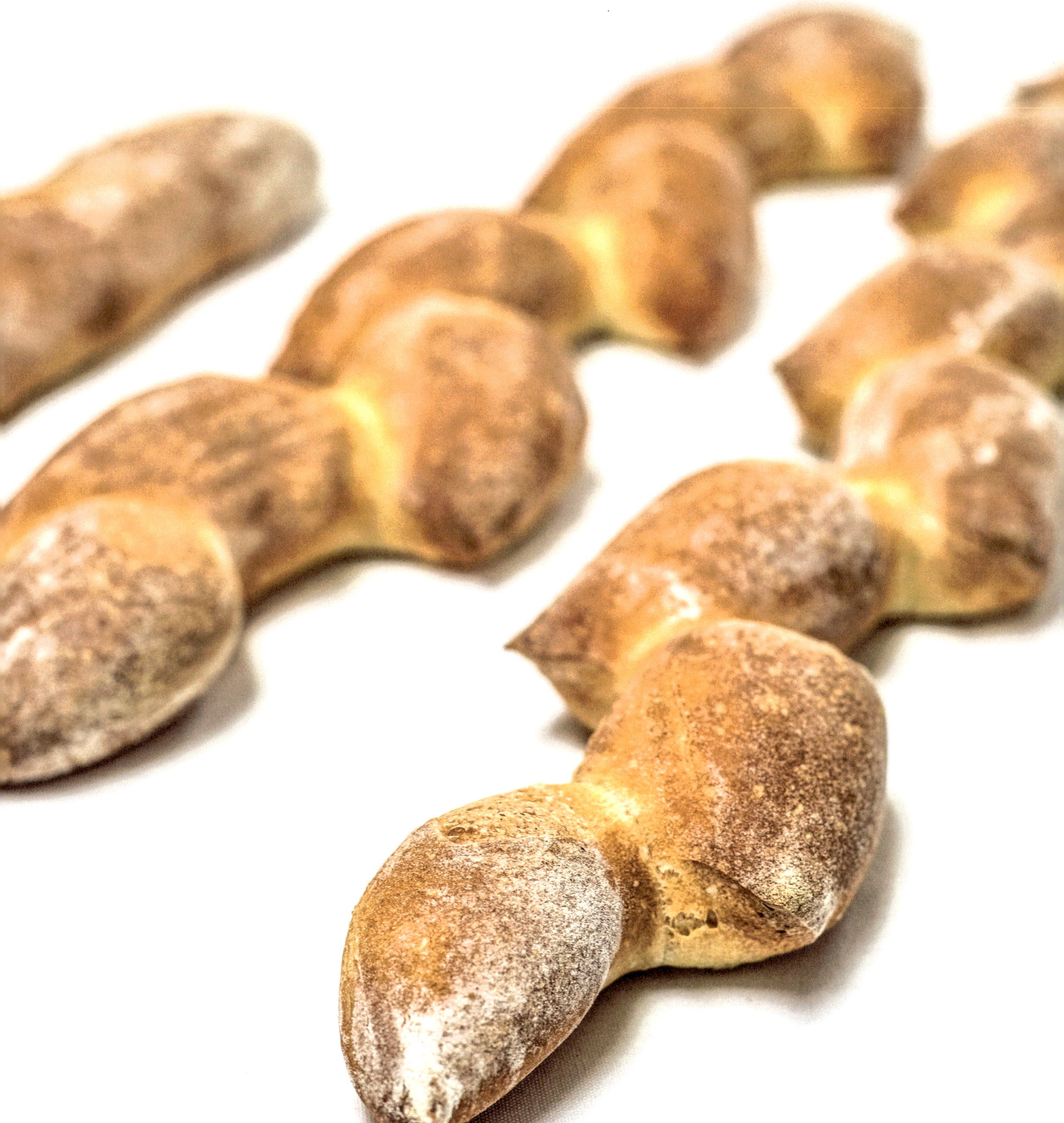

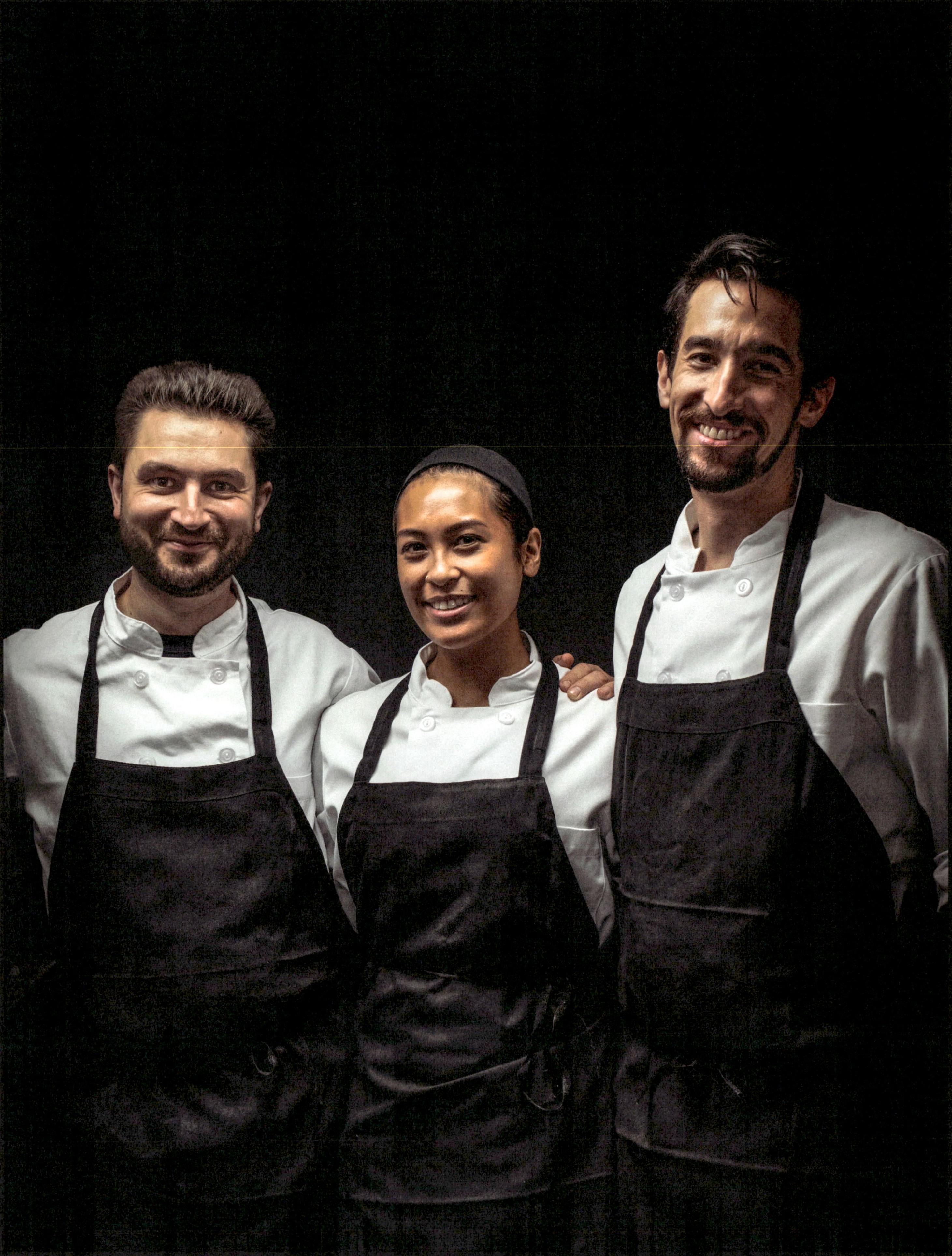

creativity is creation and creation hurts

alex stupak
justin binnie
elianne padlan

empellón
new york, ny

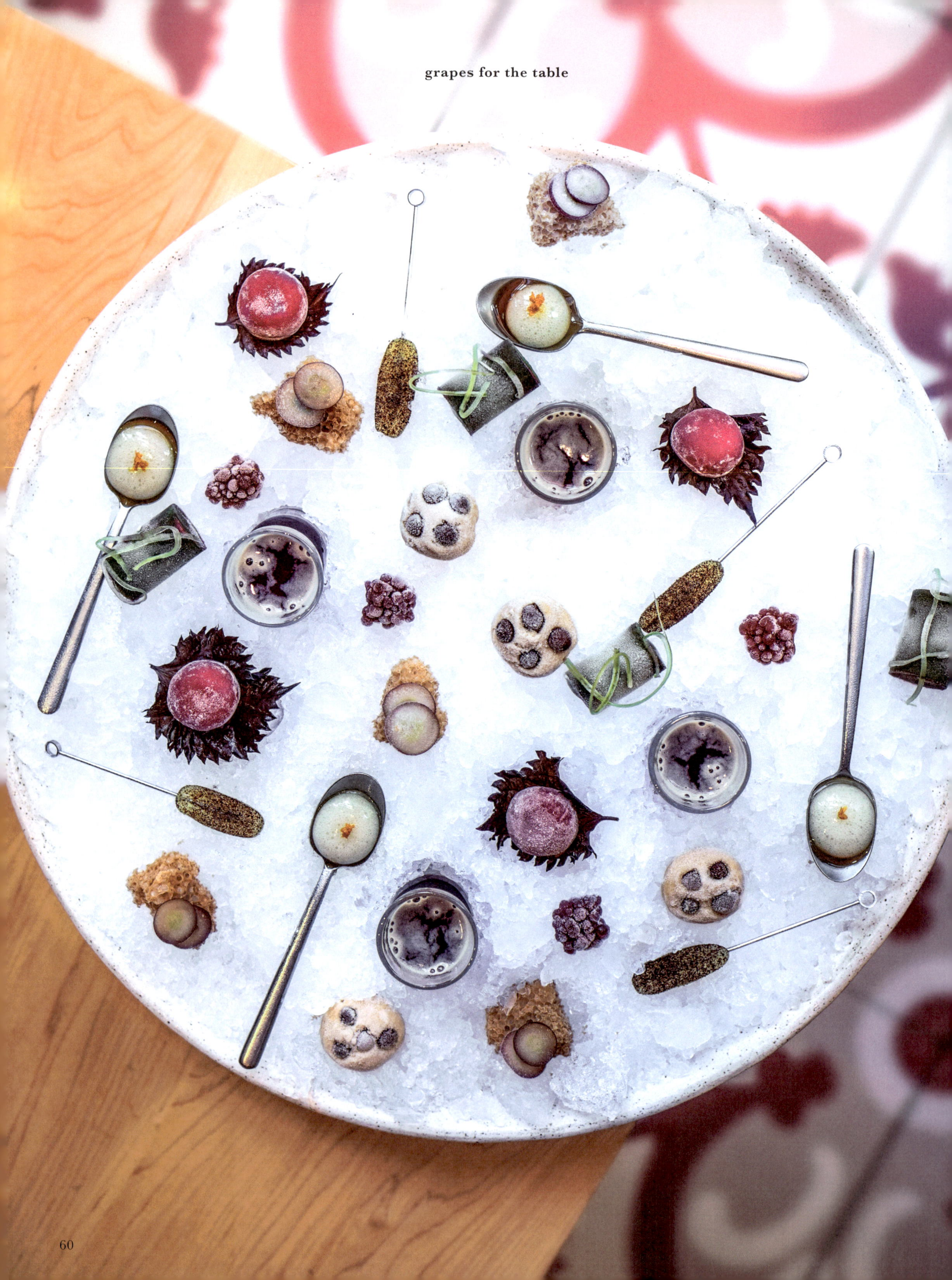

Let's just jump in. How are you involved in the day to day with all of your restaurants?

Alex: I think the classic chef's mentality we're brought up in is; If I'm not there, it's going to be fucked up. If that's the truth, you might as well live in one restaurant until you die. My role is much more directorial, inspirational, and editorial. So, how good can I be at writing the script for the restaurant and have a concept fully-baked on day one?

Who's coming up with the menus and developing the food at all of your restaurants?

It depends. I still, for the most part, write most of the menus, but that's changing. I'm a firm believer that ten people can come up with more ideas than one person. Duncan Grant is the chef here, and he just put three dishes on the menu last week.

I feel like I need to be the one to continue to define what the parameters are. It's hard for me to think about the dish anymore because, for me, the restaurant is the dish. So I can say, "Hey, we tried doing this, it's inconsistent, and here's the technical reason why." The pastry chef in me will always try to distill everything down into something, clinical and non-emotional so that we can speak about it in real terms. If something sucks, well, what does that mean? Too much and not enough are not a quantifiable metric. So, I track the menus, see what's happening with them, what direction they need to go in and work with the chefs. If I have an idea that I believe in, then I'll hand the recipes over for it, or I'll put my whites on and make the dish myself.

I've also found that lately, particularly with this restaurant, that they're better at making the dish than me. They're better at it because they don't have the same set of concerns that I have. I remember once upon a time being the pastry chef at wd-50, and I rarely checked my email. I don't even remember if I had an email. Now, my phone just buzzed five times, and I have to look at it because it might be something serious. It could be one of the places is burning down or getting hit by the department of health. Or, if you have a restaurant group with 300 employees, you're going to get sued every six months. I don't ever want that stress to infect their lives, and I want them to focus purely on making the best dish.

I feel like where I need to remain vigilant is in thinking about the big picture. None of these cooks are here because they were interested in cooking Mexican food. They were interested in Empellón, or in working for me, I suppose. Empellón is always going to be kind of a controversial restaurant because we are not Mexican. We are Mexican inspired. If the Beatles went to fucking India and took in a bunch of influences and made a new album, that doesn't make it an Indian album. It means they became inspired by something, and they incorporated it into what they were doing. My goal, in general, is to speak bitter truth. I get it; the world's in a weird spot right now, so we want to hear all this fluffy stuff. It's just never been me. I'm not down with pop music; I'm down with black metal. If I can't say it like it is, I'd rather not say anything.

For me, doing a printed magazine, it sometimes worries me about publishing something that people will dislike or are going to flip over.

What's wrong with pissing people off? Why is everything supposed to be so fucking agreeable? Just because a painting is pretty doesn't make it art. Not everything's supposed to make you feel good. So if you don't like it, don't read it. That would be my attitude. Don't go to that restaurant, don't look at that thing, or don't listen to that music. I think the world needs more things that are provocative and offensive, not less.

Why did you pick Mexican food as an inspiration? There are price perception issues and authenticity issues when you choose to cook a cuisine like that.

If I tried to explain to a weak writer what I'm about to explain to you, they would look at me cross-eyed. But if I say to them, "Well, my wife's Mexican." Then they're like, "Oh, I get it."

But that's not it. First of all, my wife's American. She was born in Santa Clarita, CA, she's half Mexican, and that's not the reason I started cooking Mexican food. It's a complicated story, so let's start at the beginning.

I didn't start my career as a pastry chef. I bullshitted my way into my first pastry chef job, and at the time, I didn't necessarily like pastry better than savory. I could be a sous chef and get annoyed by the fucking chef every five seconds, or I could be over in the corner, be left alone, and put dishes and my name on the menu. At 22 years old, that was important to me. It just so happened that I kept getting better and better pastry chef jobs. I was very attracted to the modernist movement, the molecular gastronomy movement, or whatever the hell you want to call it. I just thought that the food at elBulli was very provocative. I remember going to these conferences like Madrid Fusion in 2004, 2005, and that was a time when Ferran was famous, but there were still people in the audience scoffing at him and calling it bullshit.

But I like things that challenge things. Punk rock is supposed to piss you off, hardcore is supposed to scare you, and black metal is supposed to make you feel incredibly uncomfortable. That's what I like. So I got into that type of cooking, and I was fortunate that I got to be the pastry chef at Alinea, and then I got to be the pastry chef at wd-50. People think creativity is like this lighthearted, willy-nilly word. Creativity is creation, and creation hurts. Giving birth to a child fucking hurts. It's all pain, and in those restaurants, you're not creative when you feel like it. There's constantly a gun in your mouth, and you have to be avant-garde. But now that type of cooking is accepted, and you can turn on top chef and some dickhead with a fucking fauxhawk is pouring liquid nitrogen into a mixer. It was becoming mainstream, and I was pedigreed. I was also getting closer and closer to 30, I knew I wanted to open a restaurant one day, but to me, the third coming of molecular gastronomy seemed so depressing, you know? I wanted to do something incredibly unexpected and uncomfortable. Under a different set of circumstances, maybe it wouldn't have been Mexican. Perhaps it would've been something else.

I'm a white kid from Massachusetts who didn't grow up with any cuisine. There are all these cute stories floating around of like, "I'm me, and I'm from here, and here's my elevated version of it. Every dish has this very predictable backstory as to why it is what it is. That's fine, but I find it all to be incredibly boring and I didn't come from all that. I came from nowhere. It just so happened that I fell in love with a girl, California style Mexican cooking became our go-to in our household, and I adopted that pantry. Anytime I get interested in something; I research it a lot. Once I started looking closely at Mexican cuisine, it blew me away. It was the newness of it, and it felt as new as espuma. If you fall in love with a truffle, that doesn't make you necessarily a Francophile or obsessed with Italian culture. There are just amazing things coming from that part of the world. Guaje seeds were that for me. The idea of frying a sauce or the idea of intentionally burning things were these techniques that are so goddamn counter-intuitive. So in my spare time for five years, I wasn't doing anything other than studying Mexican cooking. As illogical as it was, I decided that my first restaurant should be Mexican. That was it.

How is it cooking savory food versus just desserts?

I fell in love with pastry after I became a pastry chef. People say you can't create new foods. That might be true, but man, you can manipulate to the point that you forget what the original thing was. When you look at a brick, you don't think about the sand that was compressed to make it. You don't think about wheat berries when you look at a croissant. Savory chefs reach for things like bread as if it were to be granted by God, like an apple on the tree. In pastry, the main component or building block of the dish can disappear, and it's okay. I can make a dessert out of strawberries for you, and even if you cannot see any berry, that's okay. But if I did that to you with a steak, you'd be pissed off. So why is that? I think it's because pastry is the one time that we only eat for pleasure, and so dessert enjoys a higher level of manipulation. It's functional in that you eat it, but again, you don't need to. So, we can wear clothing to keep ourselves warm and decent, but that's not fashion. We can build a structure to keep us warm and safe, but that is not architecture.

In the pastry kitchen, everything is exact and measured with specific steps that have to be followed. How do your savory cooks handle working with someone that is so much a pastry chef?

Everything is measured, within reason. But there's always going to be things that you have to open the drawer and grab. This restaurant has 160 seats and will do 380 covers for dinner tonight. So, why wouldn't you do as many measured, calculated, and sorted things as possible? I'm a big fan of control. If I gave you instructions and you didn't follow them, well, that sounds like insubordination to me. If I said to do something and that got misinterpreted, or it was a game of telephone, that's different. I try my hardest to document everything. What's the upside of vaguery and discrepancy?

I feel like the savory side of the kitchen isn't used to working like that, though.

Sure. It also doesn't necessarily foolproof anything. Even with the recipes, people are going to divert, miss something, or make a mistake. Our chopped cabbage salad is a measured amount of seven different cruciferous vegetables, but whether it's overdressed or underdressed is something that we have to discuss in the field. I'm not going to pre-measure your cup of sauce and dump it. You can do that, though. I remember being amazed when I saw Mugaritz's kitchen and how they leave nothing to chance.

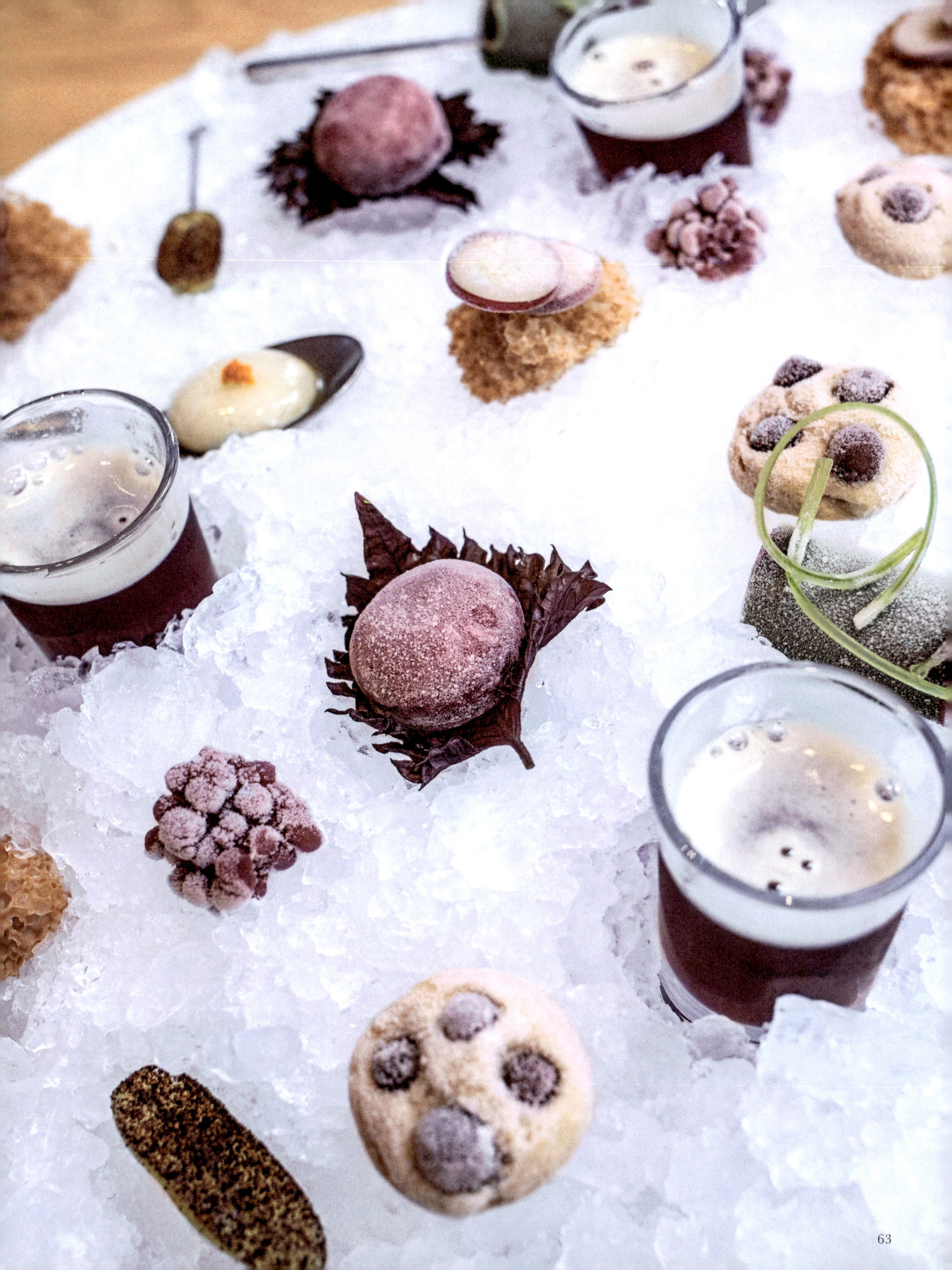

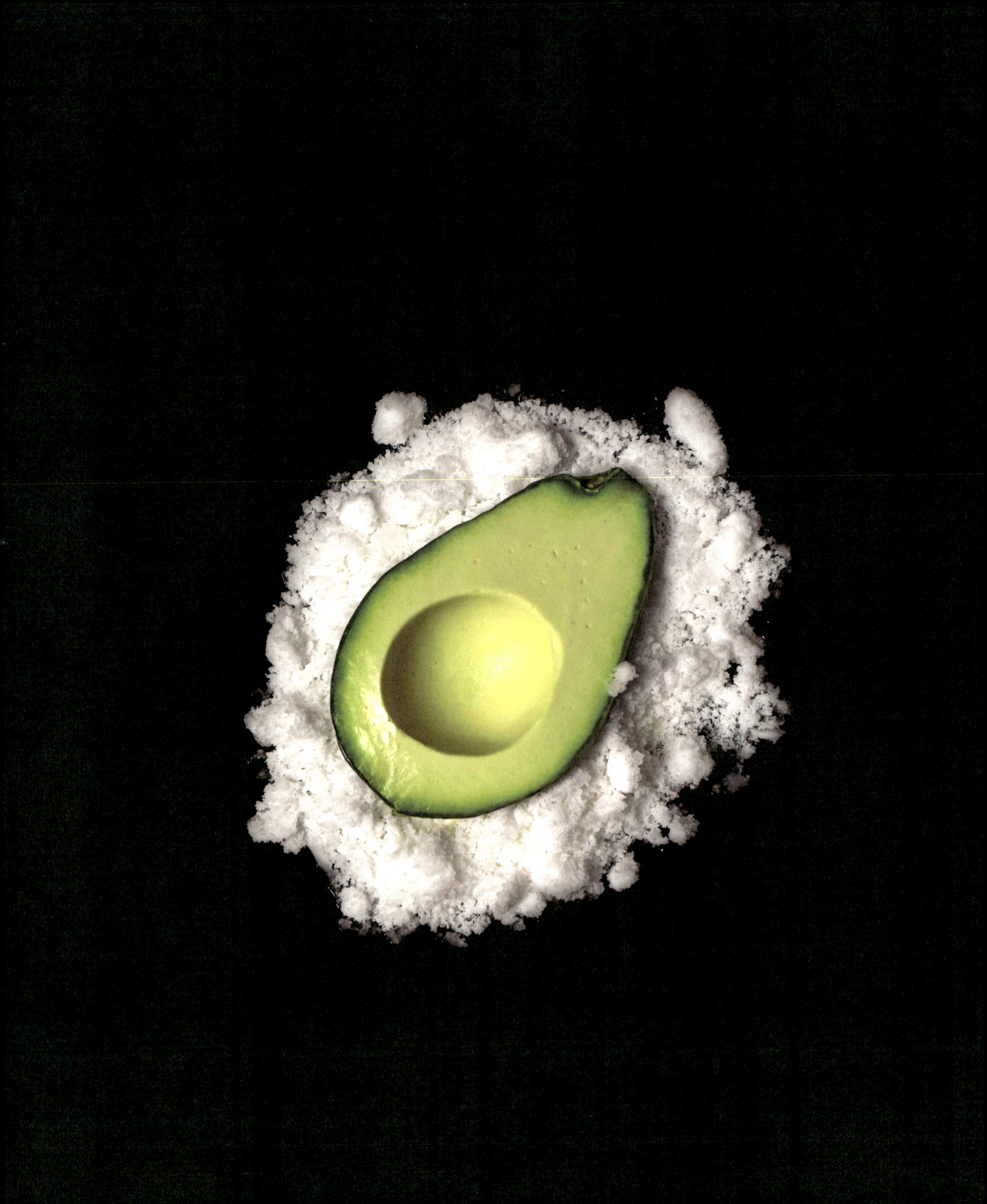

avocado, lime, olive oil, eucalyptus yogurt

If there's a broth in a bowl, it's premeasured and held in a temperature-controlled bath. But they do 40 covers. No one can argue that Albert Adria drove the entire technical side of elBulli, and he was a pastry chef. What made that cuisine so unique is that the savory side completely embraced the pastry side. I think it's interesting that he's doing arguably just as innovative, if not more innovative shit at Enigma. Yet, it's like, how do they only have 80,000 followers on Instagram? That's so offensive to me because they're doing the best shit out there.

Is it weird to go to restaurants and see pastry chefs or restaurants ripping dishes that you did ten years ago? Or, if not the dish, the aesthetics or techniques?

For a journalist, if plagiarism occurred, that's a big deal. Right? But if another musician influences a musician, it's okay. I guess what bothers me is that when the people that should be noticing it don't. I mean, I won't name names, but I'll show it to you. (*shows me a restaurant's Instagram account) This motherfucker is copying my friend Jordan Kahn. My question is, how are they sleeping at night? That's what bothers me. But, where do you draw the line? I suspect a lot of people have a problem with me making tortillas. But I would argue that if it's wrong for a white guy from Massachusetts to make tortillas, why is it okay for a white guy from Massachusetts to make a fucking baguette? I'm no more French than I am Mexican. So I would see a lot of hypocrisy in that.

I feel like a lot of people that are opening new restaurants are nervous about that kind of stuff being brought up.

I might be grandfathered into something with Empellón. If I were trying to do my book about tacos right now, maybe the publishers would be like, "Mmm, maybe not." I think that since Trump became president, everyone's a lot more sensitive, and I don't think that's wrong. But, I believe that we all should be able to cook whatever the fuck we want. I'm in love with Mexican cuisine and dedicated to it for the rest of my life. But I'm not from Mexico, and I don't have a culture to defend. I just come at it from a very different perspective. A lot of us got into Spain because we were into elBulli first. We went to Copenhagen because of Noma, and not because we were into Danish shit. Right? That's not bad. That's cool.

You know, if something artistic can lead you into learning more about culture, I think that's as good of an avenue as any. I think that has nothing to do with appropriating culture. I don't speak Spanish fluently. I'm not trying to have a tv show where I point out the interesting parts of Oaxaca to make white people feel safe about it. I'm not trying to replicate any dish, and if I am, I cite the source. I don't know how anyone could say that's appropriation. But again, it's a touchy subject, and it's an interesting subject.

What are some of the challenges of having a growing restaurant group?

We're still very small, but we have big restaurant group problems. There's a drastic learning curve when you go from being a cook to a pastry chef, to the chef of your own restaurant. Then can you become a restauranteur and then become a CEO? Can you be a big enough restaurant group so that you can hire a CEO and get back to what you loved doing at the beginning, which for me, is thinking of the ideas? I hope that's my path.

Why do you want to make this a large restaurant group versus just being the chef of one restaurant? One restaurant is way less complicated.

Everyone has a burnout point. Also, I don't personally have the discipline to do one thing forever. I get bored.

I know chefs who worked in one kitchen chipping away at it for 25 years. Then, something happens that wasn't their fault, and now they have no restaurant. Now they're 52, and what are they going to do? Something terrible could happen at any given second. Not to sound dark, but if I have one child and it dies, then I'm destroyed. If I have ten children, and one dies, I'm destroyed, but I also have nine other kids to console me. Also, unless you build a temple of constant change, you have to open new restaurants to do new things. We get a lot of flack when we change our menu. Customers feel betrayed when they've been coming here for years and having a particular dish. And you took what they love away. It's your restaurant, but it's also their restaurant, and you just fucked with it. You have to open a new thing to start housing all your ideas.

It also gets exciting because I'd like to think my next two restaurants are going to be better than my last two. When I opened my first place, all I cared about was food. Now that's just one part. I don't care how good your fucking food is, if the lighting or chairs are wrong, you're fucked. Can you build the perfect machine? But that's just personal to me. I think everyone's different, and everyone's got to do what's right for them.

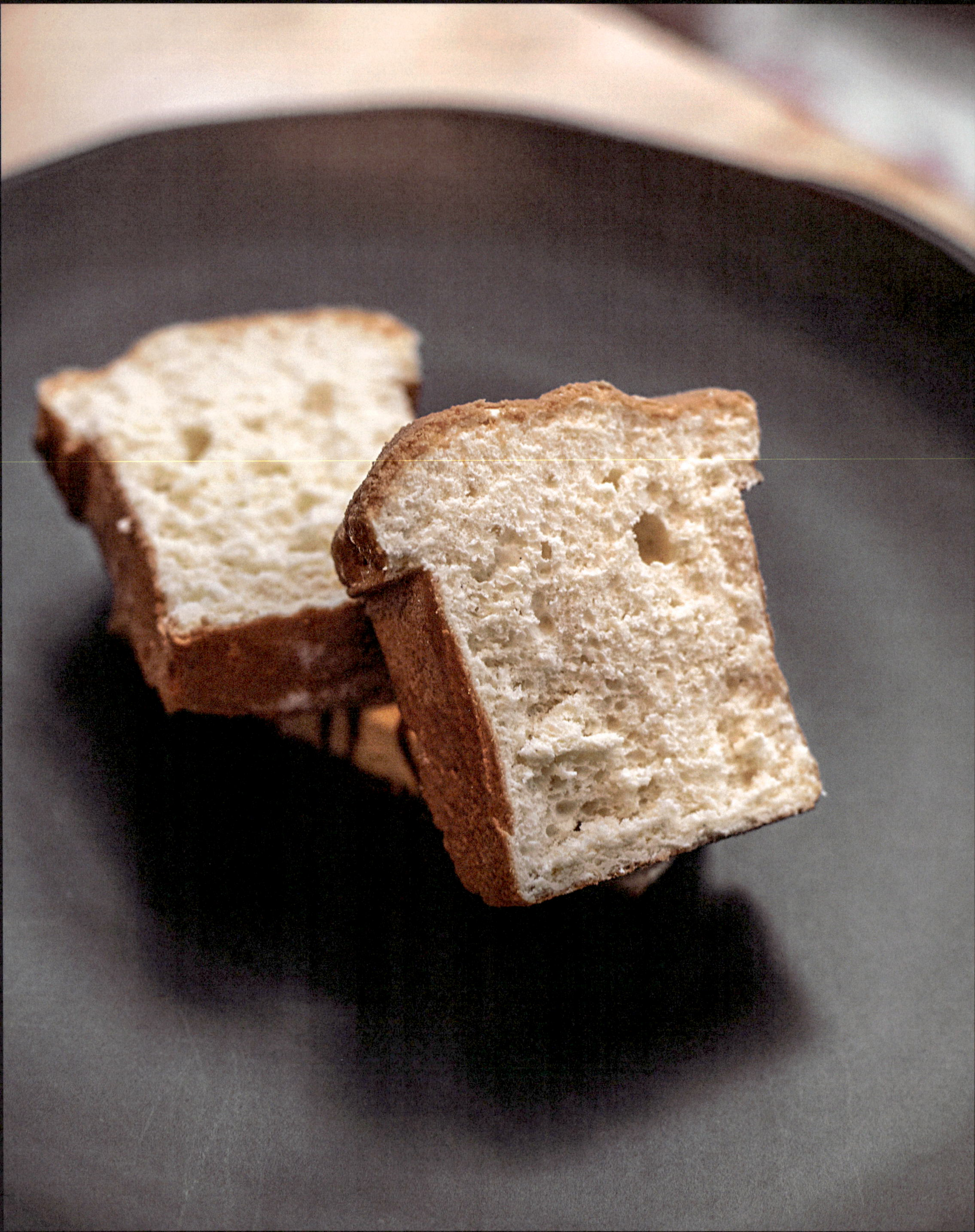

Has having kids calmed you down at all?

It forces you to realize how much time you wasted. I'm up at 5:30 every day because my kids are up then, and I take them to school. When they're ten years old, I'm not going to take them to school anymore. So as much as it hurts now, I realize how special that gift is. I want to be in my kid's lives, so I'm up early, and I'm tired. But, it forces me to prioritize. We're all so twisted as chefs that on our days off, we think we should go into work and work on the new dish. Maybe I used to work on it for 14 hours, but now I work on it for three, and then something dings in the back of my head, and I think, "I gotta get the fuck outta here. What am I doing?"

What are you working on now?

I'm focused on the mainstream. People that go into three Michelin-star restaurants, they seek that out. It's incredible, and it's the ultimate filter. The restaurant knows their allergies and preferences in advance, and they'll eat something more unusual. If that weird course was their main course in a more casual a la carte restaurant, that's a different story. But I equate that to going to a Gorgoroth concert. I'm into Gorgoroth, but I'm not a fan of Marilyn Manson. But at the end of the day, Marilyn Manson was able to inject some pretty satanic imagery right into 8:00 PM mainstream MTV and scare some 14-year-old kids. That's awesome. So, in many ways, I'm oddly focused on the mainstream because that's where I think I do the most damage and can be the most provocative.

I'm most proud of this restaurant out of all of them because everyone told me going into Midtown Manhattan wouldn't work. Midtown is famous for being conservative as fuck. People want shrimp cocktails, steak tartar, and all of that steakhouse stuff. This restaurant is weird, expensive, interpretive, and authenticity-challenging Mexican food in a place that never asked for it. I'm trying to replace your vodka soda with mezcal. I'm not trying to be your favorite Mexican restaurant; I'm trying to be your favorite restaurant.

Why is it if you asked ten New Yorkers where their favorite restaurant is, seven of them are going to name a place that's Italian. Why Italian? Why can't we replace it, and why when you mention Mexican does the conversation have to be, "How Mexican is it?" It's an interesting thing because, in French cooking, you have a technical arsenal along with tradition. But you also have originality and the ability to absorb other cultures and techniques into it. Modern French cuisine uses Japanese flavors or Thai flavors. Whereas, if you look at Mexican as a set of techniques and start injecting other things into the fold, people say it's not Mexican. And people from LA will say... well, I have a joke. Whether I'm about to receive the biggest compliment or the most scathing insult, it always starts with, "Well, I'm from LA." I get it. A great taco is every Angelino's fucking birthright.

I'm born and raised in California, and I really did grow up hearing that. That California has the best Mexican food and that there's no good Mexican food anywhere else in the USA. Especially on the East coast.

Right. We had a learning curve. When I opened up, I couldn't find a single restaurant that was grinding their masa. There was only one tortilleria that I could find that was doing it. Everything else was maseca plus water. That's insane because if we went to a great Italian restaurant right now, and they said, "All our pasta is made fresh in house." Everyone would be like, "Yeah, and water is wet, and we're breathing air." It's implicit. But we were still pulling methylcellulose ridden tortillas out of a fucking bag made from GMO fucking maseca and throwing that on a griddle to soften it. I had to grind my masa myself. I had to get the equipment made, and I had to learn all that. My masa sucked in the beginning. But I learned how to do it, and now I think my masa is awesome.

I want you to talk to my pastry chef Justin because he's been with me for three years, and the food he's about to show you is shit that I haven't touched. I'm proud of that because the type of person I was in kitchens is the type of person I want to work with going forward. And that type of person doesn't want to be told how to do everything. I want Justin to become the pastry chef of this restaurant, and five more restaurants of mine if he wants to. He's really into bread, and I want to find him his own space to open a bakery. Elianne, our pastry sous chef, is a star, and I want Justin to be out of her way so that she can progress. To allude to something, you're going to start seeing new concepts in the future that have nothing to do with Empellón.

**At this point, I sat down to chat with pastry chef Justin Binnie and pastry sous chef Eliane Padlan.*

Justin and Eliane, tell us a little bit about yourselves, and how long have you been working here?

Justin: I'm Justin Bettie, and I'm the pastry chef at Empellón. My background is a mix of bakeries and restaurants. I have a lot of experience with bread, but I was also at Jean-George for four years. We've both been here since the opening of this restaurant, so around two and a half years. Before that, we were working together at a bakery in Brooklyn, and that's where we met.

Eliane: I'm the pastry sous chef. I'm a native New Yorker, and I feel like I started cooking kind of late. I first went to college for film, but it didn't feel right, and I got into restaurants. I started in the front of the house as a hostess and then asked if I could go work in the kitchen for free. After that, I started working in kitchens full time. I first started on the savory side, and then at a certain point, they needed help in pastry, and I switch over. I've been cooking now for around five and a half years, so not that long.

What's it like being pastry chefs in a restaurant that is owned by a very well-know pastry chef?

E: I think you get more support in pastry, and he makes sure that there is a strong program.

J: He has his opinions on how pastry should be, and I get to learn what he knows and add my experience to it. Since we've opened, a lot of the reviews have focused on the desserts. I think we've built something here that people respond well to, and that feels good. It's great to have someone so engaged with all of the restaurants. The amount of detail and time that he puts into the restaurant is crazy.

Were the first few dishes intimidating to present to him?

J: Initially, everything was on paper, and we compared ideas and worked them out together. At previous restaurants, when I would show a chef a new dessert, they'd say, "Ok, looks great." I've never had that happen here. He doesn't necessarily tell me to change anything, but he gives me feedback and material to work with. Even when I think a dessert is the best thing I've made, he gives me input, and that's something I've never experienced before.

It's interesting seeing a dessert, like the avocado, blow up on the internet. Why do you think it's so popular to make desserts that look like the ingredient?

J: It gives a diner an immediate reference to what they're eating. Before they even try it, they're already identifying with the dish. Then they take a bite, and they have another reaction to it. I can see why a lot of pastry chefs do that. It's the same as when milk and cookie desserts were popular. You get people to identify with it, they love it, and then you can't take it off the menu.

Do you feel the need to play within Chef Alex's wheelhouse of techniques and desserts because, in a way, you're representing him here?

J: I find it interesting to take all of my knowledge and put it together into something new that makes sense. It's much more of collaboration here, and I think I have a lot more freedom than the savory team does. We have a very close and small pastry team here, and we talk about new dishes and feed off of each other. I love having a team this size because I enjoy working service, production, and having my hands in everything.

There's a lot of limitations to what we can do in this type of restaurant. If this were a tasting menu in a Michelin-starred restaurant, the grape dessert would be amazing. But in a restaurant like this, not everyone is here to challenge their comfort zones. People start saying, "Why is it so small? Why is it so expensive?" In the same breath, "Can I get it to go?" So we're maneuvering around all of that. It's a balance between making desserts high-end, engaging, and still maintaining our clientele.

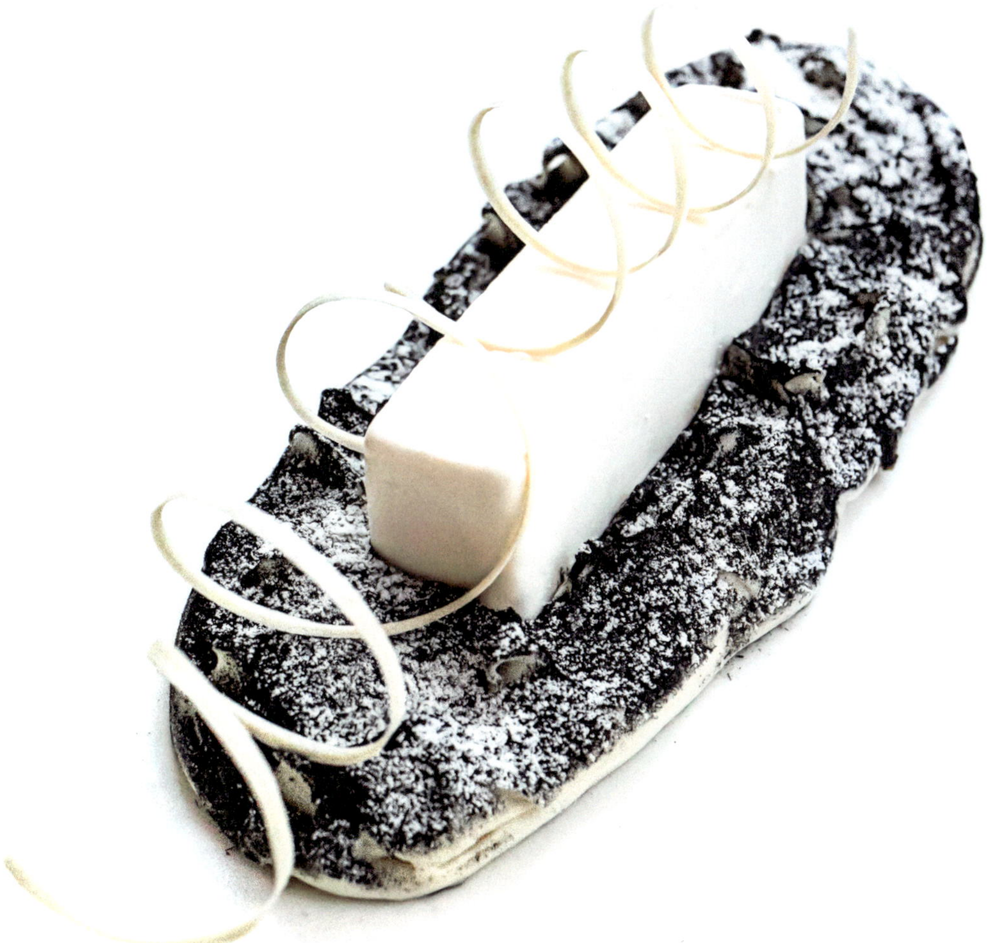

nailing the ***classics***

a conversation with

lincoln carson

bon temps

los angeles, ca

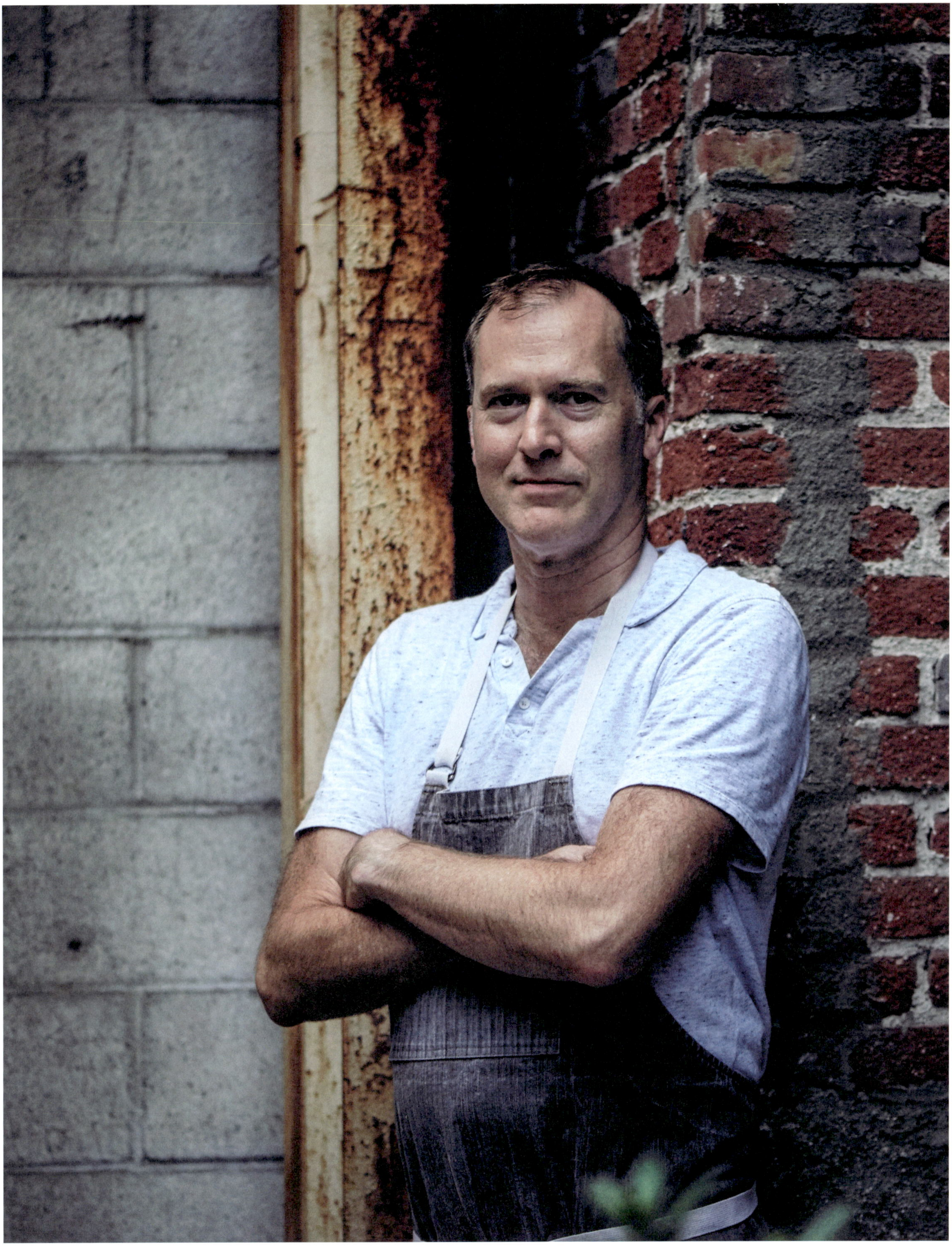

Portrait by Sierra Prescott

Tell us about yourself and your career.

I'm Lincoln Carson, and I'm the chef and owner of Bon Temps in Los Angeles. My background is in pastry, and for the past thirty years, it's the only thing I've ever done. It's probably rare to hear that, but I'm fortunate that I found it early. I took the hard line and started in culinary school immediately for pastry, and my feeling at the time was that it would be the more artistic outlet in the kitchen. Now, I don't think that's the case at all, and I believe there is artistry to be found everywhere in the kitchen. But I feel very overtly, and in a very literal sense, it can be more artistic because of the sculptural aspects of pastry. I was fortunate to work for some incredible people early on in my career. My first restaurant was Le Pactole, which was a short-lived but huge and expensive restaurant in the World Financial Center run by chef Willy Krause. There I worked for pastry chef Marc Haymon, who was very talented and old-school. I then left to work at Le Bernardin with pastry chef François Payard and quickly learned a lot. Funny enough, I had found that job by answering a blind ad in the New York Times because that's how you found jobs back then. Le Bernardin was one of a few four-starred restaurants in New York at that time. François had just become the pastry chef, Eric Ripert had maybe been there for three months, and working there kind of opened the door for me.

That's a nuts pastry chef to work for.

It was perfect for me because I was 21 years old at the time and very flexible. I would work six days a week, 12-14 hour shifts, doing everything as perfect as possible. The mindset for me was, I don't like getting yelled at, so I'm not going to fuck up as much as the other guys. I hadn't had enough other jobs to know the difference, so I just assumed that was how everybody worked. I don't know if I would say that I learned a lot of specific techniques. Instead, I learned a work ethic, how to do things precisely, and that "good enough" isn't acceptable.

I feel like not too many people, especially nowadays, get to work for those old-school French pastry chefs.

Right, and I was able to work for a couple of them. From there, I took my first pastry chef position at Peacock Alley in the Waldorf right as Laurent Manrique had taken it over. In retrospect, it was probably too early for me to take that job, but François put me in there, so I guess he saw something in me. I think I probably had a lot more to learn, but you bring yourself up and teach yourself what you don't know.

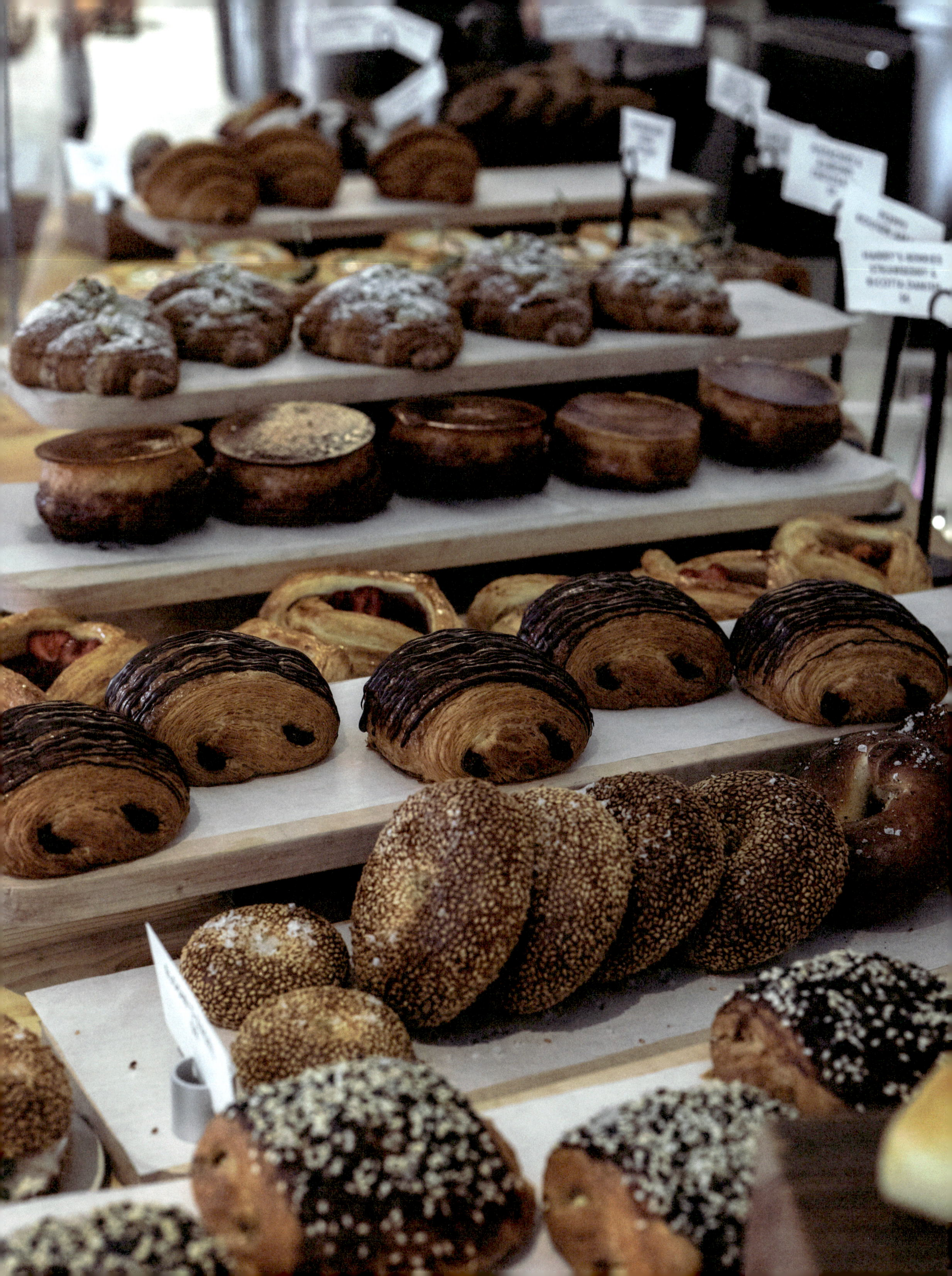

Do you think anyone is ever fully ready when they take that step to a chef position?

Some people, yes, but that job was definitely biting off more than I could chew. From there I went to a restaurant called Luxe, and then became the pastry chef at a restaurant called Cascabel with chef Tom Valenti for a couple of years. Cascabel was a perfect place for me to figure out who I was culinarily speaking and gave me direction in terms of style. I then took a pastry chef position at La Côte Basque, which had been around in form or another for fifty years. Talk about old school. The chef/owner was Jean-Jacques Rachou, and in the eighties, that's where all the prominent chefs like Rick Moonen, Todd English, and Charlie Palmer came through. So it was kind of surreal being the pastry chef there, and I was not ready for that. The pastry chef I had stepped in to replace was Richard Leach, and he's the founder of architectural desserts, right? I was trying to do slightly more modern desserts and was just getting crushed all the time with the amount of volume that the restaurant did. At that time, it was pre-hydrocolloids, and I was trying to figure out how to do things that hadn't been done. It wasn't necessarily the best stylistic fit for me there, but looking back at that, I learned about being part of the entirety of the restaurant experience and not trying to do my own thing.

Matching your style with the restaurant?

Yeah. Of course, there's going to be an inevitable progression. Two different people have two different styles, but it shouldn't be so polar opposite. After that, I went out West and was at Highlands Inn in Carmel for two years, then at Picasso when the Bilaggio opened, came back to New York for a couple of years, and then back to Vegas to open Daniel at the Wynn. Then I left to work for the Michael Mina Group, and I stayed with Michael for the better part of eight and a half years. After a good long run with Michael Mina, I moved down here to open Superba for a year, jumped around a bit, and then decided I wasn't going to work for anyone else ever again. I paid the bills consulting, which taught me how to value what I do and how to go out and hustle for work. That got me into putting together some business plans, and 4 or 5 years later, here we are with Bon Temps.

Did you ever have it in your mind to open your own restaurant?

No. I think I'm the accidental restauranteur. I had put together a business plan for a smaller-scale version of this concept with a buddy of mine up in Napa, but that space fell through, and I still had the business plan. This space came up with the investor attached, we talked about it, and this is where I wound up. It took a long time to get this all together.

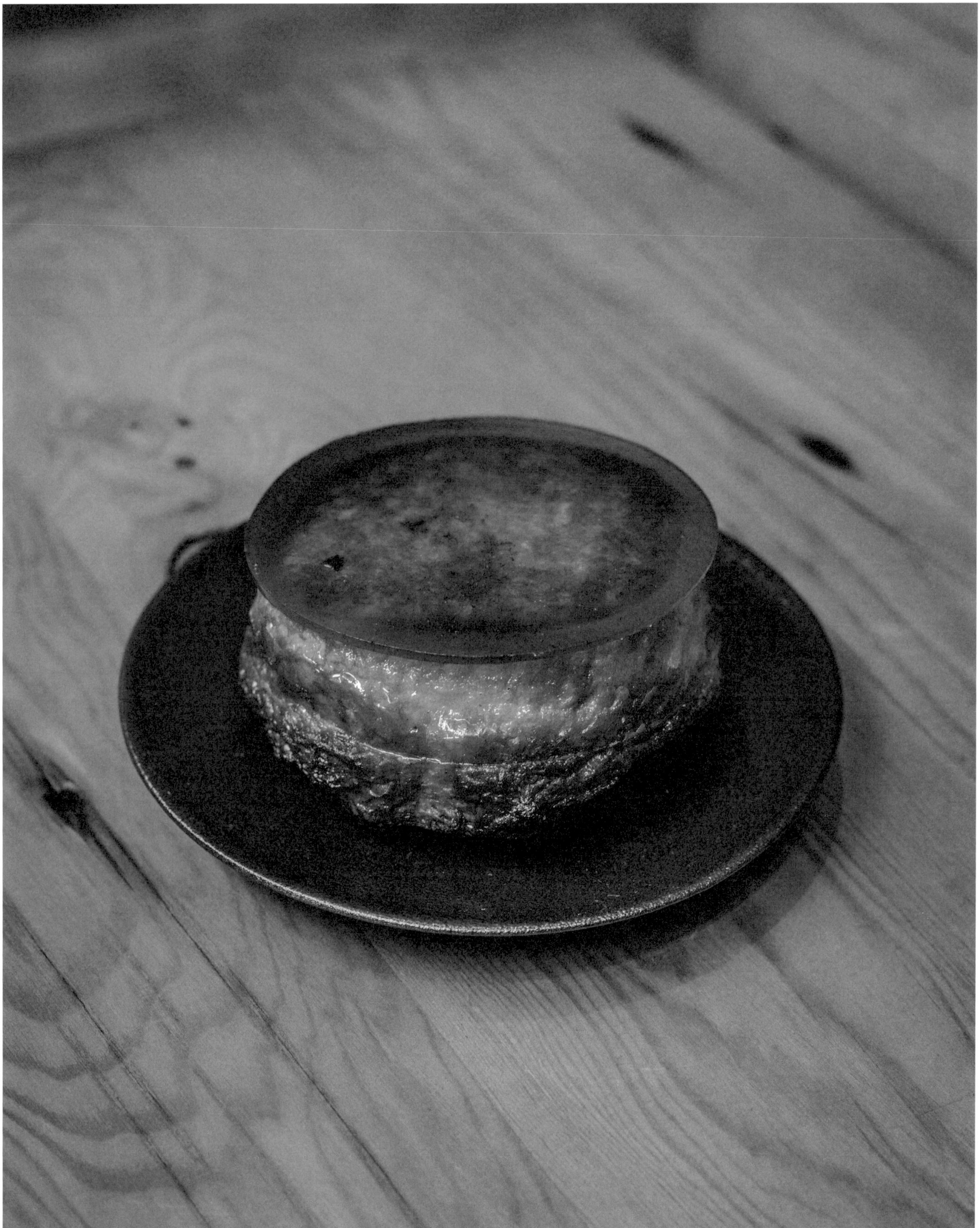

Poppy Seed Kouign-Amann

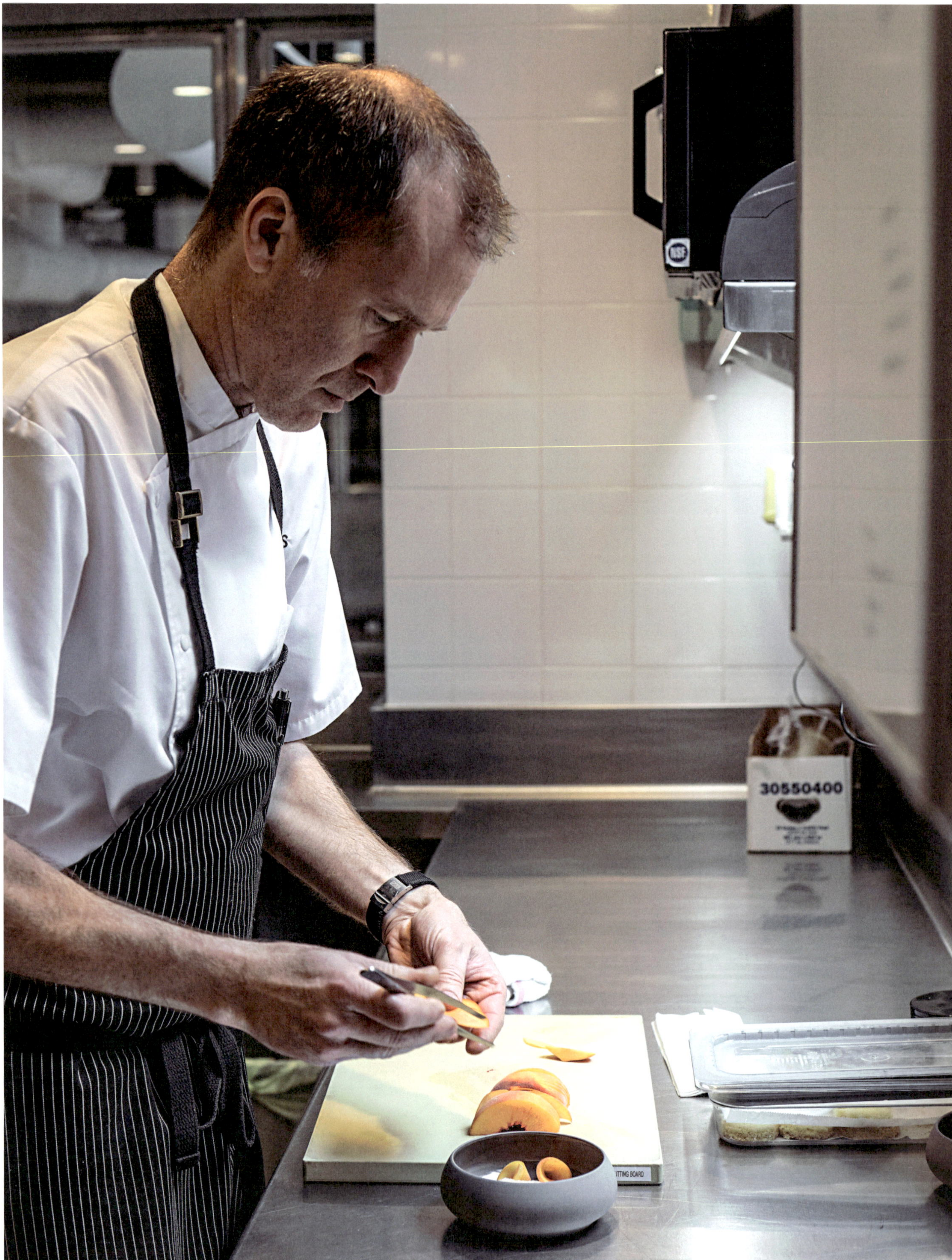
NSF
30550400

You do a lot of baked goods in the morning. Did you ever work in bakeries?

Ninety percent of my time has been in restaurants and hotels, and small hotels at that. I don't count the Bellagio and the Wynn because I was working for specific restaurants within them.

So a lot of the viennoiserie you taught yourself?

Yeah. Working on Superba was the catalyst for it, and it got me to do something different, and I developed a new skill set to a pretty high level. I still remember the first croissants I made when I was fucking around with it in the basement at Michael Mina. They were pretty awful. I had no idea what I was doing, and some might argue I still don't.

The idea here is to nail the classics, and then figure out how to fuck with it. I would put my croissant up against anyone's in the world. You might prefer a certain style or flavor profile, but from a technique standpoint, I feel mine is as good as anything else you'll find. But then we do all the other stuff with it, like the everything bagel croissant, and that's when it gets fun.

Do you think there is a lack of pastry chefs nowadays for cooks to work for? Or has it always been like this?

I think there's a lack. I think we go through these cycles where pastry gets cut first. Pastry is an amenity, right? For the most part. Here we sell a lot of desserts, especially for dinner service. I don't think there is a table that doesn't get dessert. But there isn't the same kind of mentorship that we went through. What's the Dave Grohl quote about having to suck for a long time before you get good? People don't want to suck, but it doesn't work that way. At least for me and 99% of the people I know.

Most pastry chefs that I have interviewed don't have as much experience as you. You've been in the game for a while now. What do you think of social media in food, the new food trends, and all of that?

It's changed the game completely. Instagram is probably the single most important influence on a lot of people's and restaurant's success. I think there is a lot of great things that have come out of it. The ability to share what you're doing and share other people's work is amazing. With that said, just like the advent of the internet, just because you saw it doesn't mean it's good. Just because it looks good in a photograph doesn't mean its correct. Kouign amman is a great example of that. I laughed because I saw someone posted a comment on a chef's photo about not being impressed by the lamination from an interior crumb shot. And my thought was, "What is your base for comparison?" Is it another photo on Instagram? Because it's not an informed point of view. I think the danger is moving so fast that you never master your craft. And that is what I see a lot more of. But, the positives outweigh that as long as people maintain a good self-awareness and a little humility.

"The idea here is to nail the classics, and then figure out how to fuck with it"

I find it interesting to meet chefs who are still reluctant to play the social media game.

You can't hide from it. It's part of the business. We're in business to do business. I mean, I joke with my executive chef that the ideal restaurant is one that is open one day a year, serves one guest, they pay ten million dollars for their meal, and we get to cook by ourselves for the rest of the year. But that's not reality. You need people in the door. And not only for selling your product to pay bills and your staff, but also for your own growth. If you're not busy and if you're not pushing your food and changing, you're not getting any better.

How do you like Los Angeles?

I love it. I'm continuously surprised by how much I love living here. I think the thing that blows me away is the sheer amount of diversity. Whatever you're looking for is here. You just have to find it. And I think it's a very exciting time for restaurants in this city. Not because there are all of these new restaurants openings, but because our guests are expecting better now. They're learning and know what the difference is between good and great, and that makes everyone better. You have to step your game up here.

You have opened a lot of restaurants with Michael Mina, and now your own. What would be your advice to someone looking to open a restaurant?

Find the best people you can to support you. I can't say I did it myself; clearly, I didn't do it all. But the responsibility fell on my shoulders for this. Whereas the previous 30 restaurants I've opened, I was part of a group of professionals who all had their responsibility and areas, and everyone trusted that each other had their shit together and under control. It's a very different thing when you are the main person and making sure that it all comes together. I have an incredible design firm that did all of this, but I was very involved in the build-out and had a lot of conversations and input about the design. It's important to have your hands in everything, but you can't be great at everything. I have a hard time letting go of things, and maybe that's a little bit of my nature. But it's important to get people who are good at what they do, and then let them do it. Stay out of their way. Also, it's a struggle, so pick people you like. You're going to get on each other's nerves regardless, so it might as well be with someone that you like and respect.

I have so much more respect now for anyone who opens a business. It's such an emotionally taxing and challenging thing to do. I'm learning a lot about myself and about how my job is now much more different than I thought it was going to be. It's not about just being on a station every day.

The cook working the line dreams of being a chef, and the chef's dream is to be back on the line.

The happy place is just shucking oysters, right?

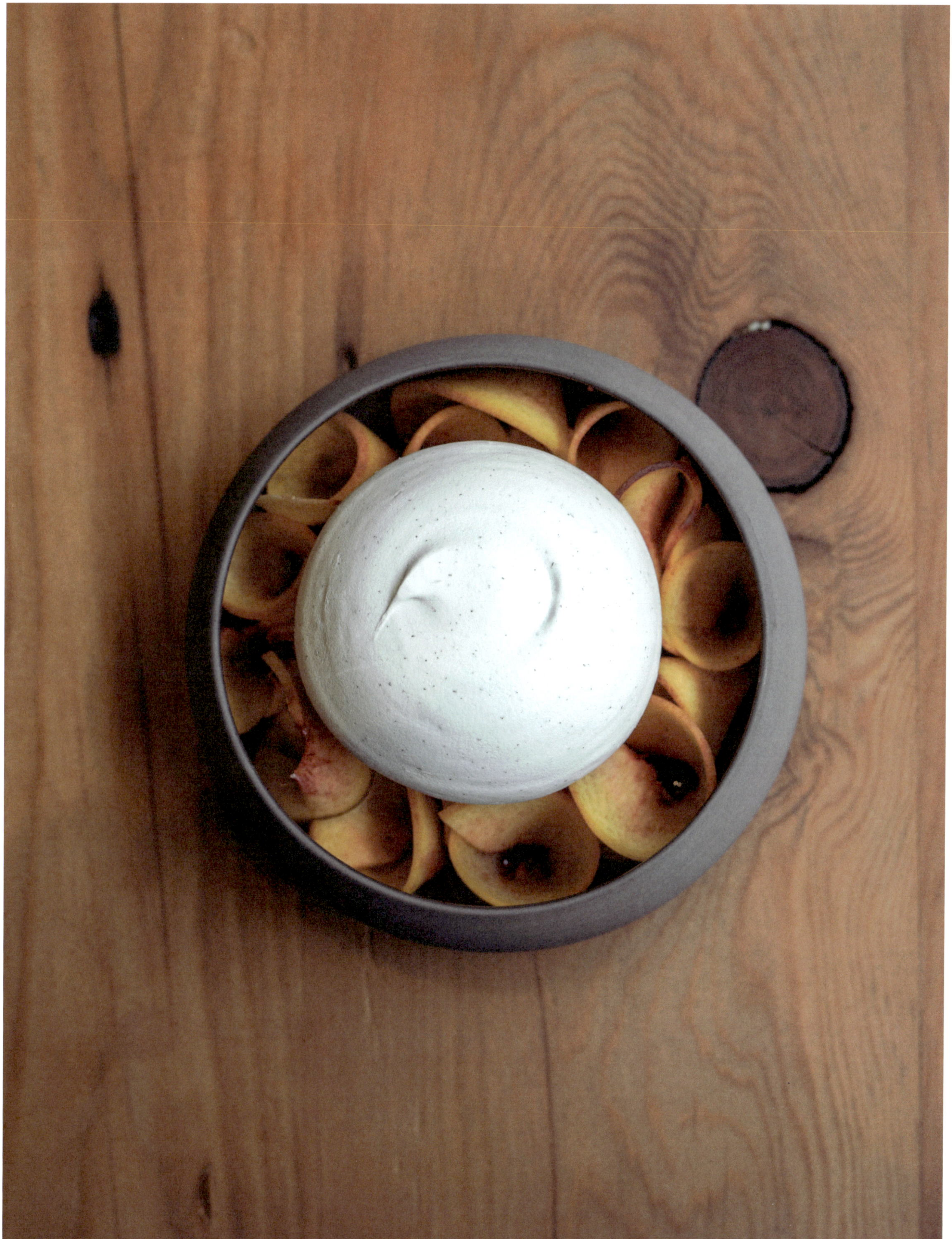

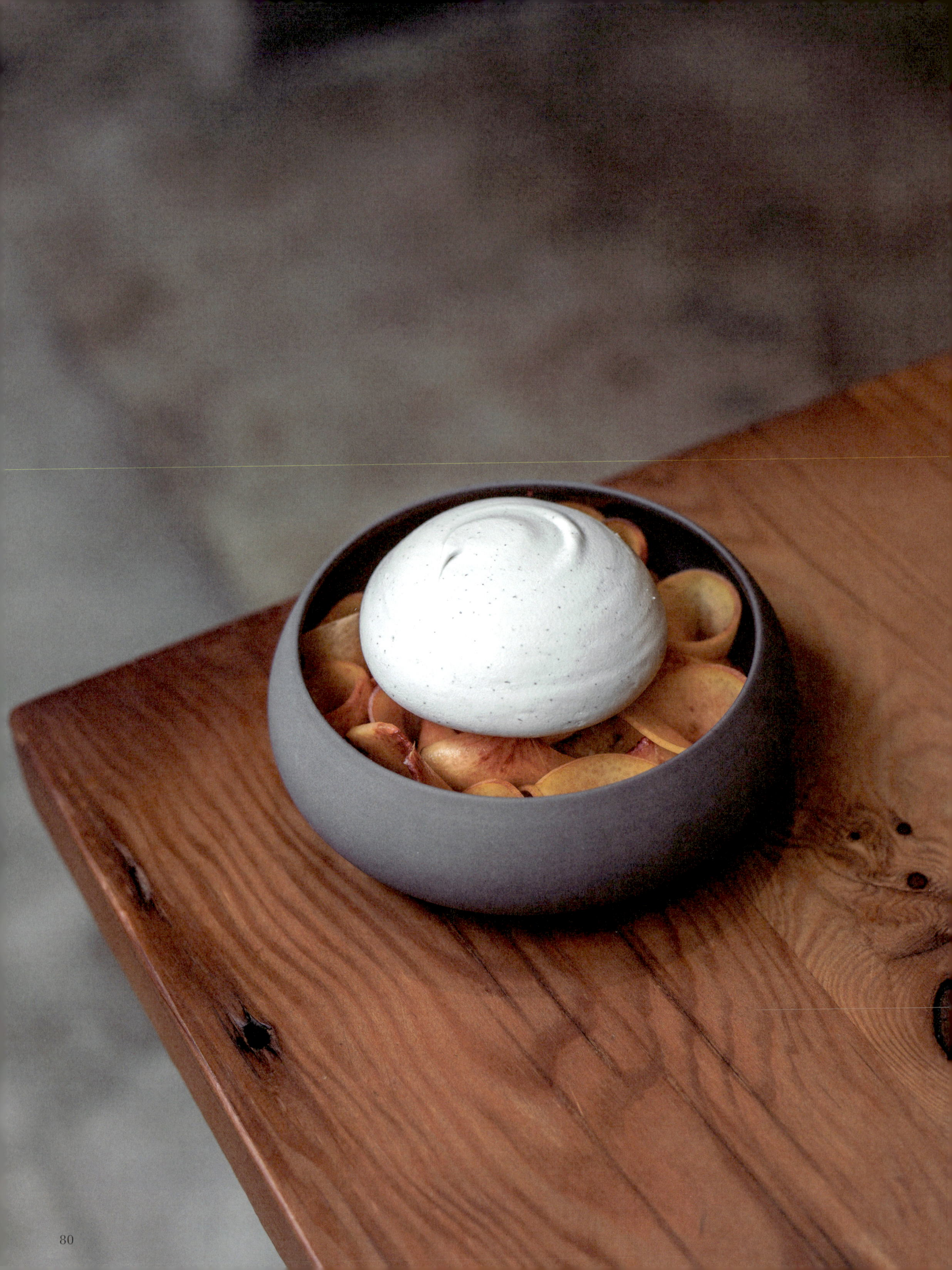

Verjus Sorbet

Ingredients:

750 ml	white fusion verjus
470 g	sorbet syrup
2.6 g	xanthan gum

Method:

In a vita prep combine the verjus and the syrup, blending well. Add the X.G. directly into the vortex created in the vita prep, and bring to high speed, shearing for one full minute. Spin as per ice cream machine requirements.

Coriander Sponge Cake

Ingredients:

330 g	whole eggs
350 g	sugar
3 g	salt
200 g	ap flour
175 g	cake flour
12 g	baking powder
200 g	milk
125 g	butter
225 g	glucose
8 g	coriander seed, toasted/ground

Method:

In Kitchen Aid equipped with a whip attachment, bring eggs, sugar, and salt to full volume. Add warmed glucose. Slowly add melted butter in a steady stream while continuing to whip on medium-low speed. Alternate sifted ingredients with warmed milk, do not over mix. Gently fill a 1/2 sheet tray that has been lined with a Silpat and lightly sprayed. Bake at 330F, 25% humidity, fan speed three. When lightly golden and cake springs back to the touch, remove from oven to cool. Make sure to wrap the cake once the sheet tray is cool enough to handle.

Blackberry Jus

Ingredients:

250 g	fresh blackberries, cleaned
50 g	sugar

Method:

Toss the blackberries with the sugar until evenly coated. If available, in a Cryovac bag under full vacuum, seal the blackberry/sugar mixture under maximum vacuum. Immerse the sealed berries in an 85C water bath for 2 hours, looking for the berries to have released a large quantity of jus. Alternately place the bag in a perforated hotel pan or on a wire rack lined sheet pan in a Rational (combi) oven set to steam only, 85C, for 45 minutes to one hour. Place the bag in an ice bath until well chilled. Remove berries and jus, and pass through a chinois. Do not push through chinois, but allow to slowly drain until the bulk of the jus has passed. Reserve liquid.

Lemongrass Consommé

Ingredients:

500 g	lemongrass
1/2 ea	vanilla bean
1 ea	zest of orange
1 ea	zest of lemon
1.5L	water
3 ea	kaffir lime leaves
400 g	sugar
375 g	Leitz Auslese Riesling
pinch	salt

Method:

Crush the cleaned lemongrass stalks. Place lemongrass, vanilla, zests, water, sugar, and kaffir lime leaf in a pot and bring to a simmer. Allow to simmer for five minutes, then add riesling and salt. Allow it to infuse for ten minutes, strain, and chill. Adjust the sugar/acid level as necessary.

Pavlova

Ingredients:

225 g	egg whites
210 g	powdered sugar
210 g	sugar
15 g	egg white powder
15 g	cornstarch
5 g	lemon juice
2 g	salt
4 g	dehydrated rose geranium

Method:

Preheat rational to 215F 0% humidity fan speed 1. In VitaPrep combine all dry ingredients with rose geranium and blend until geranium is fully incorporated and sift. In Kitchen Aid fitted with the whip attachment, whip egg whites on low speed until slightly foamy. Add sifted dry into whites in three additions while whipping at low speed. Continue whisking on low until stiff peaks are formed. Pipe meringues with the largest round tip possible, on sheet trays that have been lined with SilPats and lightly sprayed. Bake for 1hr 10min or until a thin but hard shell is formed. Allow to cool so you can handle them. Using an offset, transfer to a parchment-lined container, and cover with grip lid. Transfer directly to the freezer.

Final Dish

Place a 10mm thick by 50mm Diameter round of coriander sponge in the bowl. Using a sharp knife so as not to bruise the fruit, slice 1mm ribbons of yellow peach around the cake in such a way so as to have the edge of the slices guest-facing. Using a squeeze bottle, place blackberry jus in and under the sliced peaches, using approximately 15-20grams of jus. Place a scoop of verjus sorbet on top of the sponge cake. Place a pavlova directly atop the verjus sorbet. Serve with the lemongrass consommé in a small side pour vessel and pour tableside around but not over the pavlova.

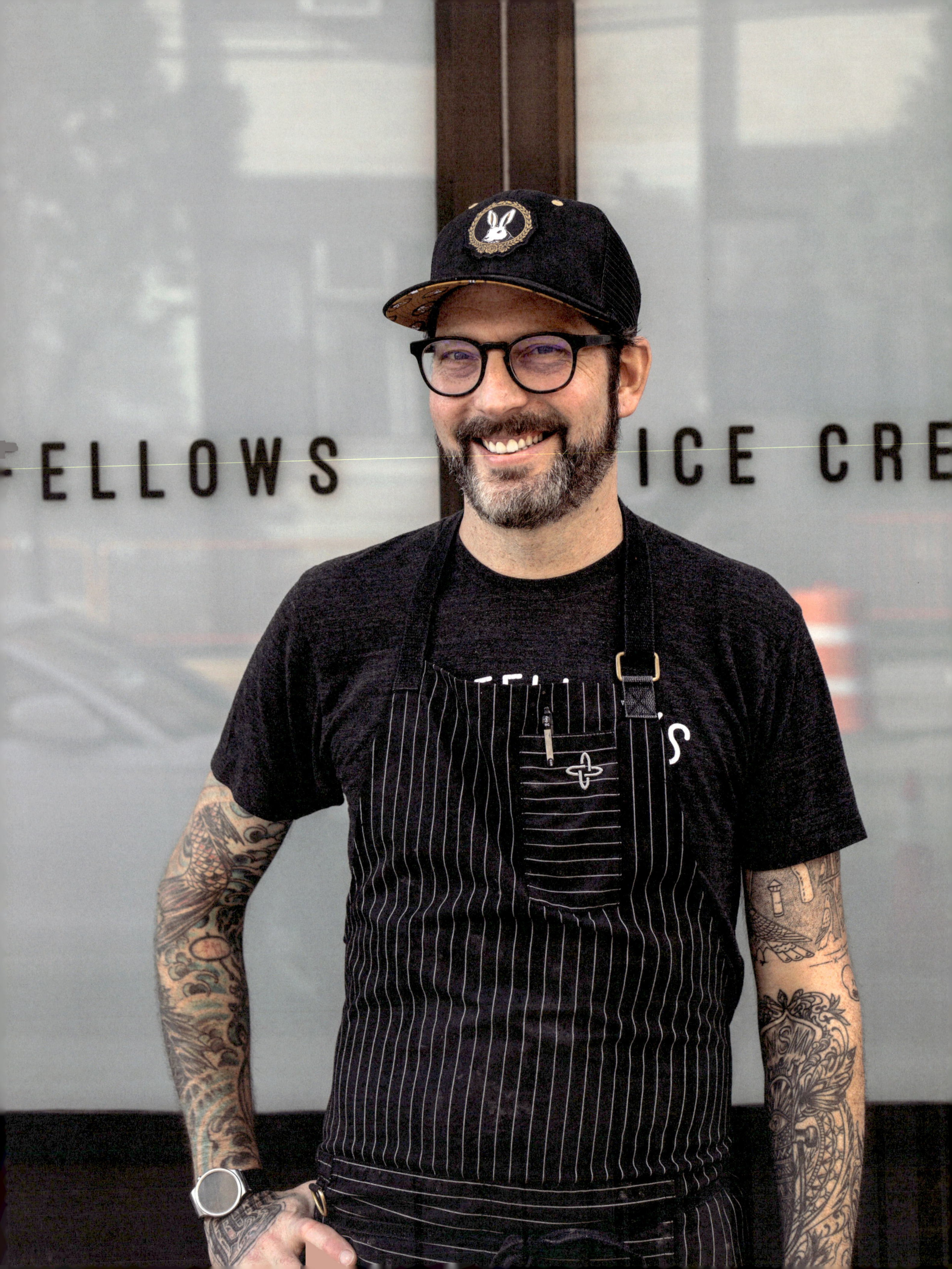
FELLOWS
ICE CRE

There are only so many things that you can shove into cream

I sat down with Sam in his Brooklyn ice cream factory to chat while we enjoyed some White Claws.

sam mason

oddfellows ice cream

new york, ny

Tell us about your background.

I'm Sam Mason. I grew up a little tot in Jacksonville, Florida. It was a strange place to grow up, and I wasn't the biggest fan. So, as soon as I threw my graduation cap up in the air, I was on a bus before it hit the ground. I went to Providence, Rhode Island, for culinary school at Johnson & Wales, and then in 1994, I moved to New York City and got my first job at Aureole, working with Charlie Palmer and Dan Rundell. I then moved over to Park Avenue Cafe, which was pretty awesome because I got to work with David Burke and Dan Budd, who was an extremely creative pastry chef. At about that time, my good friend had moved to Las Vegas to open up a restaurant called Voodoo, and he asked me to be the pastry chef. There was another restaurant opening there on the ground floor with Chef Jean-Louis Palladin. And so he's like, "Listen, I get it. You came to work with your buddy and shotgun beers on the roof. But, I should try to get you into this restaurant."

So I had my first meeting with Jean-Louis, we got along really well, and he took me on as his pastry chef. We worked together for four years, including returning to New York City to open Palladin in Times Square.

What kind of desserts were you doing there?

When I showed up, I had these sketches of these architecturally ridiculous things. It was the pastry, art, and design era. There were sugar sticks, three feet tall. Things got up on the plate and then would sit back down. He did not appreciate any of it. But after that, I reeled it back into making things that were a little cleaner and lower on the plate. You know, things that made sense.

Was it more classical stuff?

Yeah, we were doing ile flottantes and creme brulee, but he was also the first chef I worked for who made nothing in the fridge off-limits. So, it was my first time grabbing bell peppers and thinking about using them. We cooked stuff I had never thought about before, like a tomato tarte Tatin with fennel ice cream. After a few awesome years of doing that, he had become sick and was out of the kitchen, and I decided to move on.

I ended up with Rocco DiSpirito at Union Pacific, which was another very creative kitchen, but it was also the time where Rocco was exiting stage left for photoshoots and Vanity Fair covers. I started to get bored there and decided to go hang out Paul Liebrandt at Atlas, who's just another ridiculously creative human being. We did stuff that made no sense there. No sense in a good way, but we would also serve six people a night.

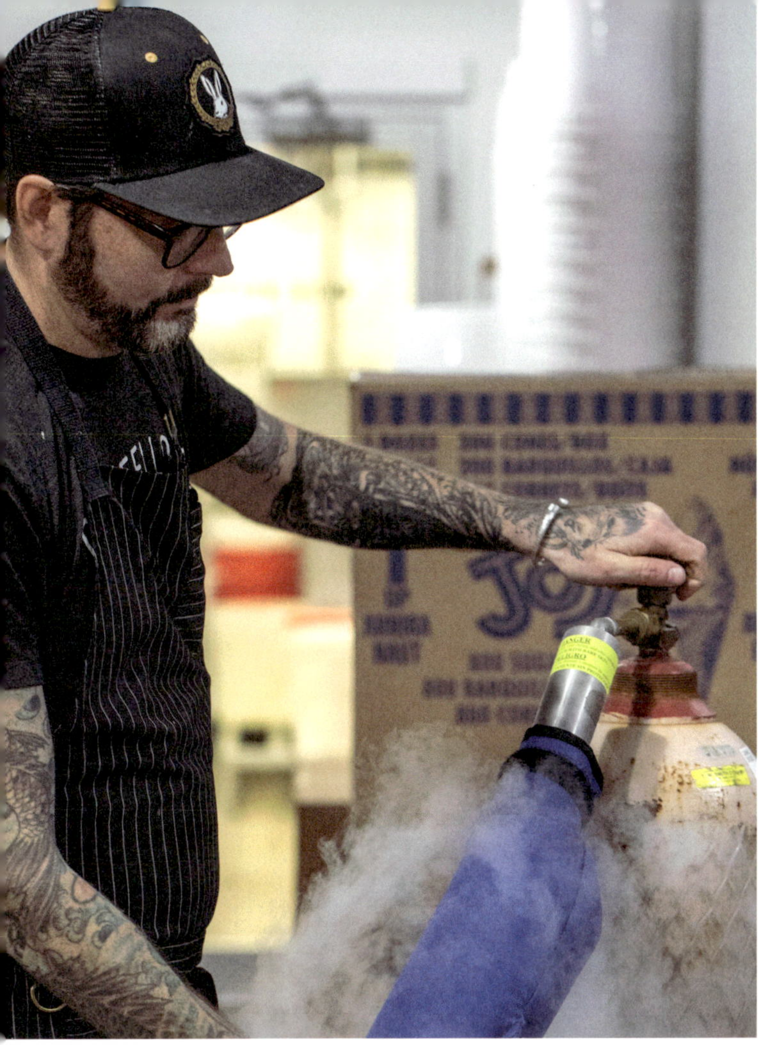

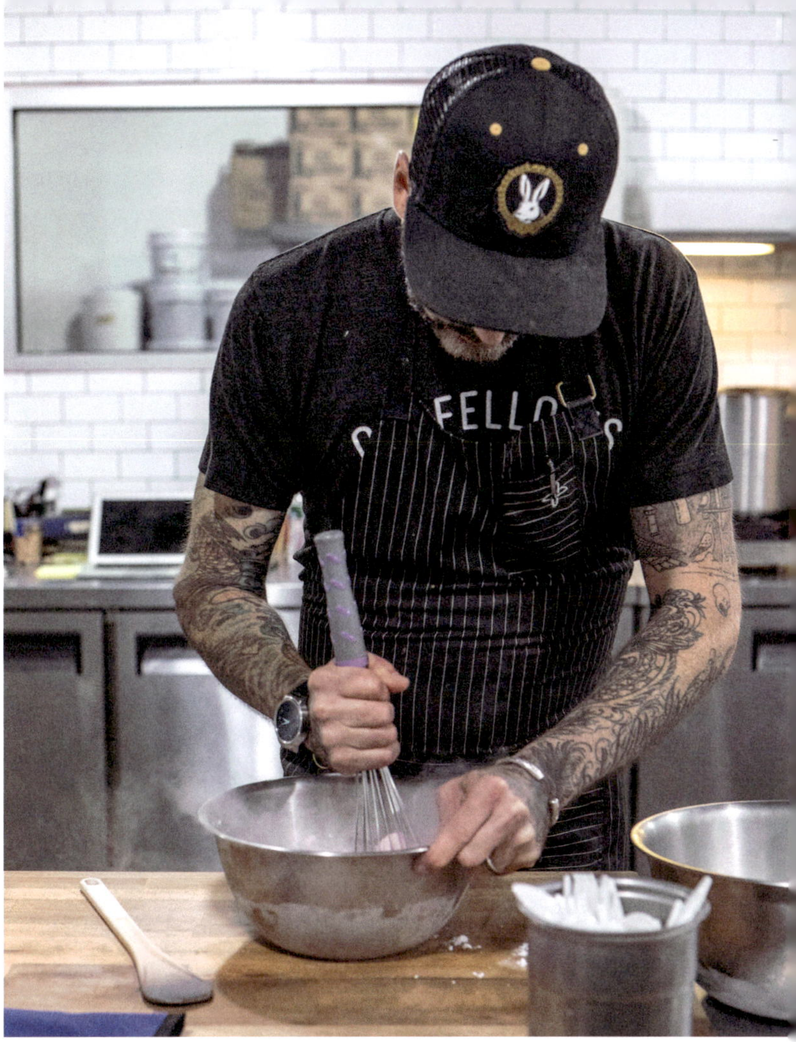

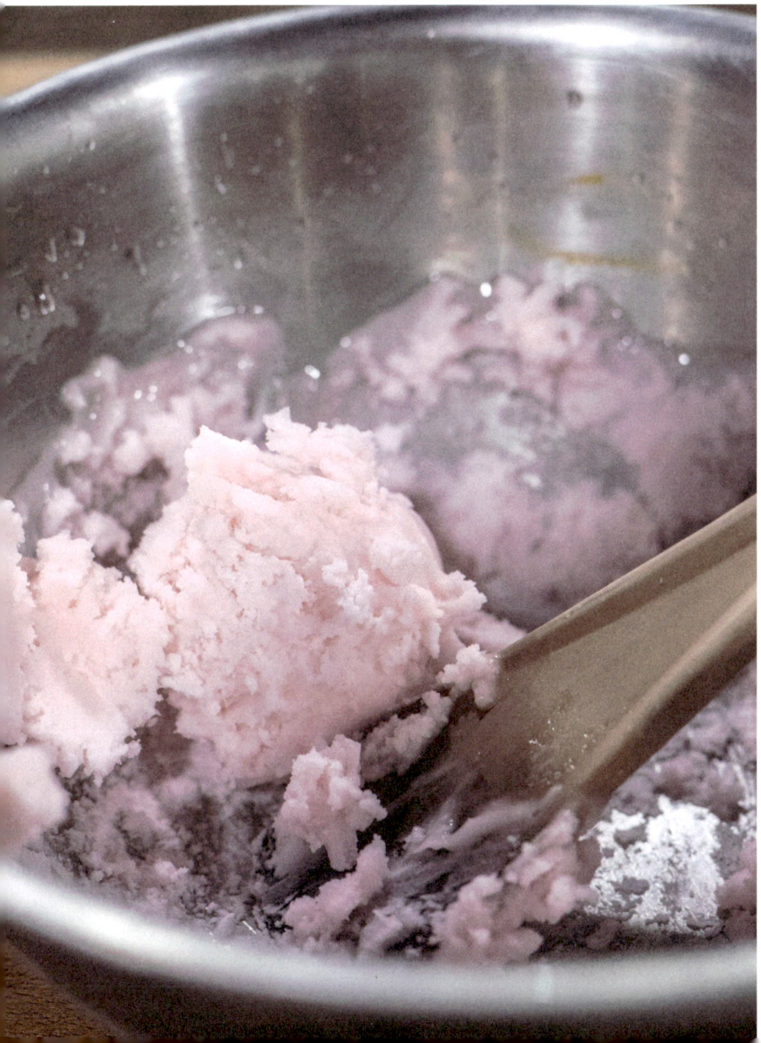

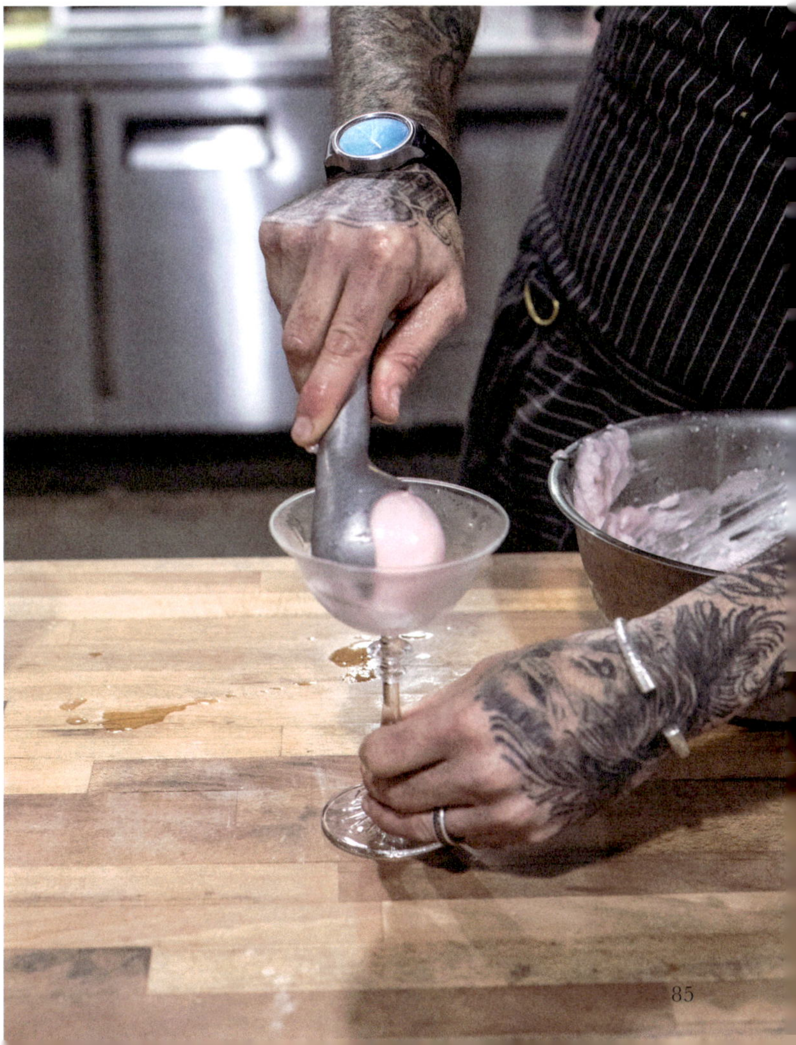

Rosé Sorbet

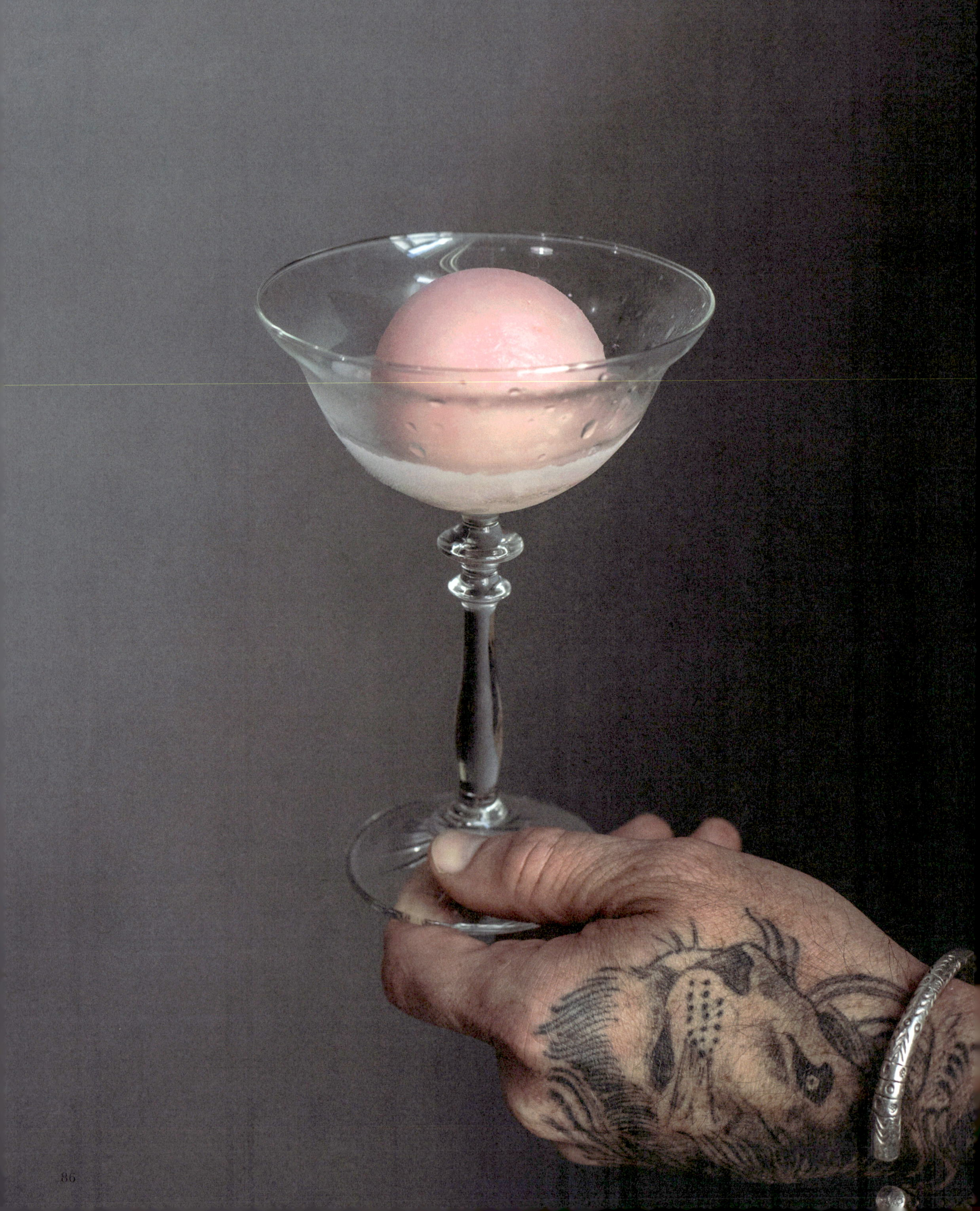

I think my last week at Atlas was the week of 9/11, and the whole world was depressed. So, I started trying to put money together to open a mechanical bull bar, and I wanted it to be this crazy, crazy thing. I soon realized that the insurance I had to get was more insane than the bar was going to be, so I ditched that idea. That six months of my life go by, and my bank account is getting down to what one White Claw costs.

I'll make sure to keep the White Claw reference in this interview.

One day everything will be equated to White Claw's price or whatever their stock is.

So, at that time, Wylie Dufresne had been calling me and asked if I could help him layout the kitchen at wd~50. By then, I'm looking at my bank account(looks at a can of White Claw), because I'm down to one White Claw. So in 2003, we opened wd~50, and we were out of our minds with stuff we were doing.

Did you know at the time that you guys were at the top of your game?

Not really, because we weren't getting a lot of people in the front door. Honestly, we were focusing more on the food rather than making people happy, and that was translating to people not showing up. You know, the hydrocolloid thing was beginning to rear its head, and we were dealing directly with these companies who would say, "We don't know how to use this stuff the way you want to use it." So we'd ask, "Well, can you send one of your little lab coat guys out here and hang out with us?" They would send us people, but we were completely self-teaching ourselves about how to use it in a restaurant. We're reading these books, which are impossible to comprehend, and trying to learn how to make these things work. A lot of that led to failures, but those failures led us in different directions that resulted in something great.

I remember one night we randomly had Heston Blumenthal at one table and Ferran Adria at the table next to him... no pressure, right? So I was making them carbonated celery sorbet, but doing it the dumbest way ever. I was pumping my chamber full of CO2, and sorbet is flying out of every seal. The machine was under all of this pressure, there is green sorbet everywhere, and I barely got enough scoops for those two tables. But then after dinner, Ferran comes in with his wife(who translates for him), and he's starts asking us all these questions about techniques. And we're like, "This is kinda cool." He ended up leaving with Cryovac bags of powders and took some of those ideas to crazy levels. That's when we started to realize that it might have been a good thing for our careers. Though, at the time, I think Wylie was about down to one White Claw as far as revenue goes.

Its gotta be nuts doing that type of "molecular gastronomy" food while someone like Ferran is also doing it. Did you feel at all in competition with them?

No, I don't think so. I think we were just enough out of the loop and on our own trajectory.

After wd~50, I decided to leave, and I opened Tailor, which was awesome. I mean, it was short-lived and was three years old when we decided that we shouldn't have spent 2.3 million dollars opening a restaurant.

I think I told you this before, but Tailor is kind of what I would dream of opening if I had to open a restaurant — having a pastry chef cook savory dishes and blurring the two sides.

Oh, it was so awesome. It was exhausting. The economy crashed, everyone was broke, and our restaurant was just too expensive. My partners were overzealous, and we were so far behind schedule. We had Paul Smith fabric wallpaper, we physically moved a staircase, and it was a mess. Like, who does that? If you gave me 2.3 million dollars, I'd give you two million back. I'd rather have 300 grand to open a restaurant. So, that shit the bed even though everyone now tells me how great it was.

Then I started my TV show, Dinner with The Band, and I got a little bit of money from that and opened my bar.

Did you have the bar idea still in your head after not being able to open the mechanical bull bar?

No, I just knew that I liked going to bars, and so it didn't seem out of the ordinary. I was sitting around with some buddies and thought we could probably open one for a couple of hundred grand. So now, at this point, Tailor is gone, and I have a shitty dive bar in Brooklyn. Out of nowhere, my current business partner, Mohan Kumar(who was a regular at wd~50) approaches me, and he's like, "Listen, I think I'm going to open an ice cream shop." Once again, its that story of someone asking me to help out and me getting roped in. Though I'm glad I got roped in, and six years later, here we are - Drinking White Claws.

How many locations do you have now?

We have five in the city, and now we have one in Boston.

How was making that step opening outside of New York?

It's easier than I thought it was going to be. One of our managers wanted to go back to Boston, and so we had a guy we trusted and understood us. It's crushing it and probably the best revenue stream out of any of our shops. It's in an outdoor mall, for the lack of a better term, and it happens to be in one of the wealthiest neighborhoods. So it's just a bunch of people buying ice cream for their kids so that they'll be quiet while they make their hedge fund phone calls.

And then we're opening in the Domino Sugar Factory, and that will have our shop between Roberta's and Other-Half Brewery.

Pizza, ice cream, and beer in one place. That's perfect.

Yeah, and we're going to do an ice cream truck. I don't know if we have anything else planned. Maybe Helsinki.

Since you're so focused on just ice cream, do you feel limited creatively?

Bored. I think we did two hundred flavors in our first year.

Two hundred?

Yeah, and we've probably done 400 since then. But now I'm running out of ideas. There are only so many things that you can shove into cream. I don't know; maybe I'm getting a little bit bored, but now that we have the farm and the factory, it's getting exciting. In January, we're going to announce the farm, announce our new partner, relaunch our new packaging designs, and go national in grocery stores. But at that point, you know, we'll be focusing on 15 flavors. We'll still have the shops doing their one-off flavors, but it's that crazy food truck idea that I'm interested in so I can do wacky stuff. I want to make people mad with my ice cream and make some kids cry. I'm kidding.

But the new farm is awesome. Our production is now vertically integrated, and we have all of our own dairy. All the production is with the Guernsey cattle, which is insane, and you can taste the grass they ate. They also have the a2 protein, which is even cooler because people who are lactose sensitive can drink it.

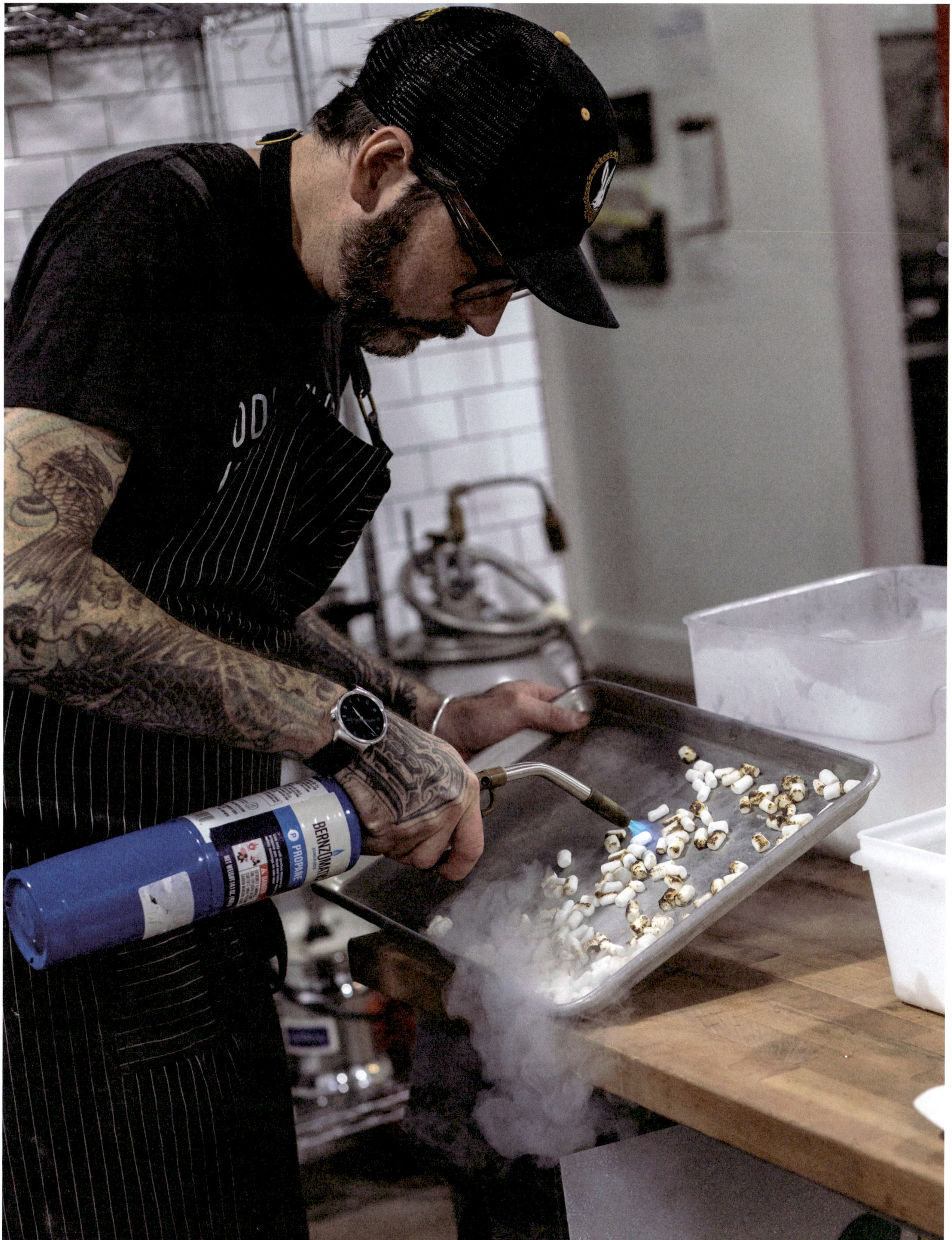
PROPANE

Producing your own dairy for your ice cream is financially feasible?

It's super expensive. But our new business partner is the guy who brought that to the table. He's like, "Listen, I've got a dairy farm, and I'm building a creamery. I love your approach to ice cream. Want to be partners?"

So do you think you'll stick to ice cream, or are you hoping this company grows to the point where it has it's systems and people in place to run itself?

I have an adult soda fountain idea that I want to put somewhere. Maybe in an awesome hotel lobby with chandeliers. But it'd be expensive. Like three White Claws shy of Tailor. But if I could get involved with a nice hotel that can handle the overhead, I could focus on some composed dishes again, because that's where all the fun is. Put things on a plate in a certain way again. You can only look at a scoop of ice cream so many times.

But are the hours here a lot different than being back in restaurants?

Oh man. I can walk out the front door and see my kid whenever I want. My wife would be super pissed if I started working the night shift again. I'm in bed by 10 pm these days, which is strange. This job has its benefits.

How has having a kid changed your priorities?

Oh, everything else has fallen to the wayside. The first few years are very important. To be around to share my first White Claw with him. I'm done... I've exhausted the White Claw associations.

You should do a White Claw Sorbet.

You know, in our Dumbo shop, I asked them to post a raspberry pink peppercorn sorbet with a raspberry White Claw pour-over and tag them in it. We got nothing. They could care less. All I wanted was a bunch of cases of free White Claw!

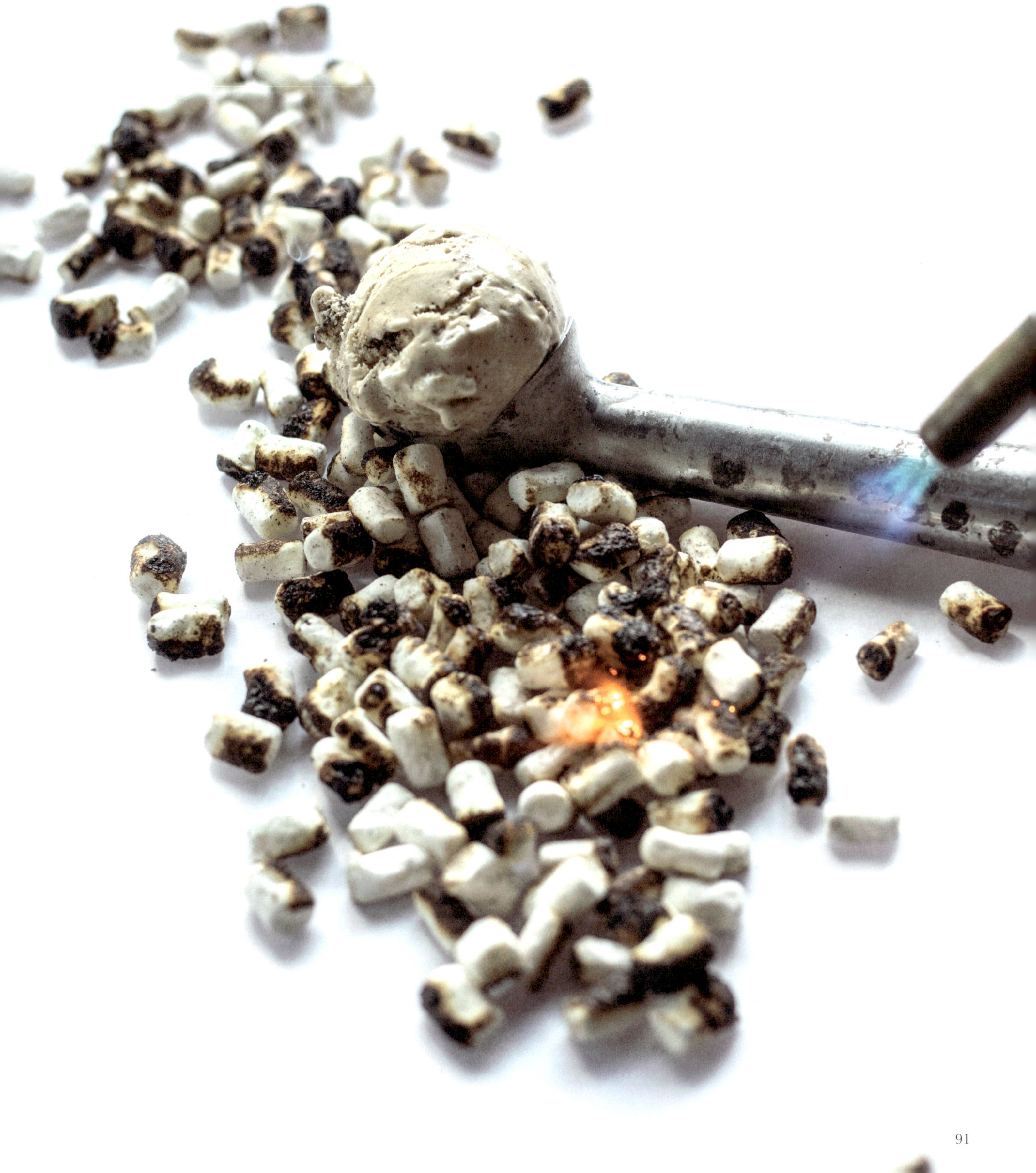

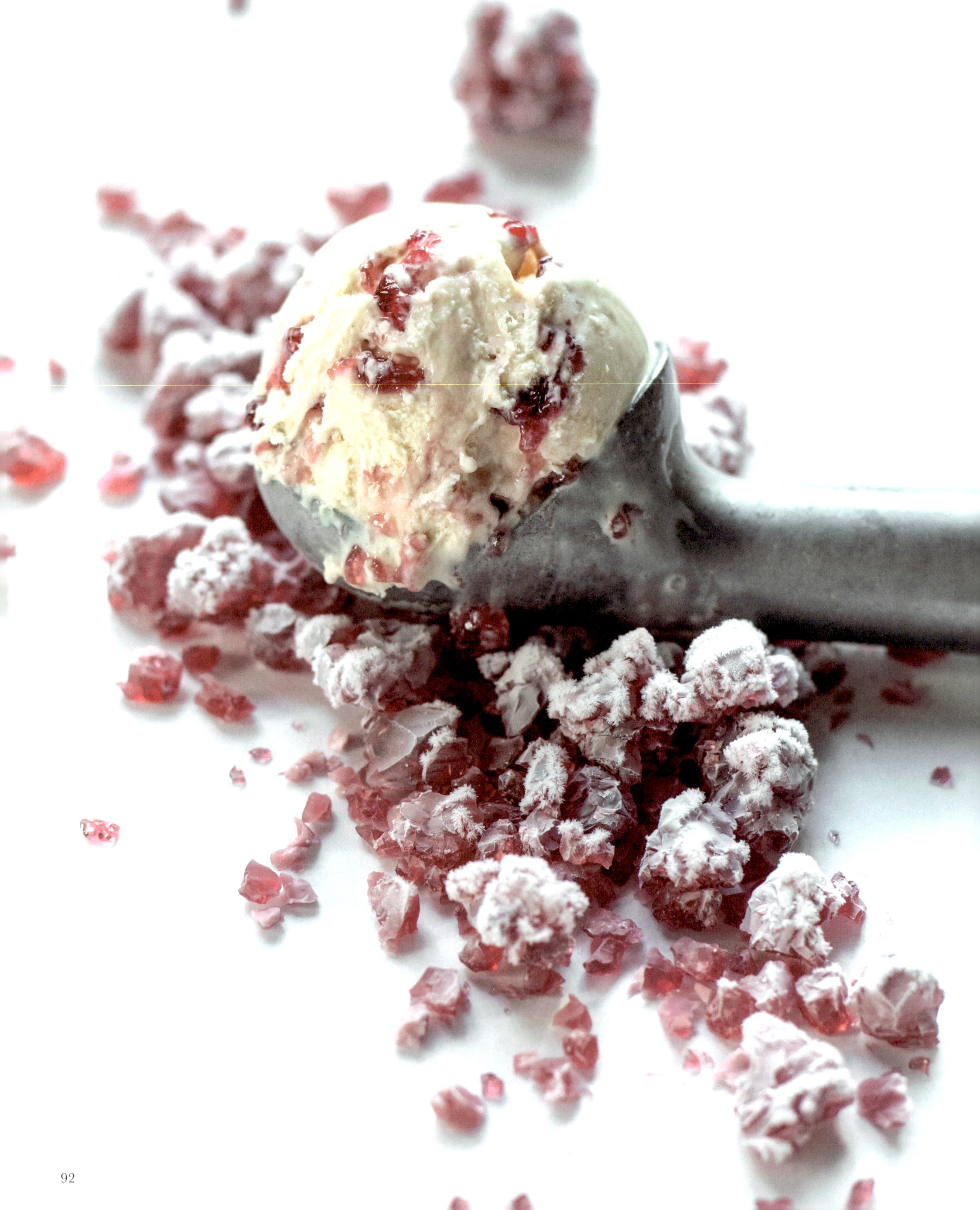

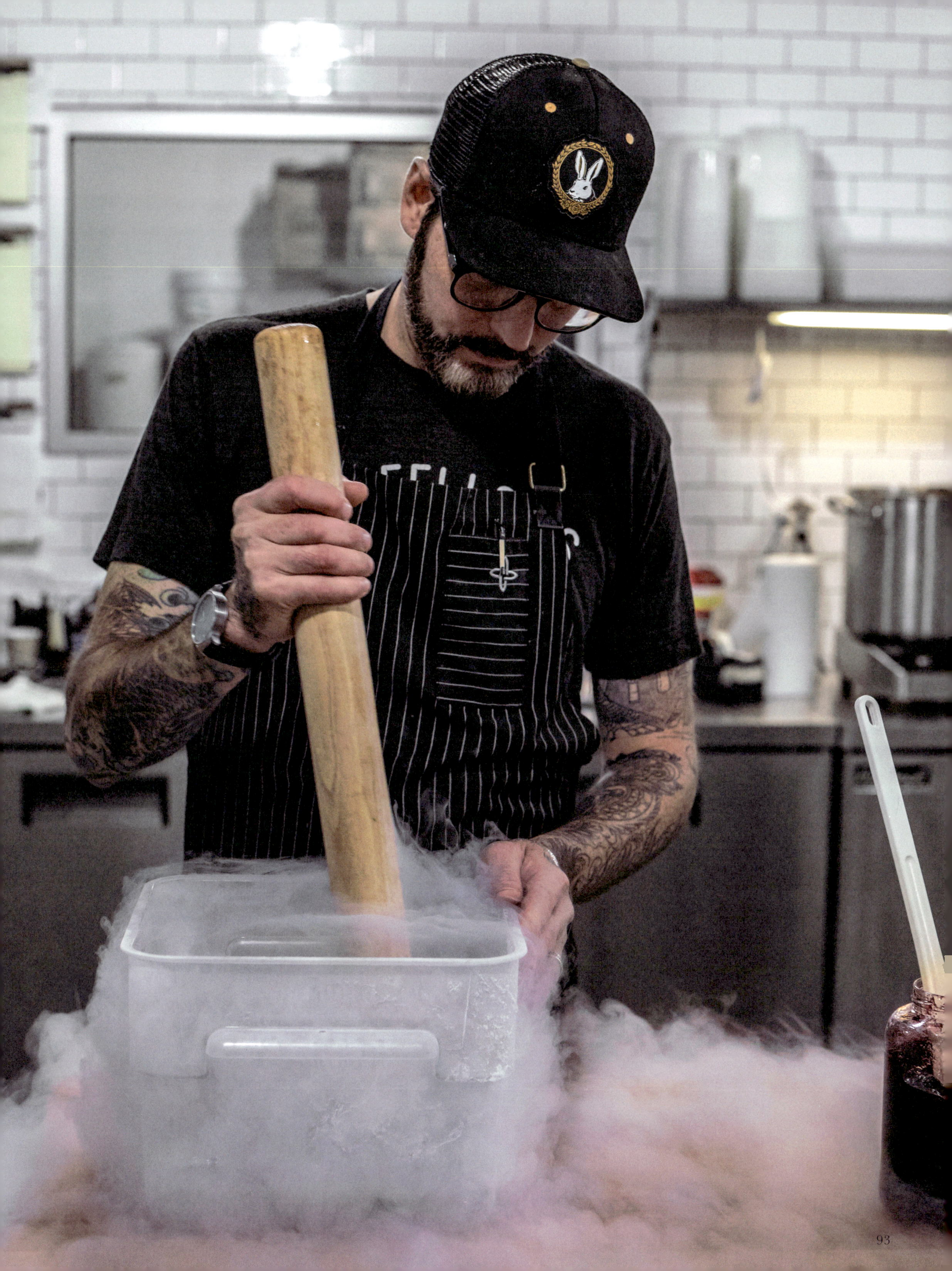

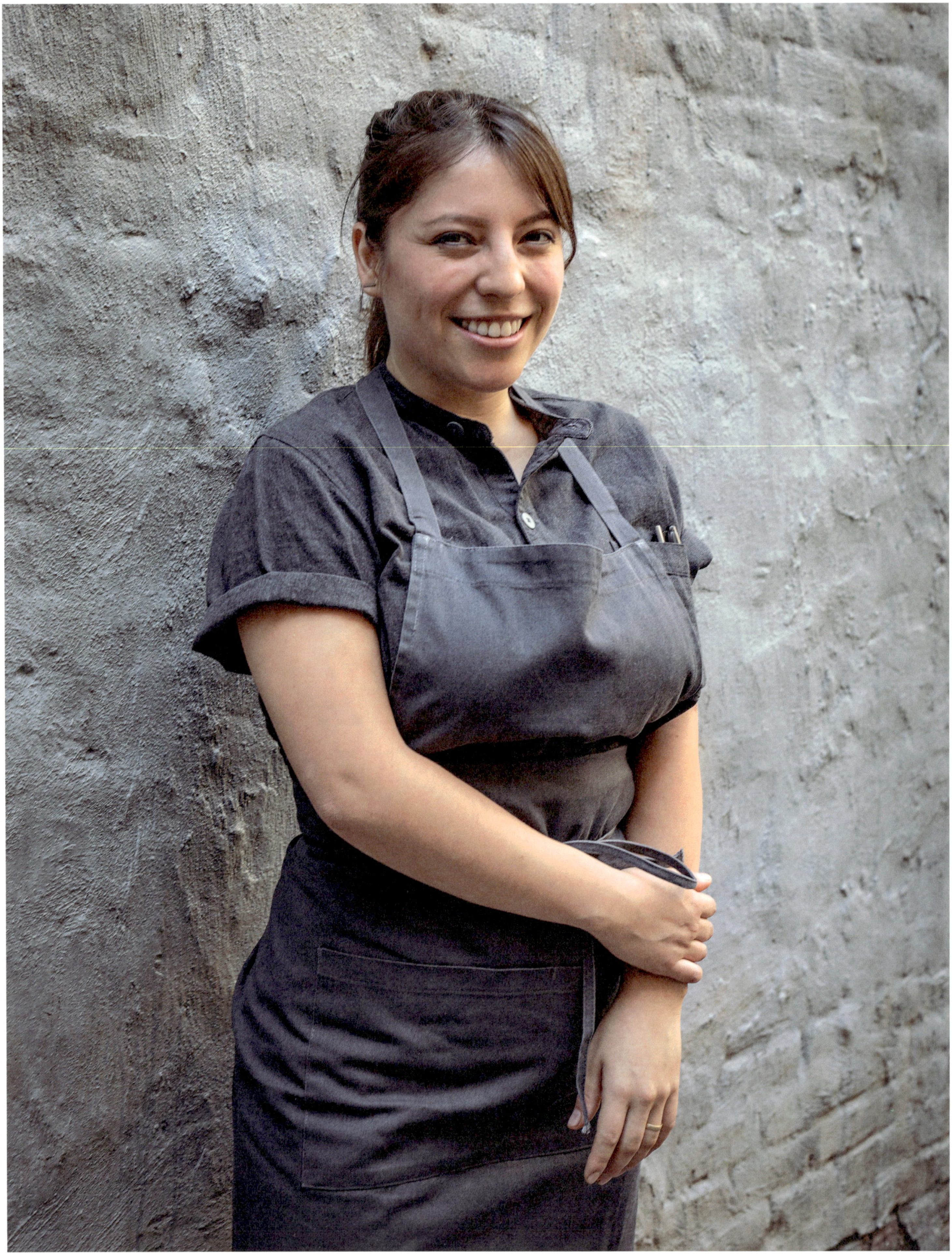

fuck it.

i'm going to new york.

isabel coss

cosme

new york, ny

Tell us about your background.

I was born and raised in Mexico City and spent years doing ballet. My parents didn't want me to become a cook, but I wanted to do something that involved movement, and I was used to the pressure from my Russian ballet teachers. They would push dancers until they cried. So, I started studying international business and graphic design, while at the same time going to culinary school. Going to school was fun, but I wanted more, and I think I found that in cooking. Right after I started in culinary school, I started working at Pujol.

So your first cooking job was at one of the best restaurants in Mexico?

I didn't know it was! I mean, I did, and I didn't. I don't know how I got a job there, but I pretended like I knew what I was doing and became their bread baker. I stopped going to culinary school after that and focused on working at the restaurant. At Pujol's 10-year anniversary party, I met Alex Stupak along with Rene Redzepi, and Alex Atala. It was super inspiring, and I decided I wanted to move to New York. I was 18 years old, and I thought, "Fuck It, I'm going."

I didn't know anybody in New York, and I went to study at the Culinary Institute of America because my parents still wanted me to be in school. Once I got to New York and saw the CIA prices, I decided against it and instead started working with Alex Stupak. I worked with him for five years, and we opened three restaurants together. It was the coolest and most educational time of my life. After that, I worked for two years at Agern in Grand Central, which was a project by Claus Meyer, and the chef was Gunnar Gíslason. Gunnar is like Santa Claus from Iceland and is the nicest guy you can imagine. He's like what a Viking would be if they didn't have to fight. He's just pure love and loves beer.

From there, how did you make your way to Cosme?

The pastry chef at Cosme at the time was my friend and wanted to go to the World Cup because we Mexicans love soccer. So they said the only way she could leave the restaurant and go was to convince me to work at Cosme. I had known Dani for seven years already, and we always wanted to work together, but it was never the right time. So my friend begged me and while I was drunk, I said yes. They actually recorded a video of me saying it and sent it to me later. So, I came to Cosme, and it's been

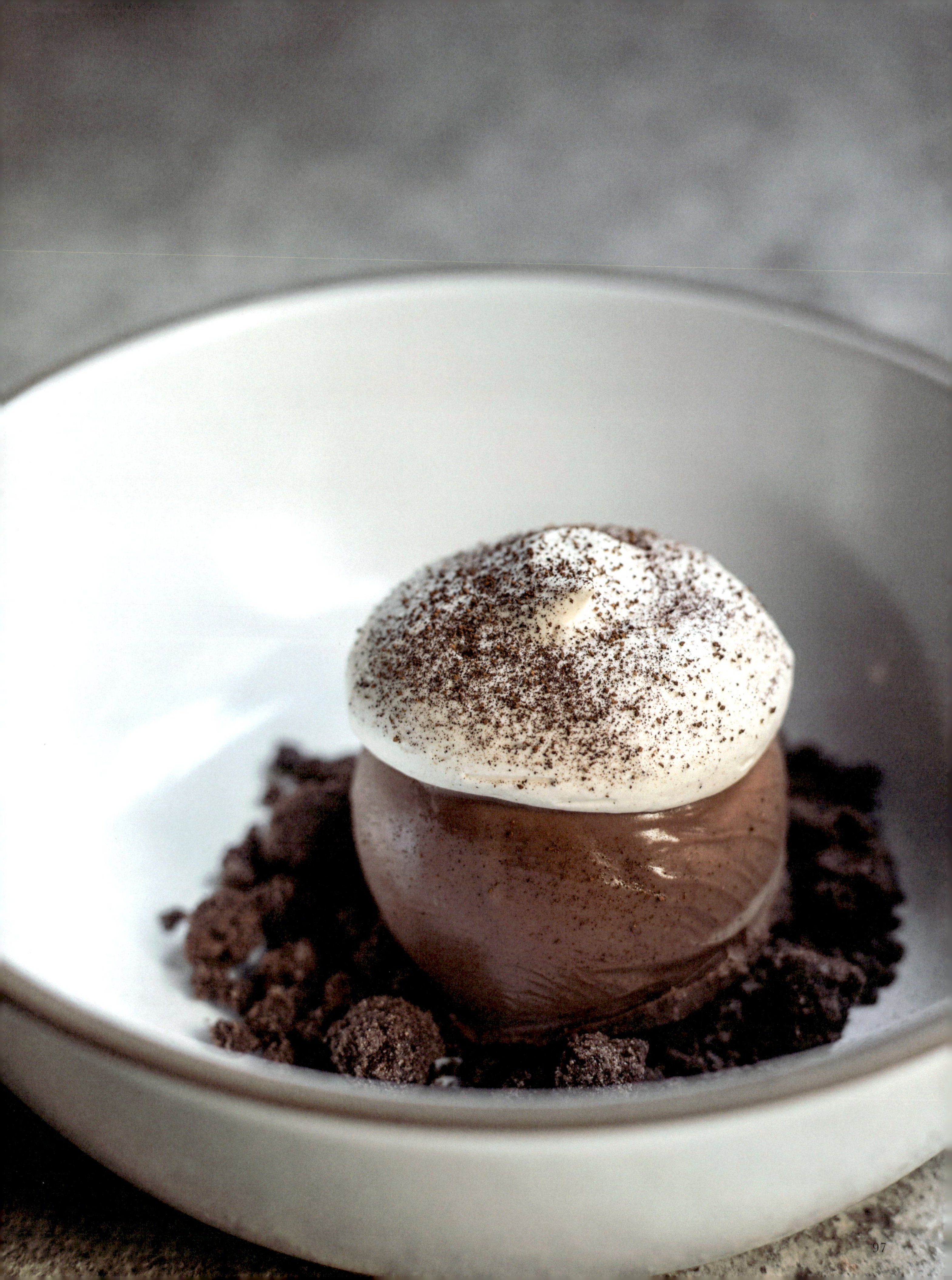

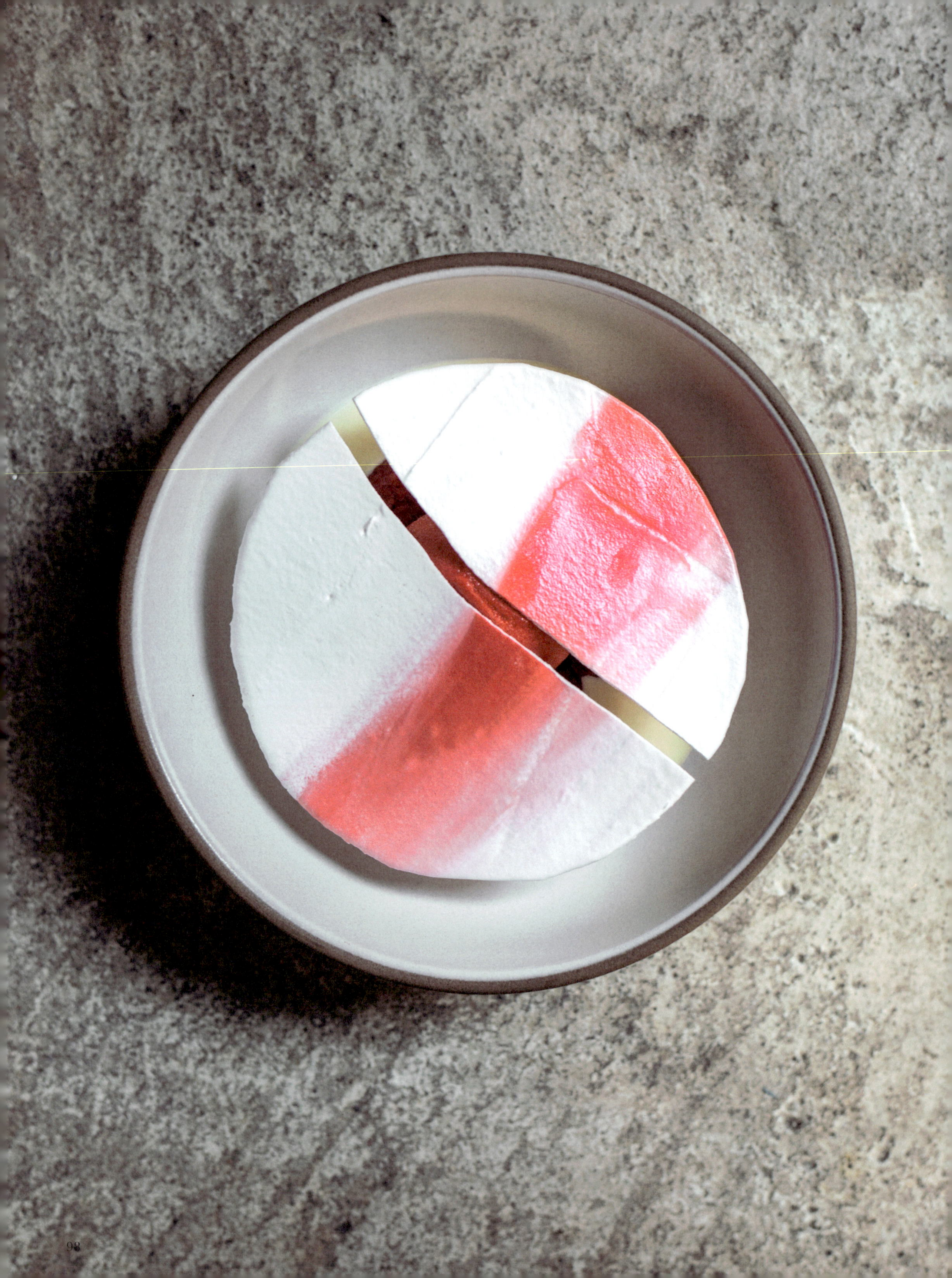

about two years. It's amazing, and I never knew I could learn so much. It's more than just a restaurant. It's like a school. I had to relearn everything because the requirements of this job are entirely different, and Dani demands fine-dining levels in a bigger and more casual restaurant. At the same time, I still have to care about myself and take care of my cooks. I started ballet again, and I also dance sometimes at night... that sounds bad. You know what I mean. At bars. Not for money. Let's make that clear. [laughs]

How was it to cook for these huge chefs like Rene Redzepi that early in your career?

It was super inspirational. It made me feel so proud to cook for them and see them love Mexican food and Mexican culture. I just did at dinner at Pujol, and the cooks there call me chef now. I'm not that interested in that, but it does feel good. To have kids looking up to you and asking about New York. If three of them end up moving to New York, I would be so proud, you know. I think the next generation of cooks is most important because they're disappearing as the glamour of being a chef fades.

How was working pastry with someone like Alex Stupak?

Working with him was a whole different switch, and that was what I wanted. I feel like when you're young, you want to learn from that kind of intensity. He's the best pastry chef that I know, and he has a lot of amazing theories. Even though I worked for him for five years and was in charge of pastry, you still cannot be a pastry chef for Alex Stupak. It's like how you cannot be the vocals for Johnny Cash, or have a Queen reunion concert without Freddy Mercury. I think the love that I have for this industry also comes from that intensity.

What do you think about the recent popularity of Mexican food?

It should have been sooner! I think it's been popular for a long time, but it's still has a misconception about its price point. If you serve the same quality of meat, but a tortilla is involved, then people think it should be cheaper. I think that's the cultural view of Mexico right now. That little border is a big difference. I think food is the most humble way to approach a culture, and Mexico is good at doing that. All of the recent political things have been making my friends nervous. But I think as long as we keep cooking our food, that is the best way to help.

It's like how mezcal has become popular over the last 8 or 10 years. You can go to any bar in New York, and each one has at least one mezcal cocktail. Some have a whole mezcal list. It's funny because mezcal is still a new thing in Mexico City. All my

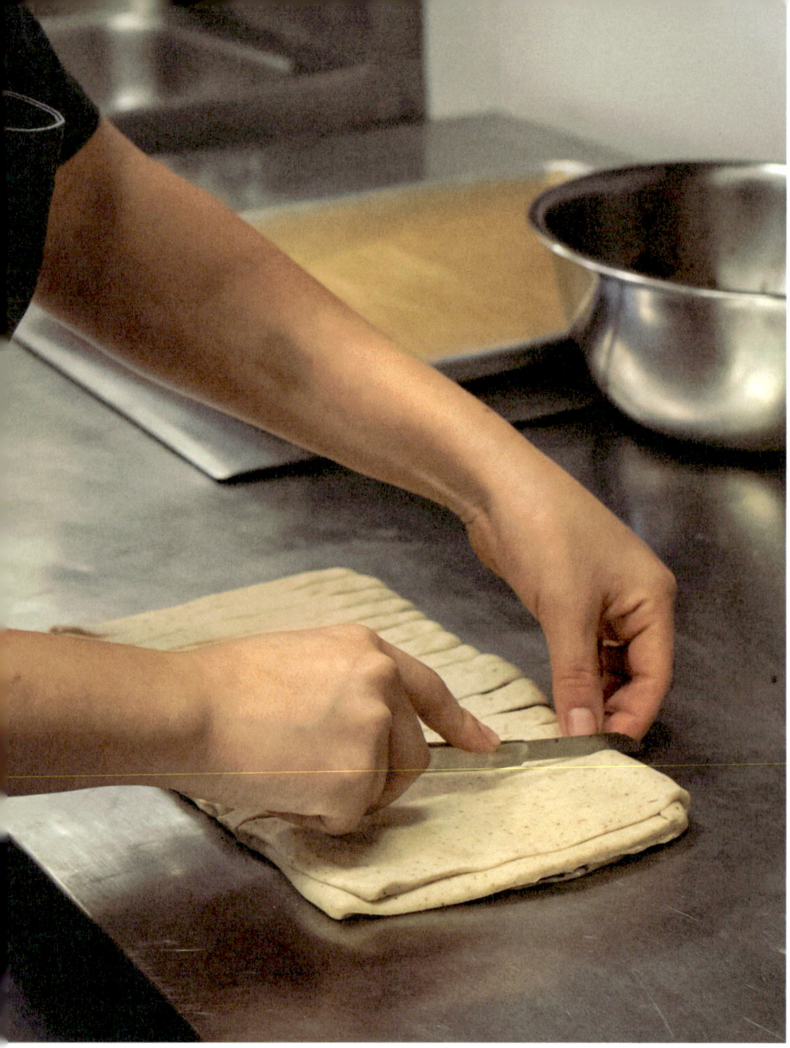

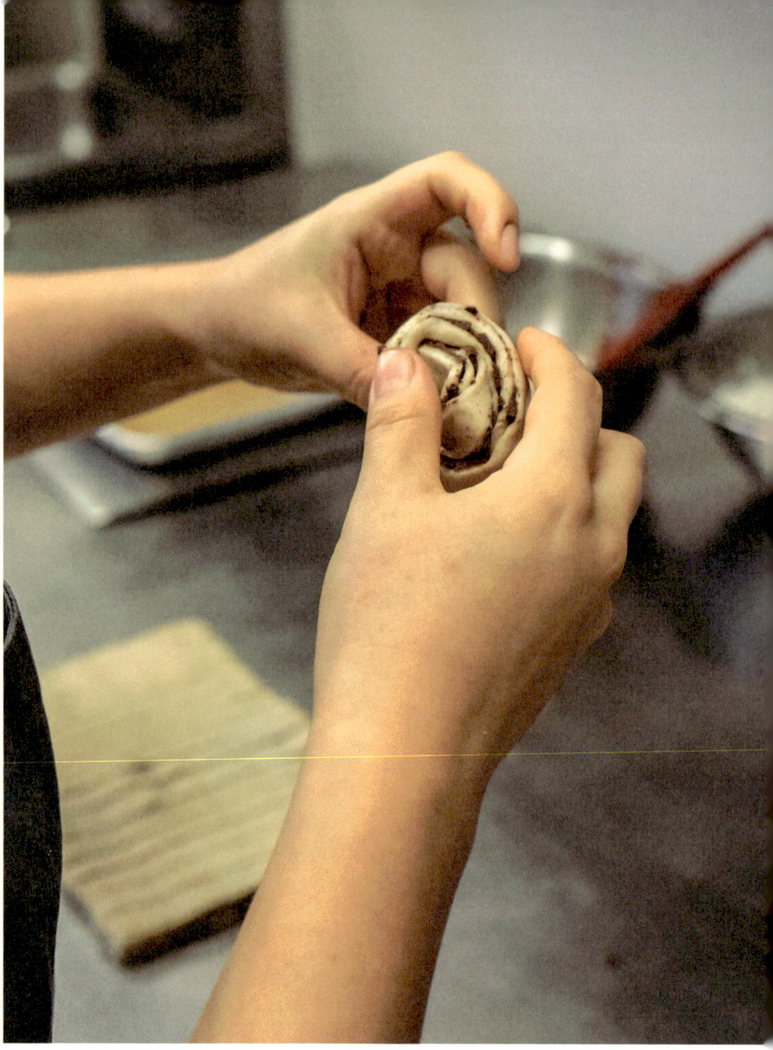

friends in Mexico look at me drinking mezcal and say, "What the fuck is that?"

What is that phrase? You don't have to be an asshole; you're not in Brooklyn anymore. It's the same. You don't have to drink mezcal; you're not in Brooklyn anymore.

How do you go about creating new desserts?

I think a lot of my inspiration comes from techniques, and I also like to have a story for each dessert. At Cosme, we try only to import chilies, corn, and maybe cinnamon. Everything else we try to use from here. So I love mangos and sapote, but I can't use them because they don't grow in New York though the amount of ingredients you can find has changed a lot in the past ten years. You couldn't find chilies or nixtamalized corn. I think at the end of the day; I like the flavors that my mother gave me growing up. I always try to go back to those ingredients. I always want to put some cajeta, Mexican chocolate, or toasted corn on them. Or I want some saltiness because Mexican food is very salty. We like salt, lime juice, and chilies on everything.

I'm also very visual and like colors. Many times the visual part is first. For example, the Fresas dessert. It has a red and white meringue with a tie-dye look, and underneath, it has a bright red strawberry sorbet, slow-roasted strawberries, and rompope made with pisco. The top is tie-dye, and after you finish your dessert, the bottom of your plate looks exactly like the meringue did.

The visual part is one of my favorite things about pastry, because you can create anything. If your cooking meat, you can't do shit with it. You can glue it and cut it a certain way, but in the end, people just want their steak. In pastry, you can create any shape or anything you want. I think that's why I ended up in pastry. Also, people would say, "Oh, you're a girl. Go to pastry." Ok, I'll take it!

The famous dessert here is the corn husk meringue. Is it annoying to keep that on the menu and reproduce it every day?

No, I'm attached to that dessert. It's a dessert from a bakery in Mexico that Dani and I went to growing up. It's also those types of flavors that I'm drawn towards. When

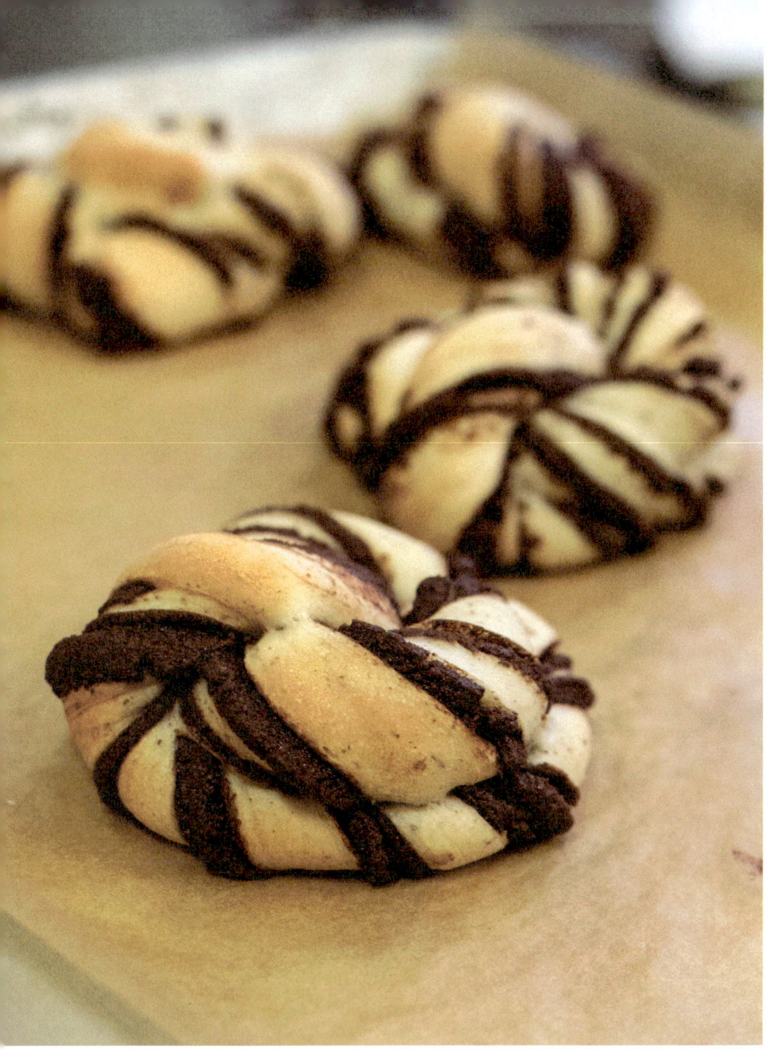

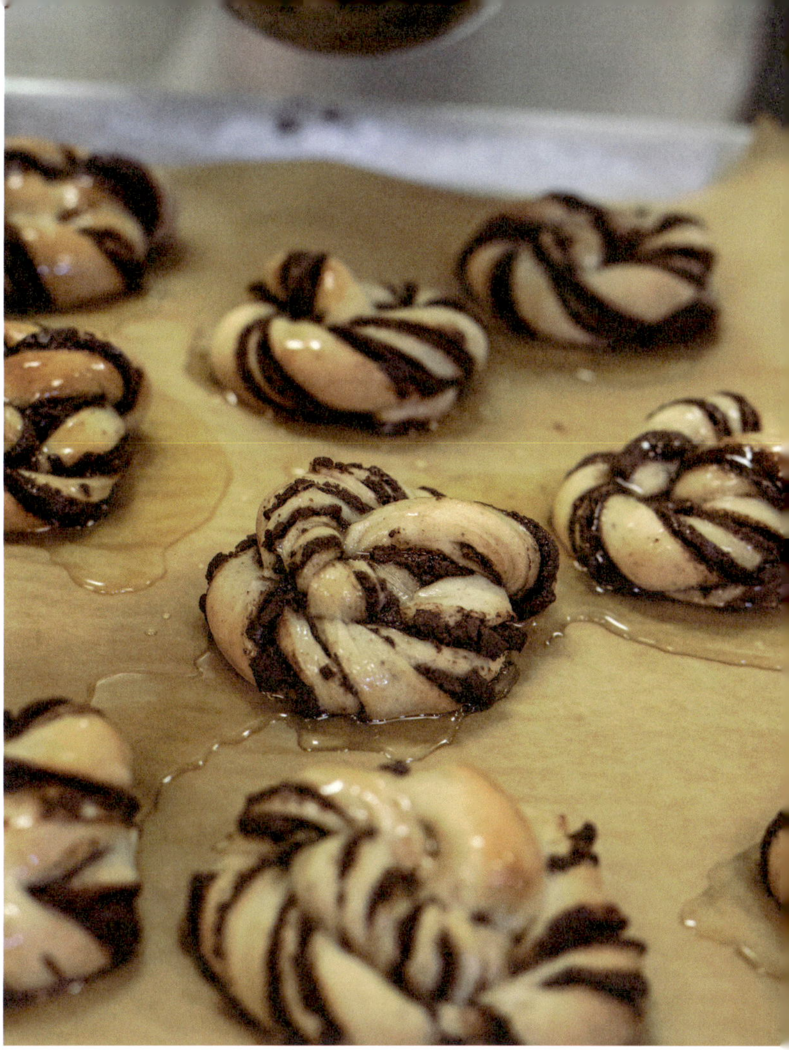

Dani was opening the restaurant, we already knew each other, and she was telling me about it. Then she went on and made it, and it's incredible. I steal one of them every day, so you could say I'm not tired of it. Maybe once I get tired of eating it, I'll get tired of making it. Also, it's one of those dishes that can't go away, or else New York will get mad.

What are your goals for the future?

I'm really looking forward to our new restaurant projects on the West coast. I'm really excited about the ingredients over there and eating all of the tacos in LA. We'll have a two-part restaurant that has a taqueria called Ditroit and a restaurant that is sort of like a hybrid of Cosme and Atla called Damian. Damian is the twin brother of Saint Cosme. They were doctors that cured people, and people called them saints. And then people killed them because they called it witchcraft, even though it was just medicine. We're also doing a restaurant in Las Vegas at the Wynn hotel.

So you'll be taking on a more corporate pastry chef role?

Yes. I'm scared of that. But I'm also excited because it's creating more opportunities for my cooks. After I left my last restaurant, one of my old cooks became a pastry chef, and that made me so freaking happy and proud. So I want my cooks now to do that, and if I can keep them in the same restaurant group, that's even better. If I can do that and make them happy, then that makes me happy. That's, I guess, why we end up in this industry.

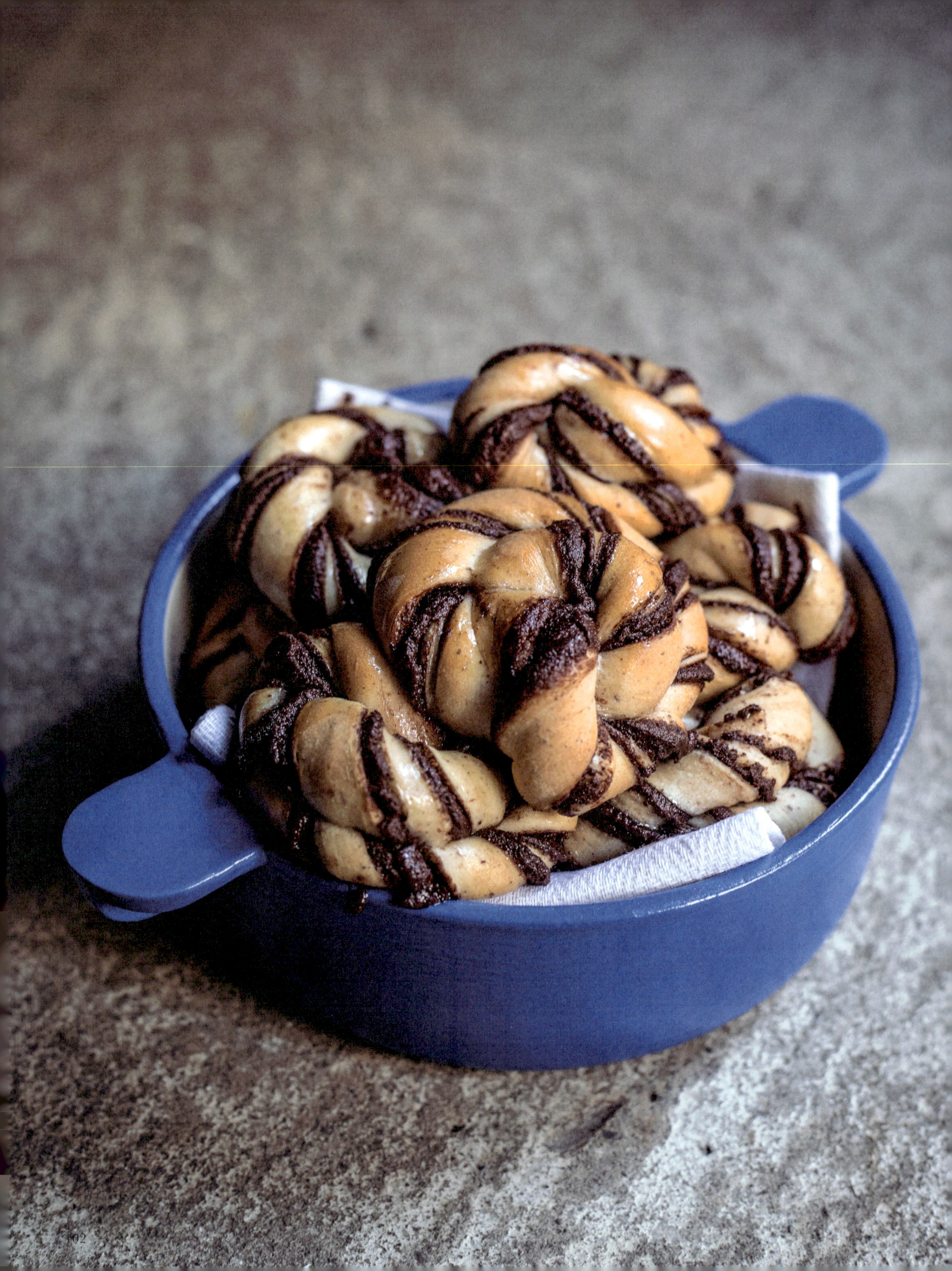

"This pan de dulce is a symbiosis of my career as a pastry chef. The idea was rooted in Kanelsnurrer, which is a traditional cinnamon swirl roll you would find at a Danish bakery. New York is my adopted home and like any respectable New Yorker: I love a good babka. That's the reason this recipe transformed into a chocolate-flavored bread. I'm from Mexico City, and indulging in pan dulce is on par with tortilla consumption there (which means it is something we eat ALL the time). It's in my DNA to have pan dulce soaked in coffee for every meal. So... that's how this Mexican chocolate babka, shaped like a traditional Danish, and soaked in carajillo was born."

Mexican Chocolate Babka

Babka Dough

Ingredients:

450 g	all-purpose flour
85 g	sugar
10 g	yeast
4 g	Mexican canela, powdered
5 g	kosher salt
200 g	whole milk
2 ea	eggs, large
85 g	butter, softened

Method:

Set a 15 minute timer. Place all dry ingredients into a kitchen-aid bowl with the hook attachment. Make sure the yeast doesn't touch the salt. Whish together the milk and eggs, and then add to the kitchen aid on low speed until the dough comes together. Slowly add the butter in pieces. Mix on speed 3, scraping the bowl occasionally until the dough starts to pull away from the bowl. Turn into an oiled tray lined with parchment paper and flatten the dough into a rectangle. Let rest in the refrigerator overnight.

Mexican Chocolate Romance

Ingredients:

100 g	butter, softened
100 g	Mexican Chocolate, melted at room temp
5 g	kosher salt

Method:

Cream the softened butter with a whisk. Fold in the melted Mexican chocolate and add the salt to season. Avoid incorporating air into the mixture.

Carajillo Syrup

Ingredients:

200 g	water
200 g	sugar, in the raw
70 g	Liqour 43

Method:

In a medium-size pot, make a simple syrup with the water and sugar. Remove from the heat and cool down. Add the Liqour 43.

Shaping The Babka

Sprinkle some flour over the baking table and remove the dough from the half sheet tray. Roll the dough into a rectangle, about 8 by 20 inches. Spread the Mexican chocolate romance evenly on the dough. The mixture and dough should be both be room temp. Fold the 1/3 left section towards the center, the 1/3 right to center like a letter fold. Cut 2-inch strips. Stretch the pieces a bit and roll towards you around 3-4 times. Roll twice around your index and middle finger, tuck in the end, and place over a paper-lined tray. (repeat with each strip)

Proof and bake at 310F , high fan, for 12 minutes. Once the bread is baked and still warm, brush them with the liquor 43 syrup and allow them to cool.

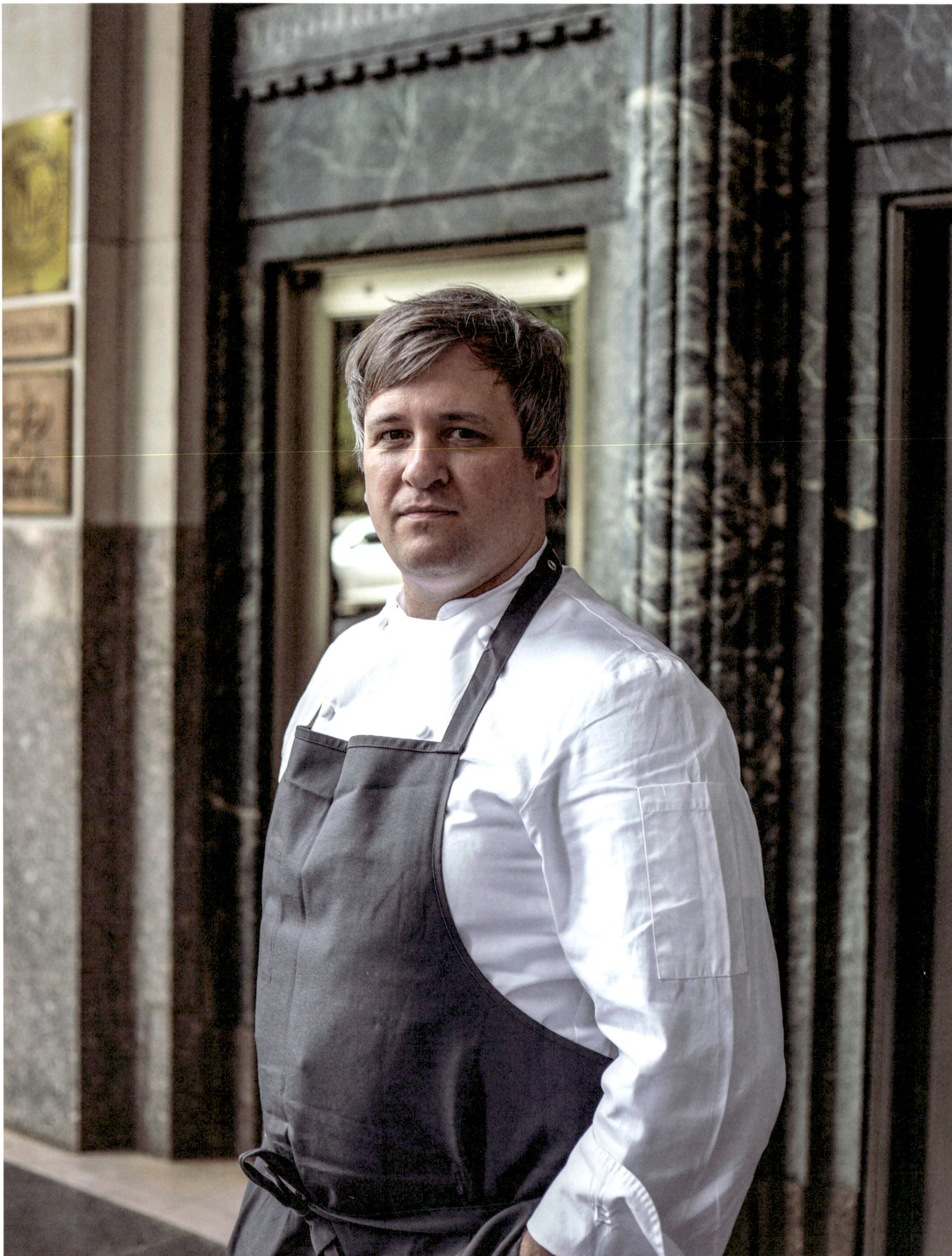

milk & honey

mark welker

eleven madison park
make it nice
new york, ny

Tell us about your background.

I'm originally from a small town in Southern Indiana called Seymour. Growing up, my family would always cook. In hindsight, it may not have been the most glamorous food, but cooking in our house was a thing, especially during the holidays. During Christmas, we would always build a gingerbread house, and I remember every surface of the house had cookies drying on it. When I was getting to the age where I was meeting with career advisers, I knew that I loved food and shows on The Food Network like Emeril Lagasse made me realize that you can make a career out of cooking. I loved the way cooking brought people together, the excitement of it, the creativity of it, and I especially loved eating it.

I went to culinary school at Sullivan College in Louisville, Kentucky, and did the baking and pastry program. In Louisville, there weren't any well-known pastry chefs or even many pastry cook positions, so I started cooking savory food. I got a job with chef Anoosh Shariat at his restaurant, Shariat's, and he quickly became a mentor and helped guide me. He taught me a lot about what it meant to be a chef and laid this great foundation down for me. He had a pastry chef there, but she would come in the mornings and bake everything, and I would plate it on the garde manger station. I remember always taking the desserts so seriously, and so I quickly stepped into that pastry chef role. I would come in early to bake the bread, and then I would work the hot-line for service, or if the sous chef was off, I would run the whole line. I think that was a good foundation for cooking and taught me how to season, how to use salt, how to do the dance in the kitchen, and how to work quickly. It was actual cooking and not arts and crafts. I have always had that philosophy since, and I think it's essential to have that pace in the kitchen.

Do you think the pastry cooks that only have pastry experience lack the intensity that you get from a cook that has worked the savory side?

Oh, very much so. I think the strongest pastry cooks do have savory backgrounds. I'm not saying that it's a 100 percent guarantee that you won't be a successful pastry chef if you don't have that, but you're going to be more well-rounded. We try to blur the lines between savory and pastry at all of our restaurants. For example, the way that we've structured our department at the NoMad in Los Angeles, the pastry cooks are starting to learn the hot-line, and they are becoming more valuable for the restaurant because we can put them wherever we need them.

So where did you go next after Shariat's?

I was in Louisville for four years and then followed a girlfriend to St. Louis. I started working at a restaurant called Chez Leon, and again I did both the pastry and the pantry. I loved that job because of all the charcuterie that I got to learn. We made sausages, patties, terrines, smoked salmon, and I quickly realized that it was in my realm of pastry and recipes.

Like following exact recipes and set rules?

Yeah, and it was prep heavy. I think that's one of the things that I love about being a pastry chef. Everything in pastry is planned multiple days out, and when you're cooking cuisine, every day, you start fresh except for stocks or sauces. I was there for two years, and it was great learning about French cuisine. When I worked at Shariat's, the cuisine was very global. Chef Anoosh was from Iran and was vegetarian, so that style of cooking was more fluid. Moving on to French cuisine was more rigid and more rules to follow.

After that, I worked for Larry Forgione at An American Place Restaurant, and I think that's where my mind and direction changed. I wanted to break free from these smaller cities, started thinking larger, and set some more substantial long-term goals outside of the Midwest. Larry, of course, came from New York and is incredible at farm-to-table cooking. He would come into the restaurant, and he would bring in stacks of blackberries. Some years I think he bought the whole farm's crop. We would preserve them, figure out ways to use all of them, and blackberries would be all over the menu. The same would happen for other things all the time, like white asparagus or other seasonal vegetables. That sparked my interest in going out more. I started taking trips to Chicago to eat at places like Charlie Trotters and Alinea, and then making trips to New York for food. I think deep down a goal of mine, since culinary school even, was to live and work in France. I felt that it was something every great pastry chef had to do. So I set up a year-long stage at a small bakery in the South of France. I quickly realized that it was more of a personal goal and challenge and that I wasn't learning that much. I did learn how to do two-hundred croissants a day rather than twelve, or how to decorate twenty cakes instead of one. I felt like it was more of a vacation and that I was learning more about French culture than cooking, so I cut my trail short.

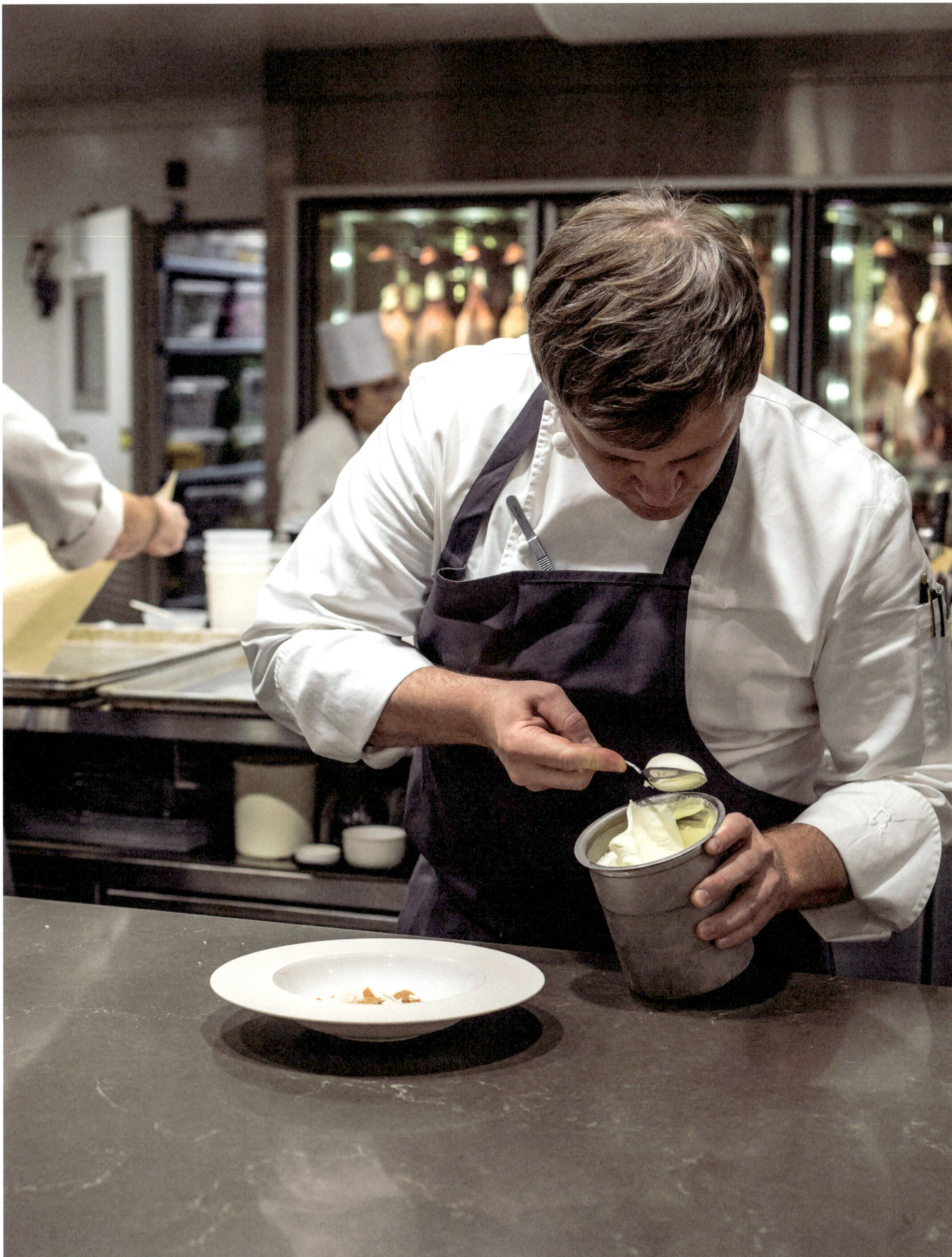

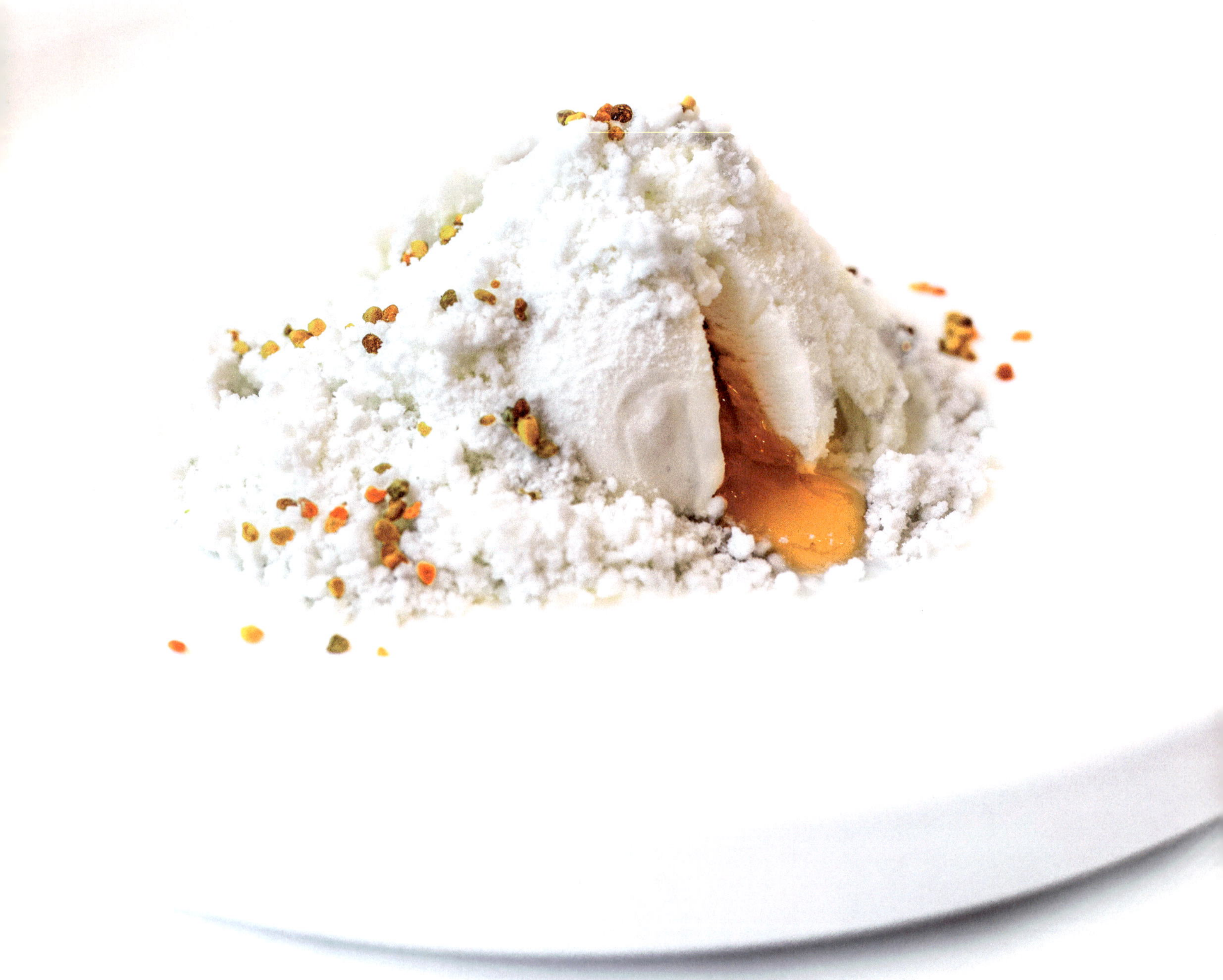

Milk & Honey

I was ready to go back to work, so I did a month and a half stage at wd-50 with Alex Stupak, Rosio Sanchez, and Wylie, of course. That was a great experience, and it was fun learning a lot of new techniques that weren't just making a pastry cream. This was in late 2008, and the economy was tanking, so a lot of the top New York restaurants weren't doing great. I realized I needed to find a job that was actually going to pay me because my savings were starting to run out. I couldn't find a job that I liked in New York, and some friends of mine bought a coffee shop in St. Loius, so I went back to help them open that. After a few months of doing that, I came back to New York, and I got a job at Eleven Madison Park. That was in 2009, and it was a lot different then. We would do ten covers on a Monday, and later on Saturday night we would get crushed doing two hundred covers. But that August of 2009, we got four stars from The New York Times, and that's when everything changed. We were fully booked every night, and fortunately, its been that way ever since.

I bet the San Pelligrino List did a lot for business also.

It's been this roller coaster that always goes back up. The first year we got on the San Pelligrino list, we started at 50, and I don't think any of the cooks knew what the list was. But we quickly learned, and we made it our mantra or motto. When I first started, and we wanted four stars, we could use it to push the team. Is this four stars? A cook could put up a quenelle with a hole in it, and we could literally ask, "Is that quenelle four stars?" No. It was quite clear, and it was either yes or no. We kind of grasp onto that, and so with the San Pellegrino list as a trajectory, we can use it as, "Is that what the best restaurant in the world would do?"

So you've been here for ten years then? Most people don't stay in a restaurant that long.

Yeah, I hit my ten-year mark in April.

Is there a reason why this restaurant is such a good fit for you?

Yeah, I'm surrounded by like-minded individuals that all want the same thing. I'm also pushed harder than I've ever been by my peers and by Chef Humm. I've always set big goals for myself, and I have been able to push to reach them. Now, my goal is to use my position to mentor the other chefs and give them opportunities to shine and reach their goals.

I think most restaurants of this caliber would have a pastry chef, and that person would stick to focusing on just the one restaurant. You're doing all the others. How did that happen?

So I started at Eleven Madison Park in 2009 when Angela Pinkerton was the pastry chef. By 2010, I was a sous chef, and then by 2011, we were planning the NoMad Hotel, which opened in 2012. I left EMP and was the opening pastry chef at the NoMad. That was a real wake up call for me because at the time I was very cocky and had a huge ego, I realized that I wasn't ready to be a pastry chef, but everyone on that team was the same way. Everyone was in these growth roles, as we say, and we all learned together. After a few years, I found my stride, and I started to get comfortable. Angela Pinkerton left in 2014 or 2015, and at that point, we were planning other NoMads, and it was kind of apparent that I worked well with Chef Humm and could execute his vision. So I came back as the corporate pastry chef, essentially, and that was a whole world of challenges itself. It's tough to manage pastry chefs, who, by all means, have the talent to run their own department. But I think it's so that Chef Daniel doesn't have to be here all of the time and he can focus on what he needs to. I can be the liaison between Chef Daniel and the pastry chefs and help execute the vision.

Now I'm not working services and much more involved in the r&d process. Now that I've lost that stress of service, my creativity has gone up. I can now manage my stress and manage the other pastry chef's stress so that we can all achieve the same goal and get to the places we all need to be.

That's the dream role when you don't have to worry about the daily production or service at the restaurant.

The only reason I don't have to worry about that is that I have such talented people in each restaurant. If at Eleven Madison Park, we weren't able to hit the finish line, I would step in. But expectations have to be set so that people aren't leaning on me too much. I want the chefs to feel comfortable being vulnerable enough to say, "Hey, I need help." I can manage my schedule and projects to give them the support that they need or talk them off the ledge.

Are the desserts and all the different locations your creations, or are they collaborations with the pastry chefs?

It's very much collaborative all around. We have scheduled tastings where the cooks can work on dishes and receive feedback from the whole team of chefs, including Chef Daniel. Every quarter we have what we call Cook Battles. There is a formatted template where they have to come up with a dish concept, draw pictures, and shpeal the idea.

We have four fundamental words that we use when we create food. It's got to be delicious, beautiful, creative, and have intention or a story. For the story element, that would be, let's say, a strawberry farmer who also grows rhubarb, and so we put the two ingredients together. So each dish we judge through the lens of those four words, and we decide which one is best. After we pick a winner, the cook is assigned a mentor to help them with the dish, and then they usually get to present the dish to Chef Humm. It's pretty nerve-wracking for them, but the idea is that something makes it onto the menu. It might not be a full dish, but maybe a technique of a component.

At that level, everyone is expected to be creative in our kitchens, to learn how to take criticism, and, most importantly, to criticize themselves.

What was the intention behind the milk and honey dessert? Why is that a dessert that you've continued to evolve in all of the restaurants?

It started because Chef Humm is from Switzerland, and it's comfort food for him. His mom used to give him milk sweetened with honey when he didn't feel well. Back in 2010, when Chef Angela was still here, he wanted a dessert of milk and honey, and she developed the original version. It was a huge hit, and people loved it. It's actually my favorite one as well. It was also super refined and felt like Eleven Madison Park food did at that time.

Then when the NoMad opened up, chef Humm wanted a version there, so I developed the one with the quenelles and stripes. That version took on more of a frozen cereal vibe, and felt more organic and more like the Nomad's food. That version has a mix of rustic and refinement. I don't care where the ice cream goes on the plate, but the quenelles have to be perfect, and the stripes need to be parallel because the rest of the dish is all the cookie crumbs and crunchy things.

After that, it was a snowball effect. For each new project, we need a new version of the milk and honey dessert. It's a challenge creating different dishes with such few ingredients. It's working with only two main flavors, but it forces me to be creative. You'd be surprised how many different things can you do with milk. Now we have fun with it. We started doing the ice cream sandwich version in Los Angeles at the NoMad, and now we do them at all of them. When we did the summer house pop-up, we did a milk and honey soft-serve.

Do you feel like at this point you're starting to get a work-life balance?

No. We're opening up three restaurants this year, so this year is a bit crazy. I'm very fortunate, and I'm able to take time off, but I don't take advantage of it. If I don't have to be in the kitchen immediately, I can wake up, make coffee, and get some of my admin work done at home. I have Saturday and Sundays off at this point, and that helps. Chef Humm preaches the importance of work-life balance, but he also says that figuring that out is up to you and that it's your job to manage. I always have the mentality of doing whatever it takes to be successful. When we opened the NoMad in Los Angeles, I think I worked 35 days straight. But I didn't care or even really notice because I was opening a restaurant with my best friends and we made each day exciting and fun.

Is there a process for your creativity?

I read a lot of cookbooks. I like to go out to eat, but I try not to focus too much on what other people are doing so that I don't lose track of my own style. I just like to see what other people are doing so that we don't mimic it too much. But obviously, this industry is incestual, and other people always inspire people. My brain is always moving and doesn't turn off. It races when I'm in bed, in the shower, and I'm always writing down ideas. I think most of the creativity comes from times when we're just having fun and experimenting in the kitchen. If my chefs are working on a new strawberry dish, I want their hands to be stained red every day from constantly dissecting and manipulating strawberries to understand them better. It can be frustrating, but I think it's important to push others beyond what they believe they are capable of.

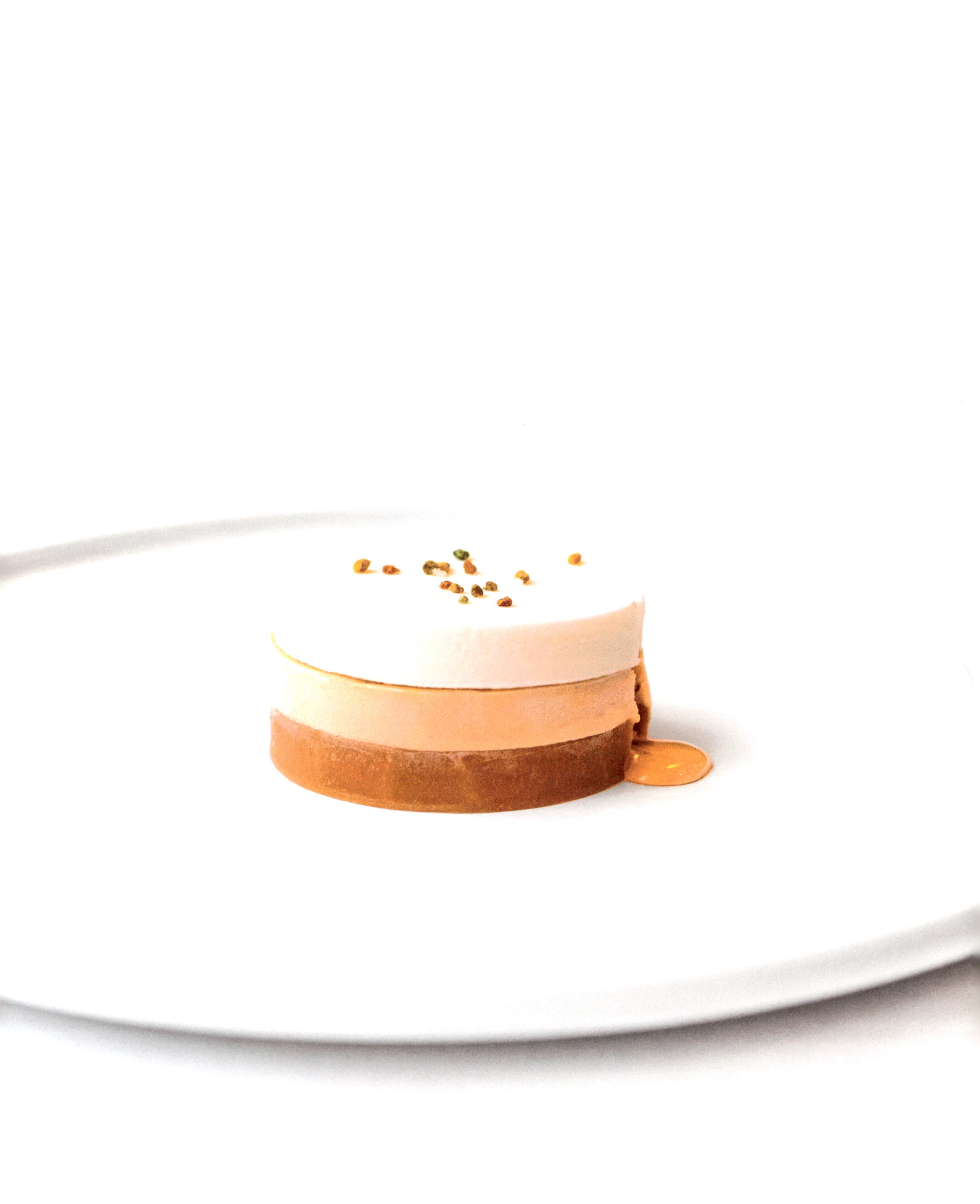

Milk & Honey

Milk and Honey - NoMad

Milk Ice Cream

Ingredients:

42 g sugar
9 g Cremodan ice cream stabilizer
791 g milk
240 g cream
28 g trimoline
140 g powdered Glucose
87 g milk powder
6 g salt

Method:

Prepare an ice bath. Combine the sugar, powdered glucose, and ice cream stabilizer in a mixing bowl and stir to combine. Combine the milk, cream, trimoline, and sugar mixture in a saucepan over medium heat and whisk until combined and fully dissolved. Cook the mixture to 85 C / 185 F, whisking constantly. Whisk in the milk powder and cook to 91 C/196 F. Strain the base through a chinois and season with salt. Chill over the ice bath and freeze in an ice cream machine. Keep frozen for up to 24 hours.

Honey-Oatmeal Crumble

Ingredients:

145 g butter, softened
65 g sugar
80 g honey
3 g salt
2 g vanilla extract
150 g flour
50 g rolled oats
1 g baking soda

Method:

Preheat the oven to 149 C/300 F. In a stand mixer fitted with the paddle attachment, cream together the butter, sugar, honey, salt, and vanilla. Add the flour, oats, and baking soda, mixing until just combined. Roll the dough on a parchment paper to 6-mm/1/4-inch thick. Transfer the dough to a baking sheet and bake in the oven until golden brown, about 15 minutes. Turn the oven down to 66 C/150 F and continue to bake until crunchy throughout, about 30 minutes. Remove from the oven and let cool to room temperature. Break into small pieces and reserve in an airtight container for up to 5 days.

Honey Brittle

Ingredients:

200 g sugar
50 g water
60 g butter
50 g honey
8 g salt
3 g baking soda

Method:

Line a baking sheet with a nonstick baking mat and set aside. Heat the sugar, water, butter, and honey in a heavy-bottomed saucepan over medium heat. Bring to a boil, while stirring with a rubber spatula, until the sugar is fully dissolved and turns amber colored, about 6 minutes. Stir in the salt and baking soda. Once fully incorporated, remove the pan from heat and turn the caramel out onto the prepared baking sheet. Evenly spread the brittle thin and let cool to room temperature. Transfer to a food processor and pulse several times for a coarse crumble. Reserve the brittle in a dry, airtight container.

Dehydrated Milk Foam

Ingredients:

500 g milk
100 g glucose syrup

Method:

Combine the milk and glucose in a large saucepan over medium heat and bring to just under a boil. Remove the milk mixture from the heat. Froth the milk using an immersion blender until a thick foam has developed. Scoop the thick foam onto a 33 by 22.9 cm (13 by 9-inch) rimmed baking sheet lined with soft acetate. Place the baking sheet on a dehydrator tray and dehydrate at 65°C/150°F for 5 hours. Gently break into large pieces and store in a dry, airtight container throughout, about 8 hours. Let the foam cool to room temperature. Break into small pieces and reserve in a dry, airtight container for up to 2 days.

To Finish

Buckwheat honey
Milk ice

Divide the dehydrated milk foam, honey brittle, and honey-oatmeal crumble in each of 4 bowls. Scoop 2 quenelles of milk ice into each bowl. Drizzle lines of buckwheat honey across the top of one quenelle in each bowl.

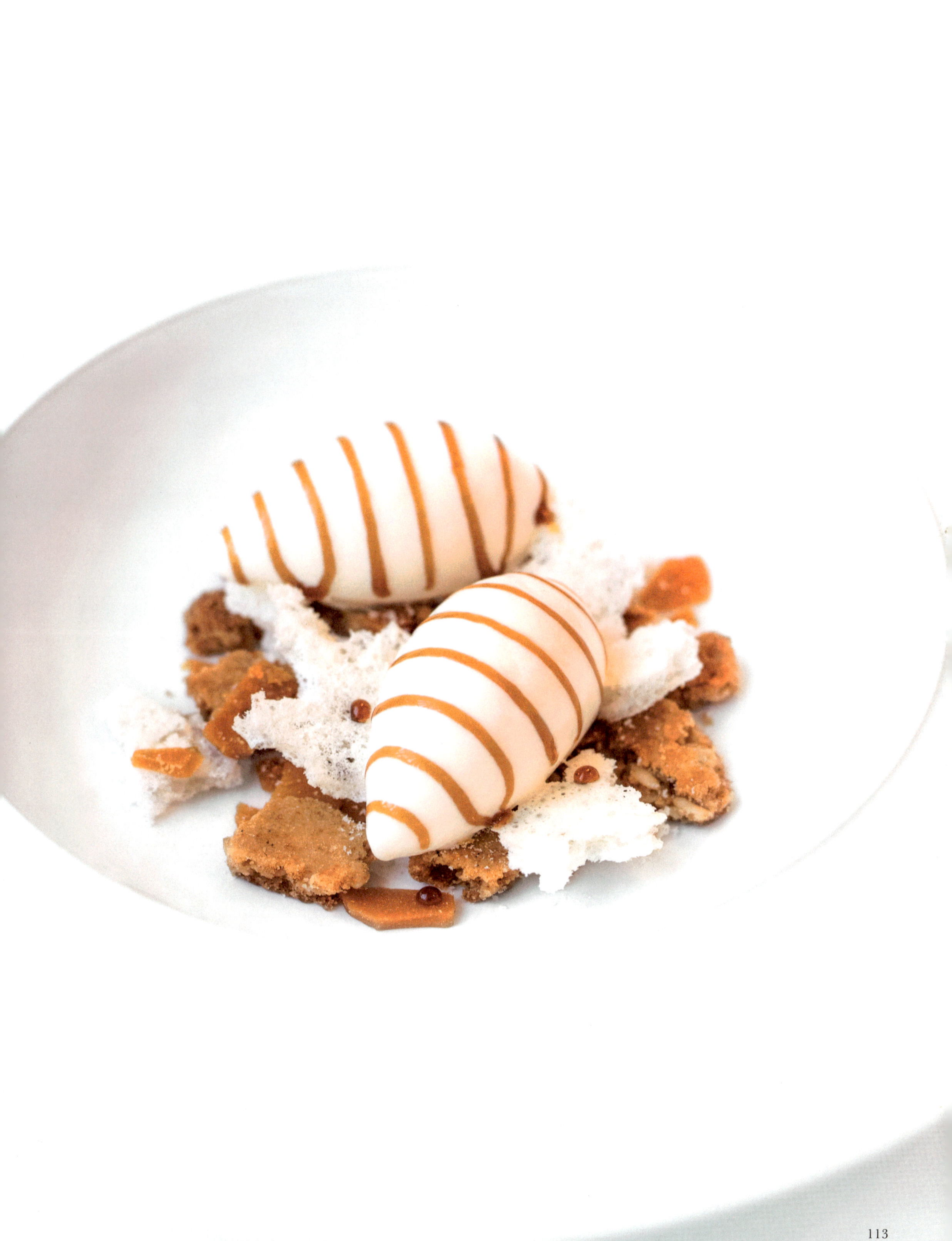

Milk and Honey Ice Cream Sandwich

Honey Center

Ingredients:

400 g	orange blossom honey
242 g	glucose syrup
600 g	heavy cream
37 g	white chocolate
150 g	butter
12 g	salt

Method:

Combine the honey, glucose, and cream in a large pot over medium heat. Cook the mixture, without stirring to 108 C/226 F. Remove the mixture from the heat and immediately pour into a mixing bowl. Using a hand immersion blender, blend in the white chocolate, butter, and salt. Let cool to room temperature and transfer to a piping bag. Pipe 10 g into the base of each of 8 cylinder silicon molds, 4.1 cm (1 5/8 inches) in diameter, 2 cm (3/4 inch) tall, and freeze for 3 hours.

Dehydrated Milk Foam

Same as on Page 64.

Milk Ice Discs

Ingredients:

1035 g	milk
333 g	cream
100 g	milk powder
100 g	glucose powder
116 g	sugar
50 g	trimoline
12 g	cremodan ice cream stabilizer
8 g	salt
8	Honey Centers

Method:

Prepare an ice bath. Combine the sugar and ice cream stabilizer in a mixing bowl and stir to combine. Combine half of the milk and cream in a saucepan over medium heat and bring to 65°C/150°F. Add the trimoline and glucose powder. Continue the cook the mixture, while whisking until it reaches 74°C/165°F. Sprinkle in the sugar and stabilizer mixture and continue to cook while whisking until the mixture reaches 85°C/185°F. Whisk in the milk powder and cook to 91°C/196°F. Mix in the remaining cold milk and cream. Strain the base through a chinois and season with salt. Chill over the ice bath and freeze in an ice cream machine. Immediately transfer the ice cream to piping bags. Pipe 15 g into the base of each of 8 cylinder silicon molds, 5.7 cm (2 1/4 inches) in diameter, 3.2 cm (1 1/4 inches) tall, and freeze for 3 hours. Keep the remaining milk ice frozen. Submerge the honey centers in the silicon mold in liquid nitrogen for a minute. Remove the honey centers from the mold and center one on each of the milk ice cylinders. Pipe additional milk ice to surround the honey center, so that the top of the milk ice is even with the top of the honey center. Then pipe an additional 15 g milk ice over each honey center to cover completely. Using an offset spatula, smooth the tops. Freeze for 3 hours.

Shortbread Rounds

Ingredients:

600 g	flour
360 g	confectioner's sugar
440 g	butter
8 g	salt
300 g	grapeseed oil

Method:

Preheat the convection oven to 163°C/350°F, low fan. Combine the flours, sugar, butter, and salt in the bowl of a stand mixer and paddle until crumbly. Spread the mixture onto a parchment-lined baking sheet in an even layer. Bake in the oven, cutting and stirring the mixture every 5 minutes until dried, about 20 minutes. While still warm, transfer the mixture to a food processor and process until the shortbread is all in uniform pieces and all the large pieces have been ground down. With the processor running, slowly add the grapeseed oil. In three batches, transfer the mixture to a blender and blend on high speed until very smooth. Strain through a chinois twice. Line three 45.1 by 33 cm (17 3/4 by 13 inch) rimmed baking sheets with hard acetate, cutting the corners to that the acetate lays perfectly flat. Pour 375 g of the liquid shortbread into each of the prepared baking sheets, tilting the pan so that the shortbread fills the trays evenly. Refrigerate the trays for 1 hour, then freeze overnight. Working one tray at a time, invert the liquid shortbread onto a clean sheet of acetate. Using a 5.4 cm (2 1/8 inch) ring cutter, punch rounds from the sheet of liquid shortbread. Keep the rounds frozen until ready to assemble.

Bee Pollen Coating

40 g	milk foam
80 g	bee pollen

Method:

Coarsely chop the milk foam and mix with the bee pollen.

To Finish

16 Brown Sugar Tuiles

16 Liquid Shortbread Rounds

Method:

Preheat the convection oven to 150 F/300 F, low fan. Warm the brown sugar tuiles in the oven until they just begin to soften but do not get any additional color, about 2 minutes. Immediately press one tuile onto each liquid shortbread round. Unmold the milk ice discs and sandwich one disc between two liquid shortbread rounds, keeping the tuiles on the outside of the sandwich. Roll each sandwich in the bee pollen coating. Keep frozen until ready to serve.

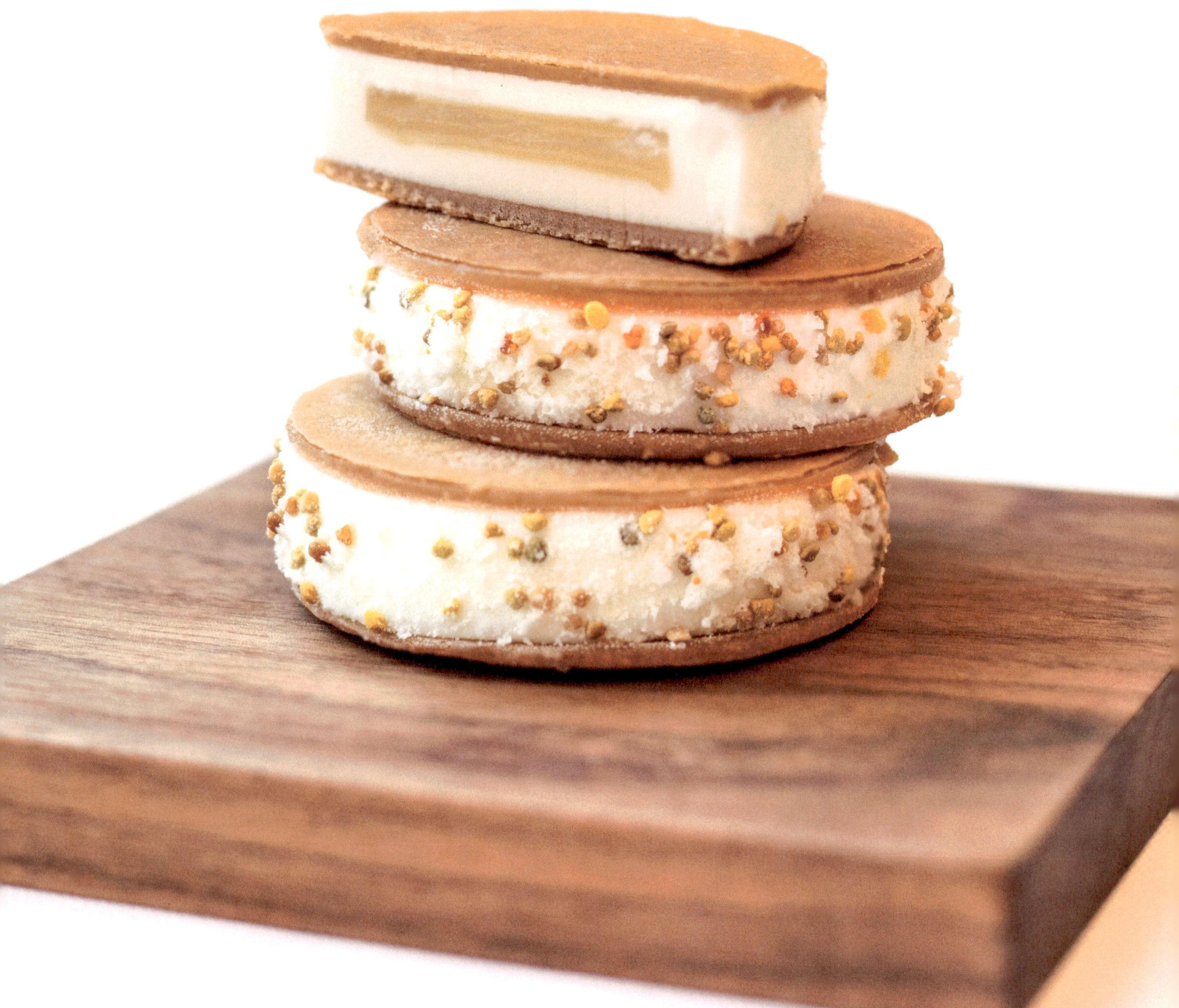

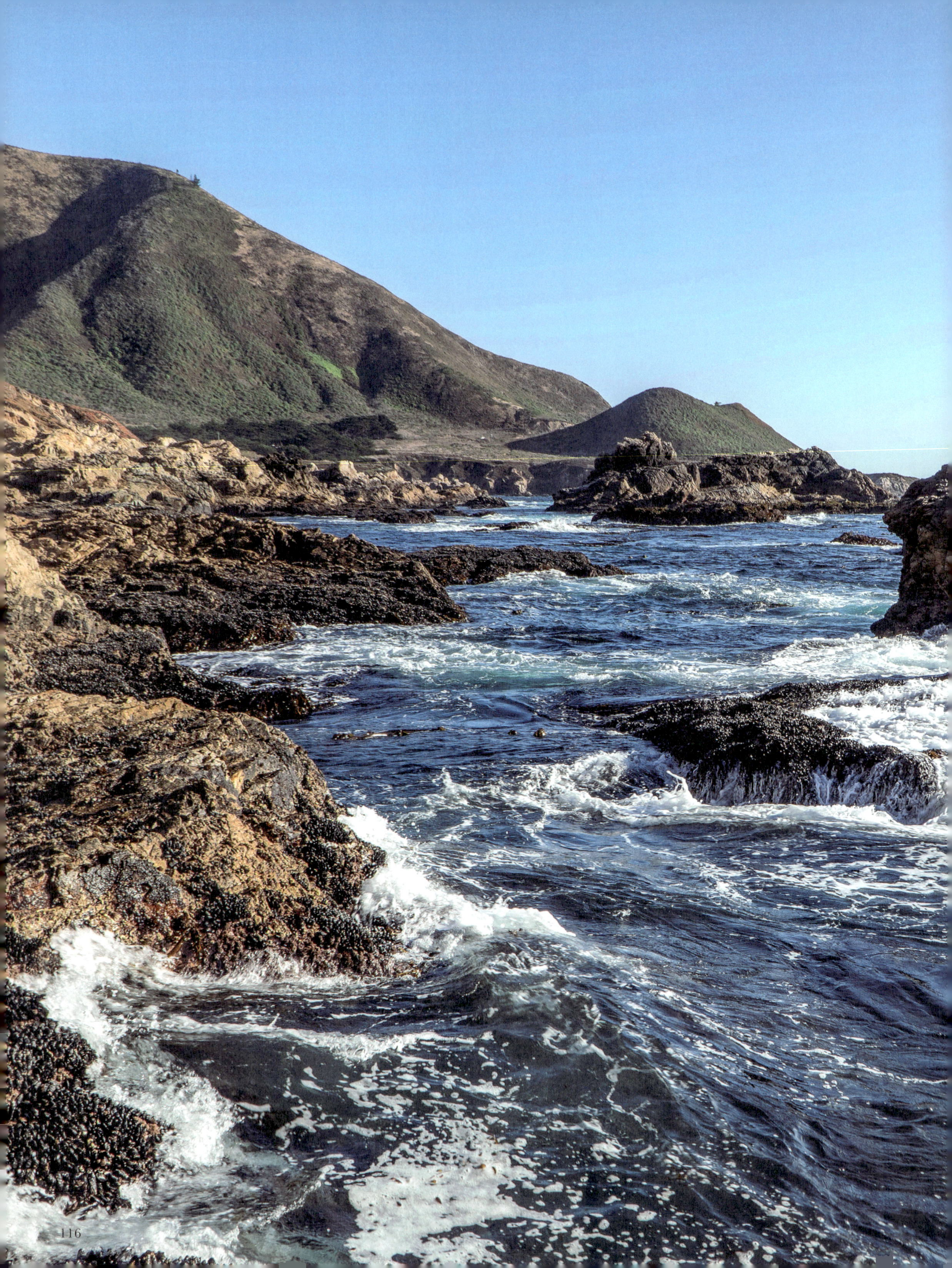

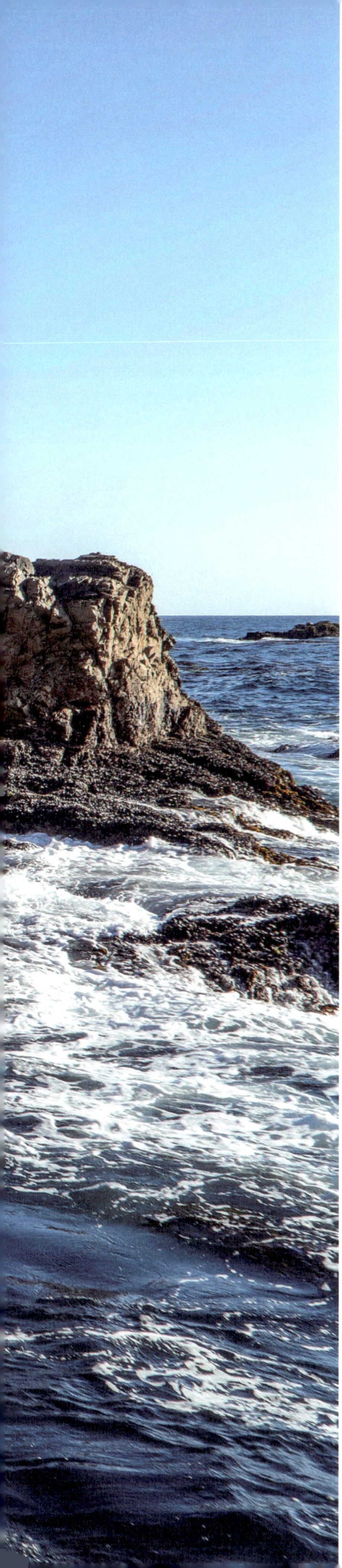

terroir to table

cooking in big sur

written and photographed by chef

alexander r. terrazas

big sur, ca

It was my last day in San Francisco after my tenure as executive pastry chef of Jane the Bakery. Just hours away from a flight that would take my wife and me to our new life in Lyon, I was filled with excitement for everything to come. Then everything changed... I got a message from a friend I met at the bakery, Chef Jonny Black. We had met in San Francisco, where he had been the corporate executive chef for the Crenn Group. With a new family in toe, he packed up and moved to Carmel Valley to begin his project with Sierra Mar at Post Ranch Inn. He reached out to me to see if I'd be able to revamp the bread program and get things in line with his vision for the restaurant. Here was a friend who also needed a hand; staffing is an ongoing challenge for Big Sur restaurants, and they were in a transition period at Sierra Mar. I knew the opportunity was too good to pass up, but it was more than one of prestige, it was an opportunity of place. Despite the remote location, flaky wifi, and limited pool of qualified staff, talented chefs are making their stake in Big Sur. There's no foot traffic or city bustle to bring guests. Diners and chefs alike are there with shared inspiration. They're there to absorb the energy from the place where land meets the sea, where a diversity of life flourishes at every turn, and where ancient trees tower over everything. Because there is nowhere else in the world like Big Sur.

The expansive Post Ranch Inn has its own community of caretakers. Generations of families have grown up there, adding their piece to the story of the property. Like a small Midwestern town, you come to know the faces quickly, and everyone says hello when you pass. In all of this, you have a luxury resort at the edge of the world. Guests travel from all over to remember the feeling of presence. There is only one television on the entire property, and if you're stuck on your phone, you might miss the dozens of magical moments that flourish during a short walk on the 100-acre property. At the center is a chef's garden that produces a palette for cooking with colors of the season. Tended to by farmers that know and love the land, it's easy to draw inspiration by merely passing through. The region decidedly influences the cuisine at Sierra Mar, sourcing as much as possible from local purveyors and farmers, though much of the produce comes from the chef's garden itself. Seafood is a staple. Jonny's presentation has always shown life and purity. The tasting menu draws influence not only from local produce but also from the land itself. Ranging from the bold & briny flavors of the sea to deep, earthy dishes, the seasoning is always precise, which further gives the cuisine life & elegance.

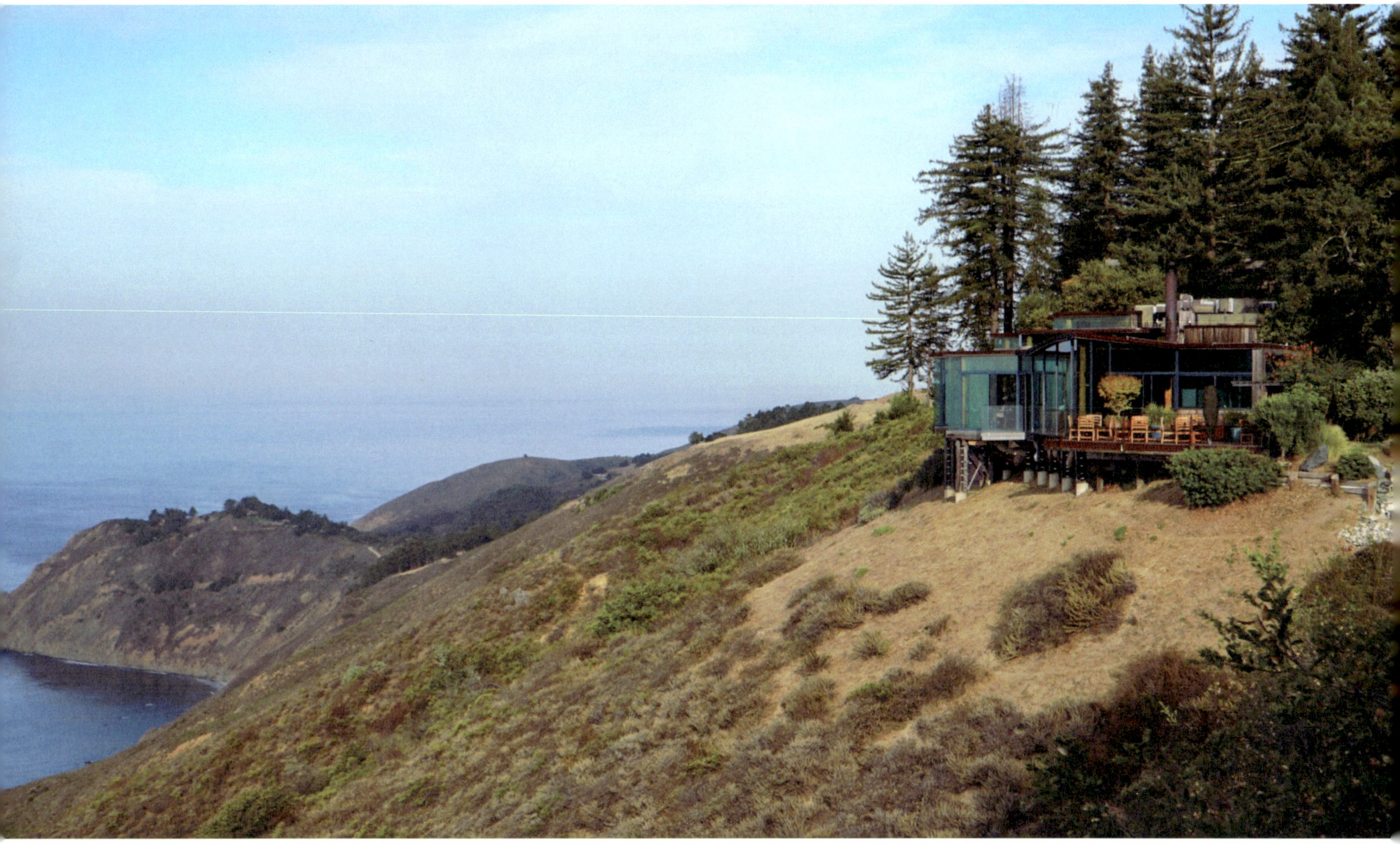

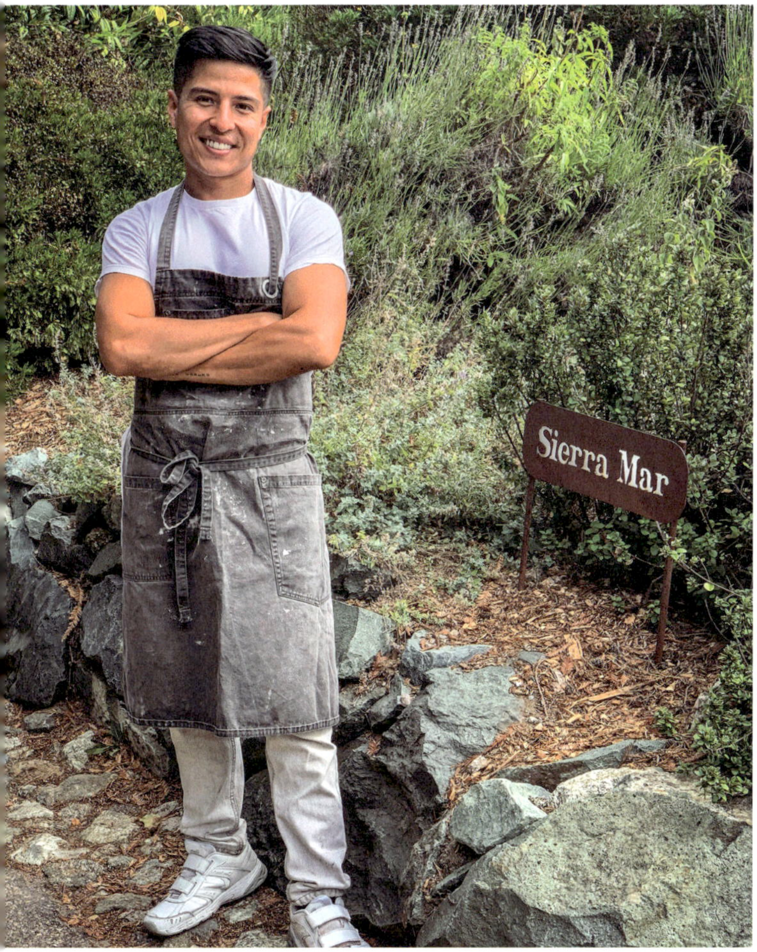
Sierra Mar

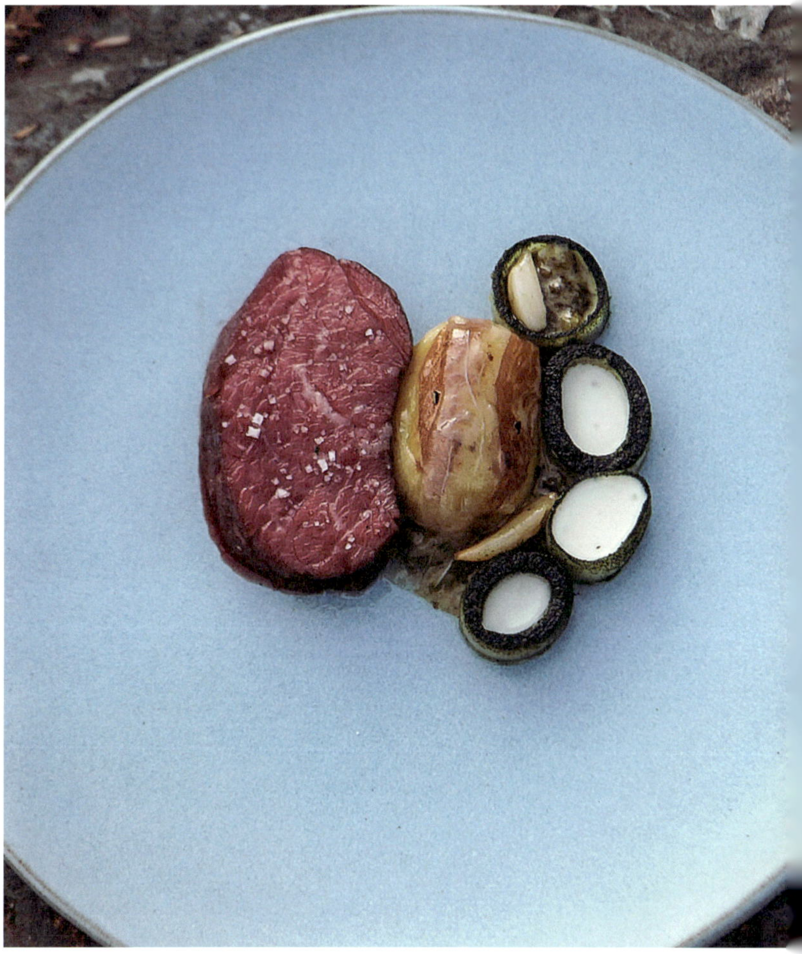

Sierra Mar Restaurant sits on the horizon, teetering on the edge of a cliff over an endless ocean. Its glass facade reflects the water's shimmer like a diamond atop the Redwoods that encircle Post Ranch Inn. Wild turkeys and deer run freely, almost to signal that you've found someplace safe from the claws of urban sprawl. Famous for its sunsets, the sky touches the ocean here, which is one of the most magnetic draws for guests, who time their dinner to sky-gaze through the glass walls. As a baker, I had the good fortune of being able to watch the sunrise daily. Like the guests, I benefited from this quick reprise before the call of the oven timer as a moment where I could forget about everything and awe in the beauty. The crackling of the bread, hot from the oven with wisps of steam rising, was reminiscent of the fog drifting on the coast.

During my time at Sierra Mar, I had the fortunate coincidence of meeting Sherry Mandell of the Tehachapi Grain Project. She is a warm spirit with a passion for heritage Californian grain, of which she is reviving a direct trade with chefs and bakers in California. She introduced me to Raquel Bagatini, the lead baker of Big Sur Bakery. The bakery, café & restaurant is a renovated homestead with an Alan Scott wood-fired oven at the heart of its cuisine. Raquel offers a satisfying assortment of wood-fired bread, laminated pastries, and other treats, both savory and sweet. Full of character, the fire gives her lofty bread a blistered crust. The aroma is sweet, and the crumb is moist and flavorful. Raquel spoke of the challenges and successes of being a baker in Big Sur, from up-keeping the historic Alan Scott oven (which will last for generations), to the hour-long commute from Carmel that she and other morning cooks take at 3 am in order to start their production in time for service. By night, the space transforms into a cozy dining room that mirrors the warmth of the kitchen, with a fireplace as the focal point.

After meeting with Raquel, I drove north up Highway 1 to harvest salt with Carlo Overhusler, the founder and owner of Big Sur Salts, an artisan salt company that produces salt using ancient methods and solely from the water from the ocean. We stopped at an unmarked path on the side of the road and hiked down steep cliffs, dodging sagebrush and poison oak. It's easy to see where Carlo finds inspiration for his salt blends, as he foraged wild herbs during our hike to the ocean. His salts are always inspired by the terroir of specific trails and places in Big Sur, such as his Lost Coast blend with orange, sage, and fennel.

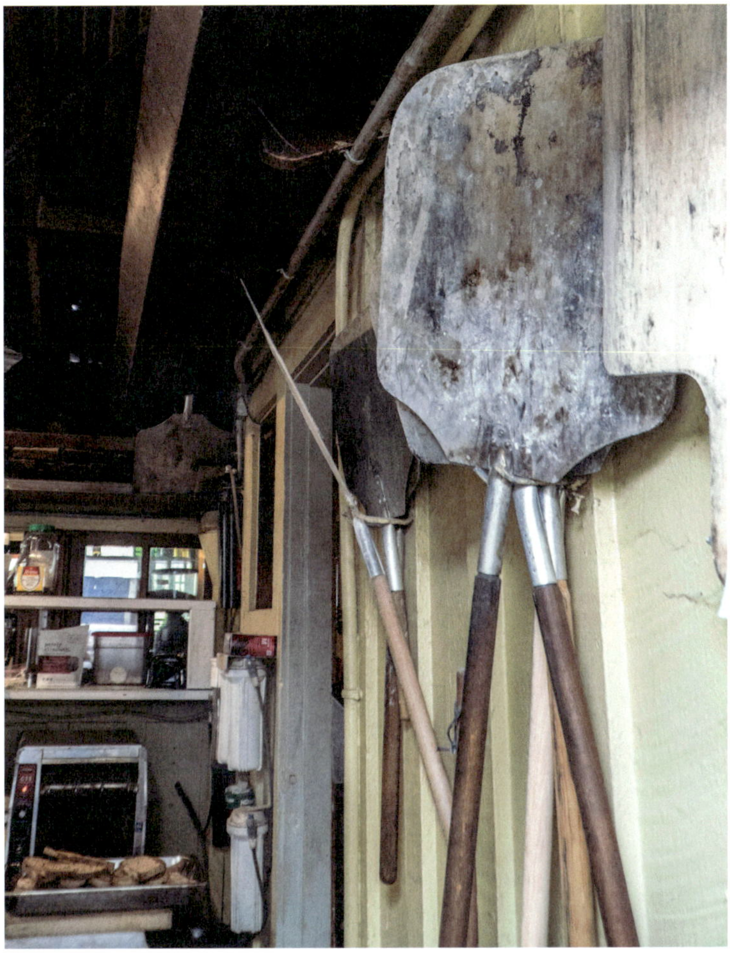

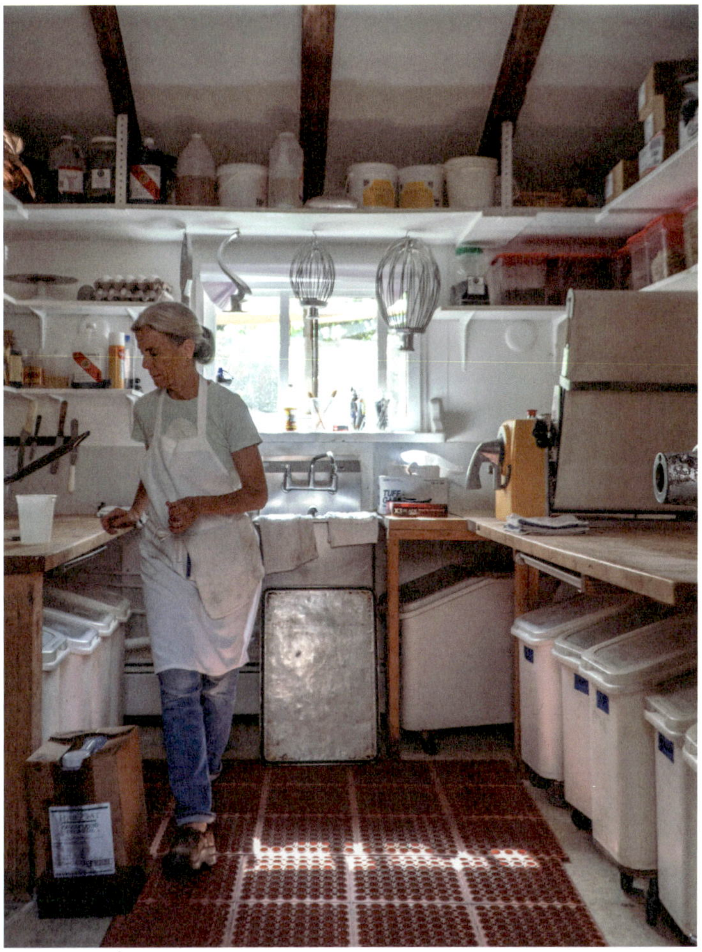

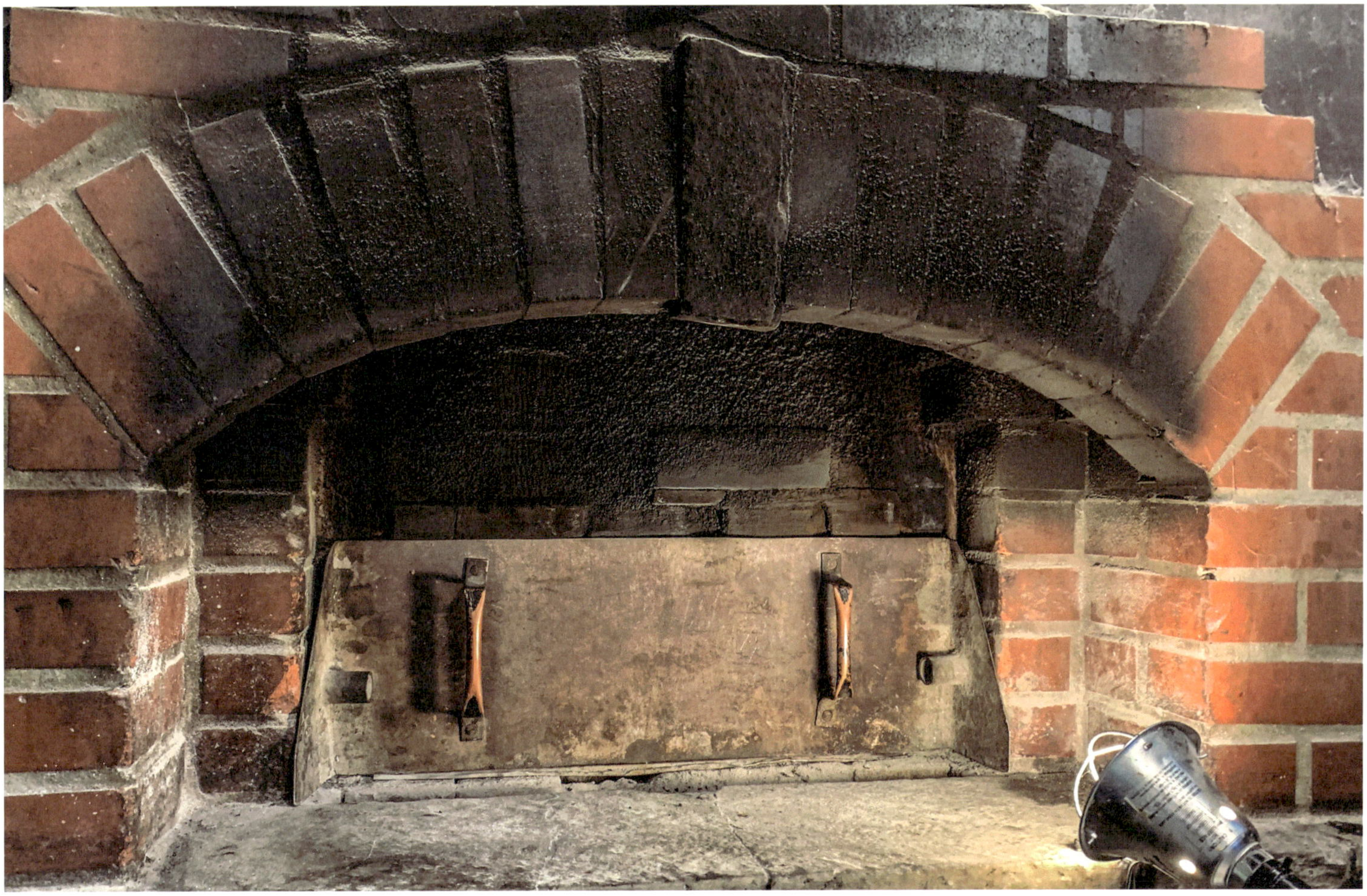

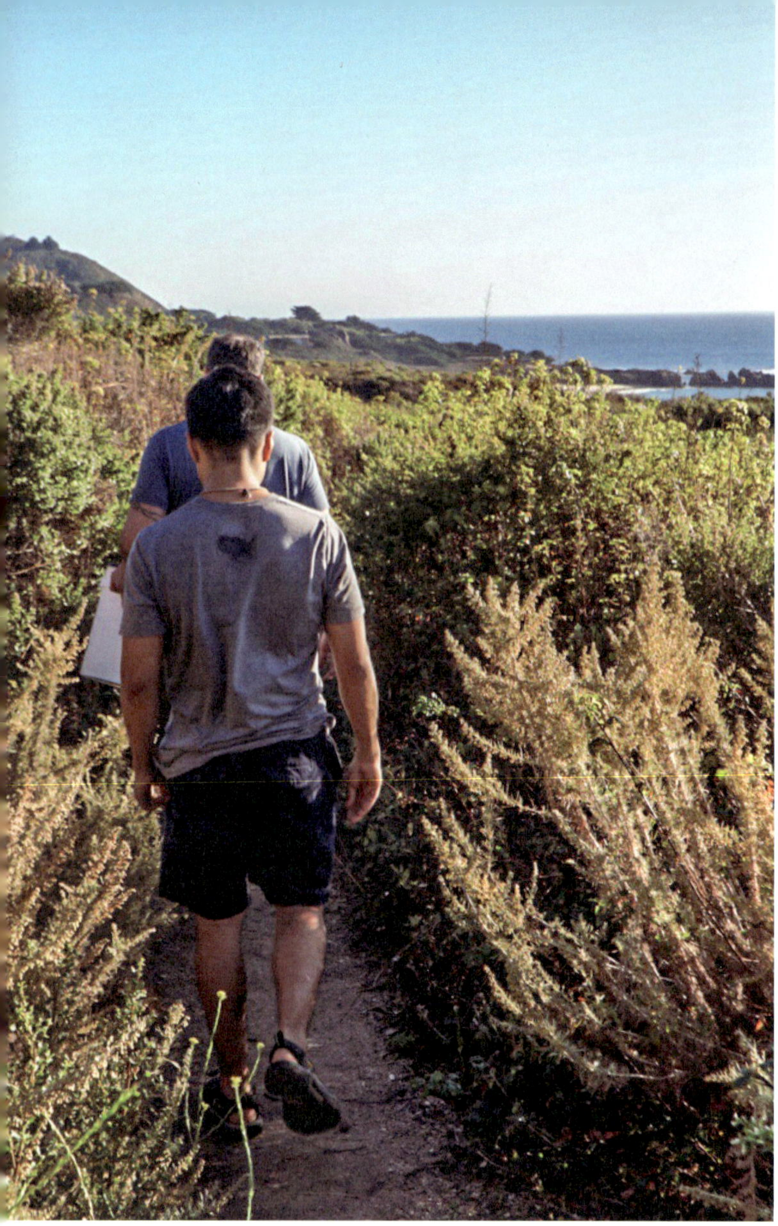

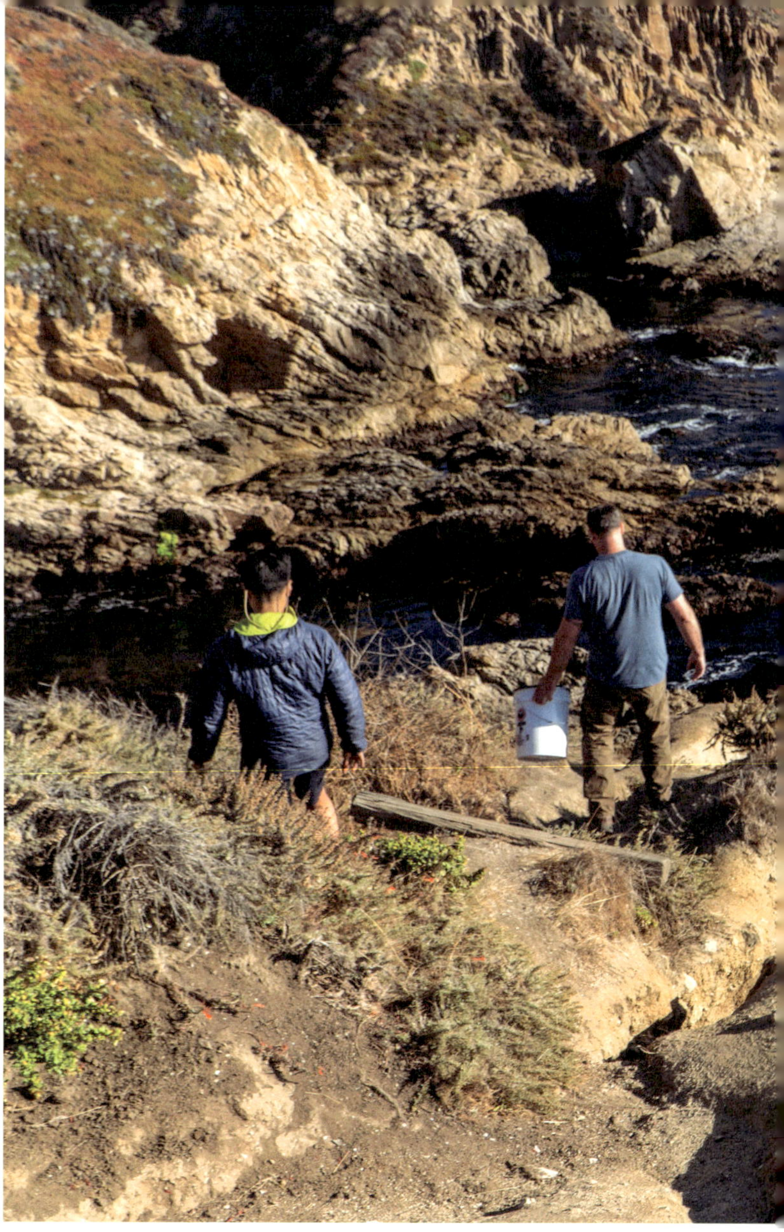

I asked him, "How do you choose these spots to harvest your salt?" He began to explain that he looks for places that are not very accessible, not heavily trafficked, often down paths lined with poison oak. This is all in an effort to find a spot where he is able to maintain the integrity of his process. He also looks for places where you can access the coast to harvest water. An important step is finding a shallow natural basin above tidal pools where the seawater won't spill in. Over the course of a season, he adds water to the basin and allows it to reduce and go through the natural formation of salt crystallization. The process is complex and works within the natural lifecycle of salt shrimp and algae. All of this adds to the terroir of the salt, giving a unique character and minerality to the finished product. The process, which is not temperature controlled, results in a crunchy, medium-sized grain.

Carlo navigated his way down the rocky cliffside with ease that indicated experience. We passed along tide pools filled with an urchin, anemone, and starfish. The waves crashing against the rugged coast splashed saltwater on our faces. His process involves braving the cliffs and an intense tide to gather ocean water and deliver it to his chosen basins. This is a surprising feat for someone that almost lost his life to the ocean; Carlo's original inspiration for Big Sur Salts came from surviving a near-death experience when a massive tidal wave sucked him under.

The salt can be used in a variety of ways, from a finishing salt, to a brine for fish, or even in bread. The trip with Carlo to the tidal pools got my wheels turning as to how could I capture the terroir of Big Sur and translate that into a loaf of bread.

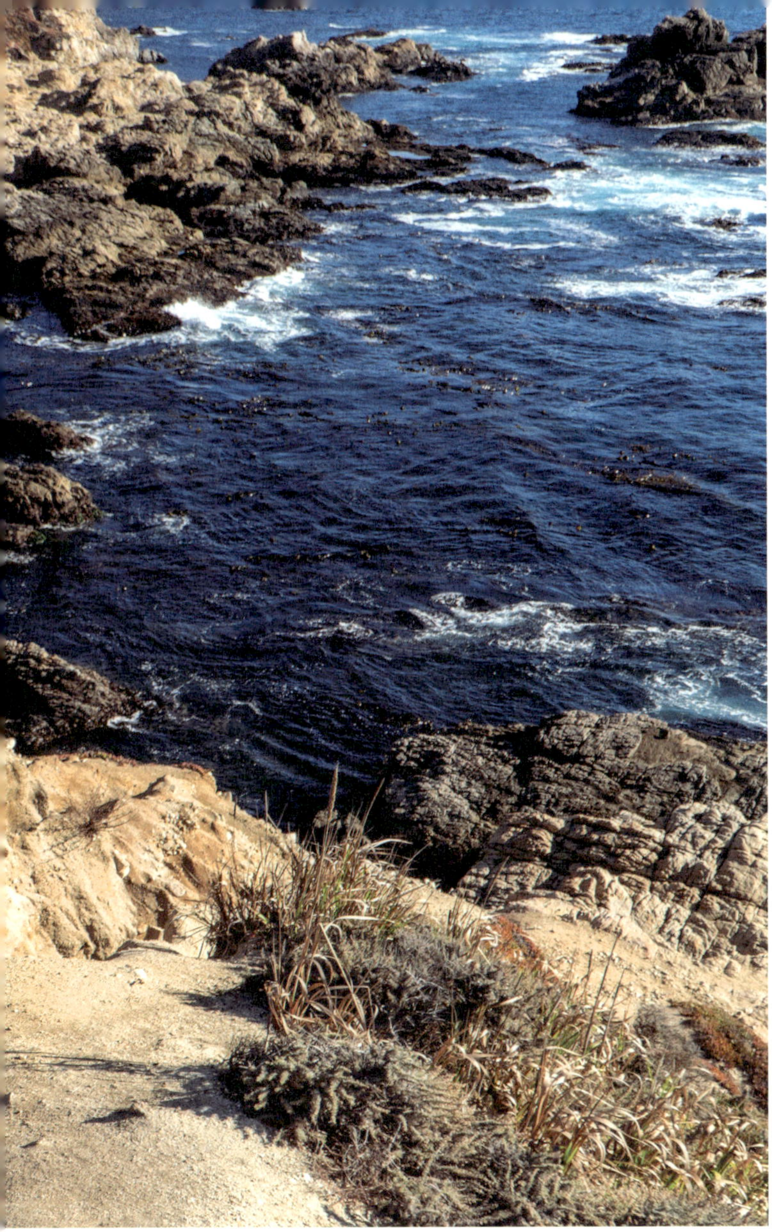

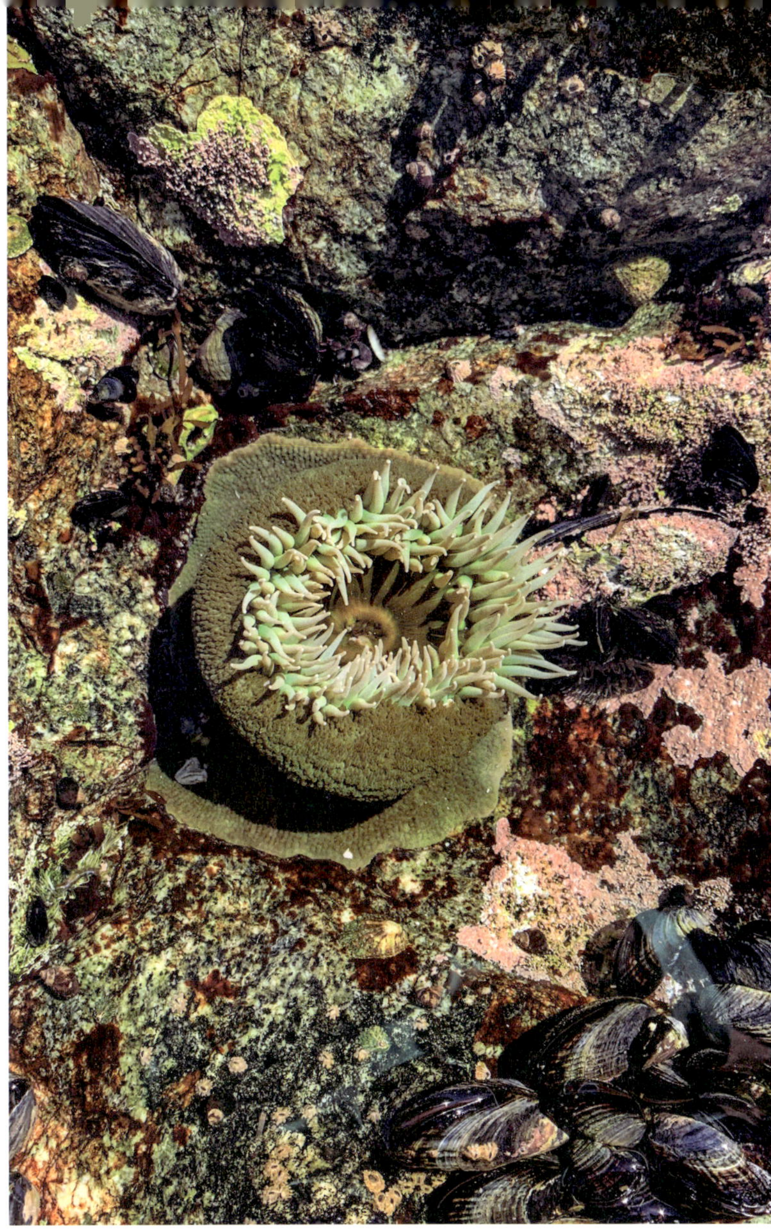

The result: Sprouted Grain Porridge Loaf with foraged coastal seaweed. I decided to call this bread le pain de mer, the bread of the ocean, and used Carlo's salt to impart a true essence of time and place. I wanted the loaf to be reminiscent of the sea life that I found in the tidal pools, so I coated it in a 50/50 mix of poppy and black sesame and scored it in a pattern mimicking the pinate structure of an urchin or sand dollar.

I asked myself, what is the draw to this place? Is it the natural beauty or a sense of adventure? For me, it's a place where beauty is never lost, no matter how many times you watch the sunrise on the coast. The expansive horizon of the endless sea washes away any and all distractions, forcing you into the present moment. It's a place that revives you day in and day out. Big Sur is a place that cultivates creativity and inspiration.

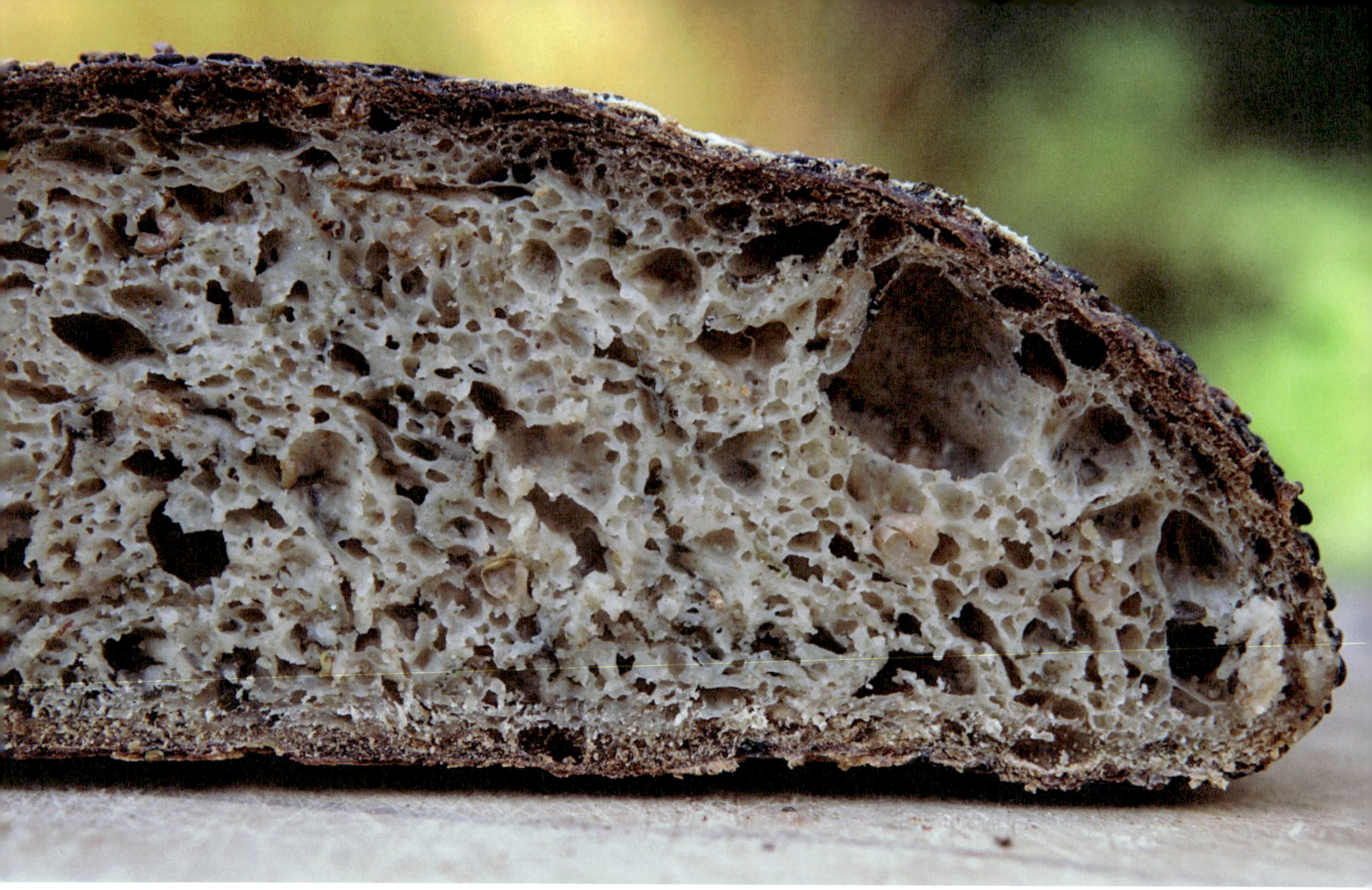

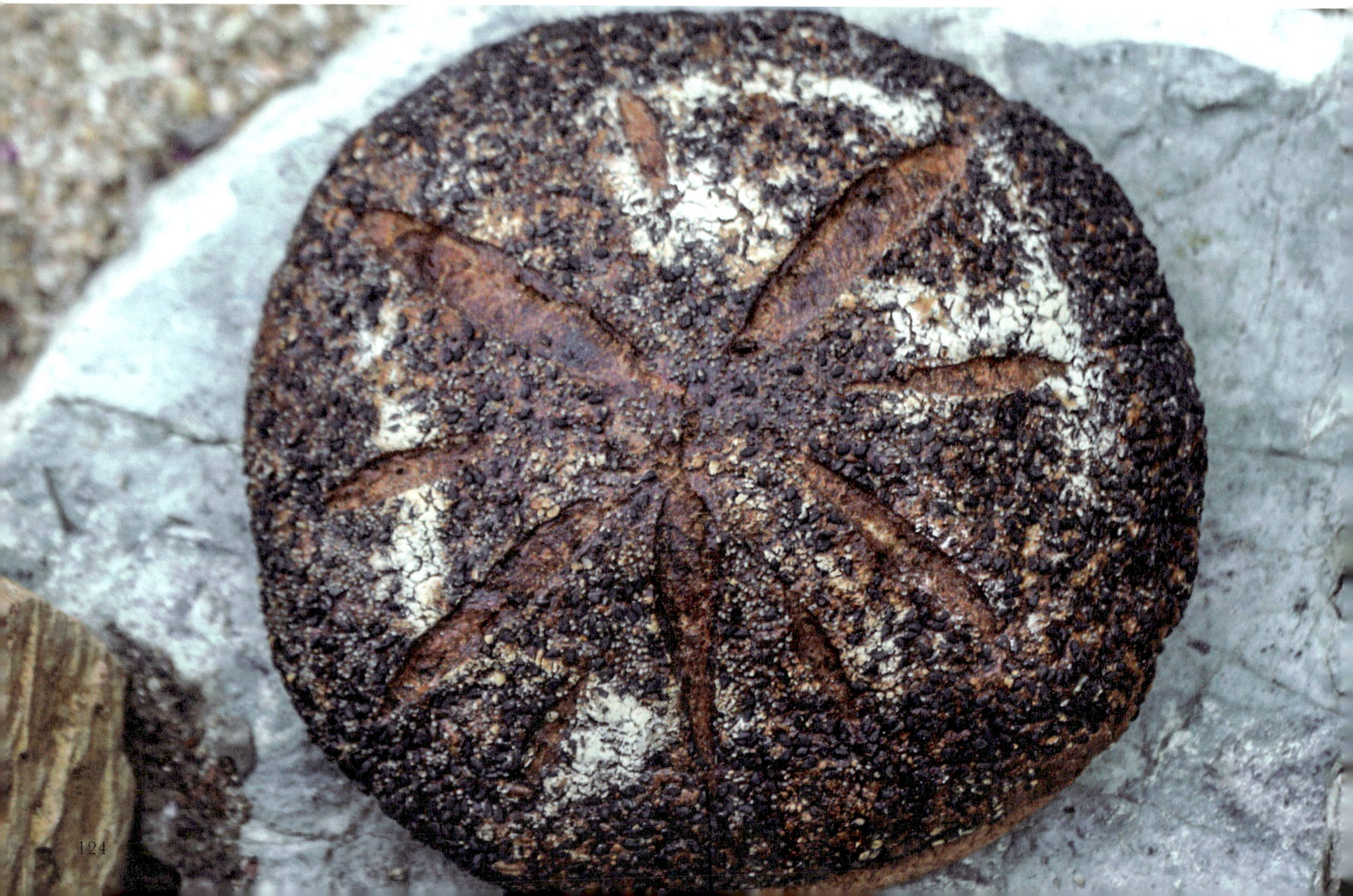

Pain De Mer

Dough:

Ingredients:		*baker's %*
341 g	T70 flour	90
38 g	whole wheat flour	10
303 g	water	80
76 g	levain	20
9 g	Big Sur sea salt	2.5
19 g	sprouted spelt	5
19 g	sea lettuce	5
45 g	oat porridge, toasted	12

Method:

Mix and ferment levain for 12 -16hrs before using in the dough. Mix the flour and water holding back salt and levain and mix until the flour is hydrated and evenly incorporated. Autolyse for 30 minutes. Add the salt and levain, and then mix on speed 1 for 5 minutes. Scrape the bowl and continue to mix for an additional 2 minutes. Increase to speed 2(medium), and mix for 1:30-2 minutes. Move the dough into a lightly oiled container and take the temperature of the dough (DD: 81F)

Rest the dough for 30 minutes. Add the porridge, sprouted grain, and sea lettuce. Mix by hand until fully incorporated into the dough. Give a clean up fold.

Bulk ferment for 2 hours, while giving 5 folds at 20 minute intervals. Pre-shape the dough into a boule rest for 15 minutes. Final shape into a boule and roll the dough in a 50/50 mix of black sesame and poppy. (Note: use a bench knife and lightly watered hand to shape the dough)

Proof at 78F to 81F until dough relaxes and becomes light to the touch. Retard at 41F-45F overnight (12-18hrs). Preheat deck oven to 520 and bake with steam for 20 minutes. Vent the oven and continue to bake for another 25 mins. Tap the bottom to check for a classic hollow sound. (minimum internal temperature 202F)

Focaccia

Dough:

Ingredients:		*baker's %*
359 g	bread flour	50
359 g	whole wheat sanora flour	50
474 g	water	66
21 g	salt	2.9
287 g	levain	40
1 g	yeast	1

Method:

Mix all ingredients on the first speed for 5 minutes. Scrape the bowl and mix for an additional 2 minutes. Turn speed up to second speed and mix for 6 -8 minutes until intensive. Pull a window to check for smooth gluten development with some streaks. Put the dough in a bowl rubbed with olive oil.

Bulk ferment for 2 hours, folding the dough three times in half-hour intervals. Add the dough to a well-oiled half sheet pan and spread into the size of the pan in three 20 minute intervals. Begin by spreading to 60% of the size of the pan and then rest 20 minutes. Spread the dough to 80% size of the pan and rest another 20 minutes. Spread the dough to the full size of the pan. Final proof for 20 -30 minutes.

Heavily dimple the dough, pressing your fingertips into the dough from the bottom to the top. Top the dough with desired toppings and generously season with salt.

Bake at 480F for 25-28 minutes or until the bottom is caramelized and golden.

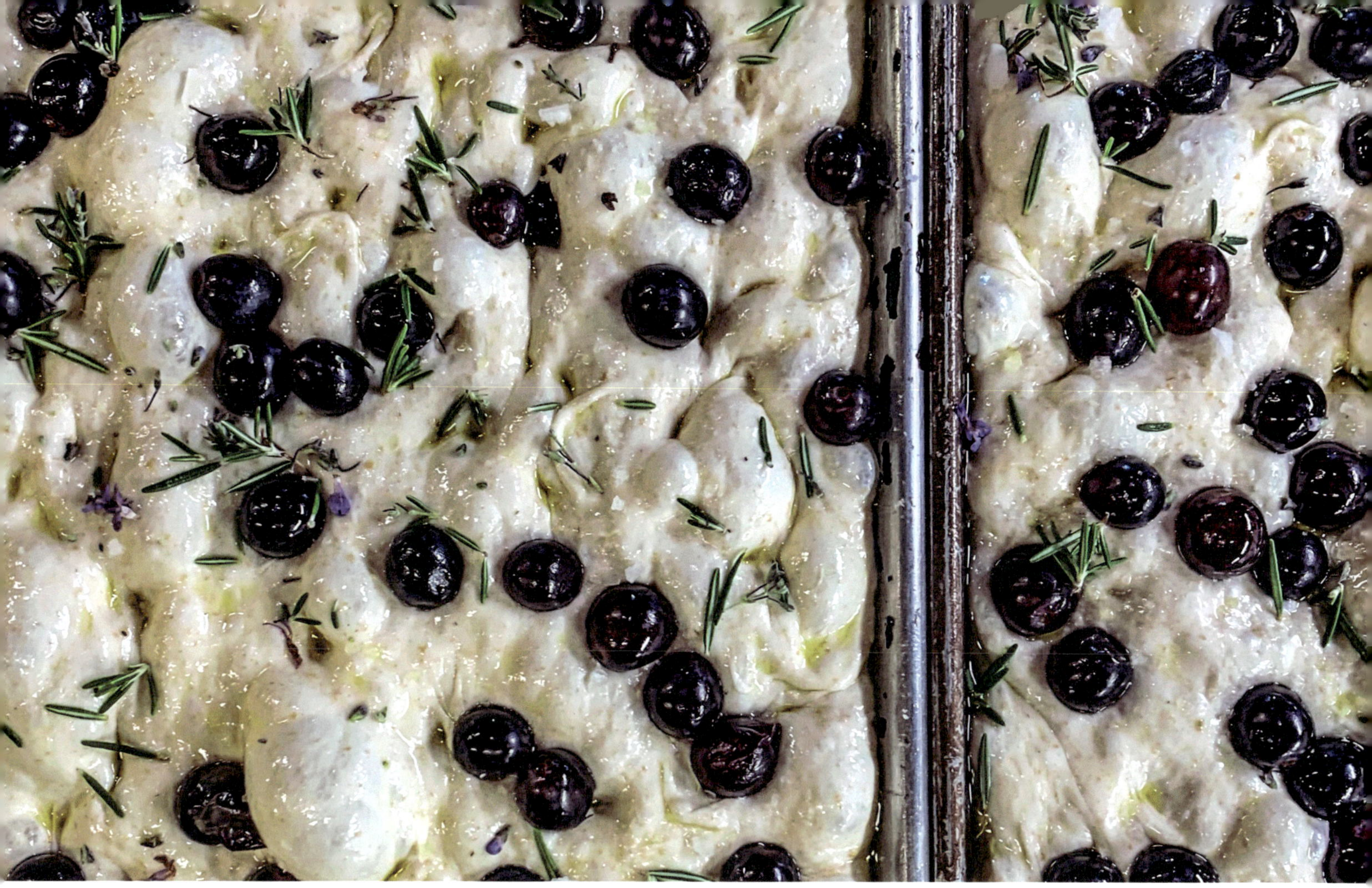

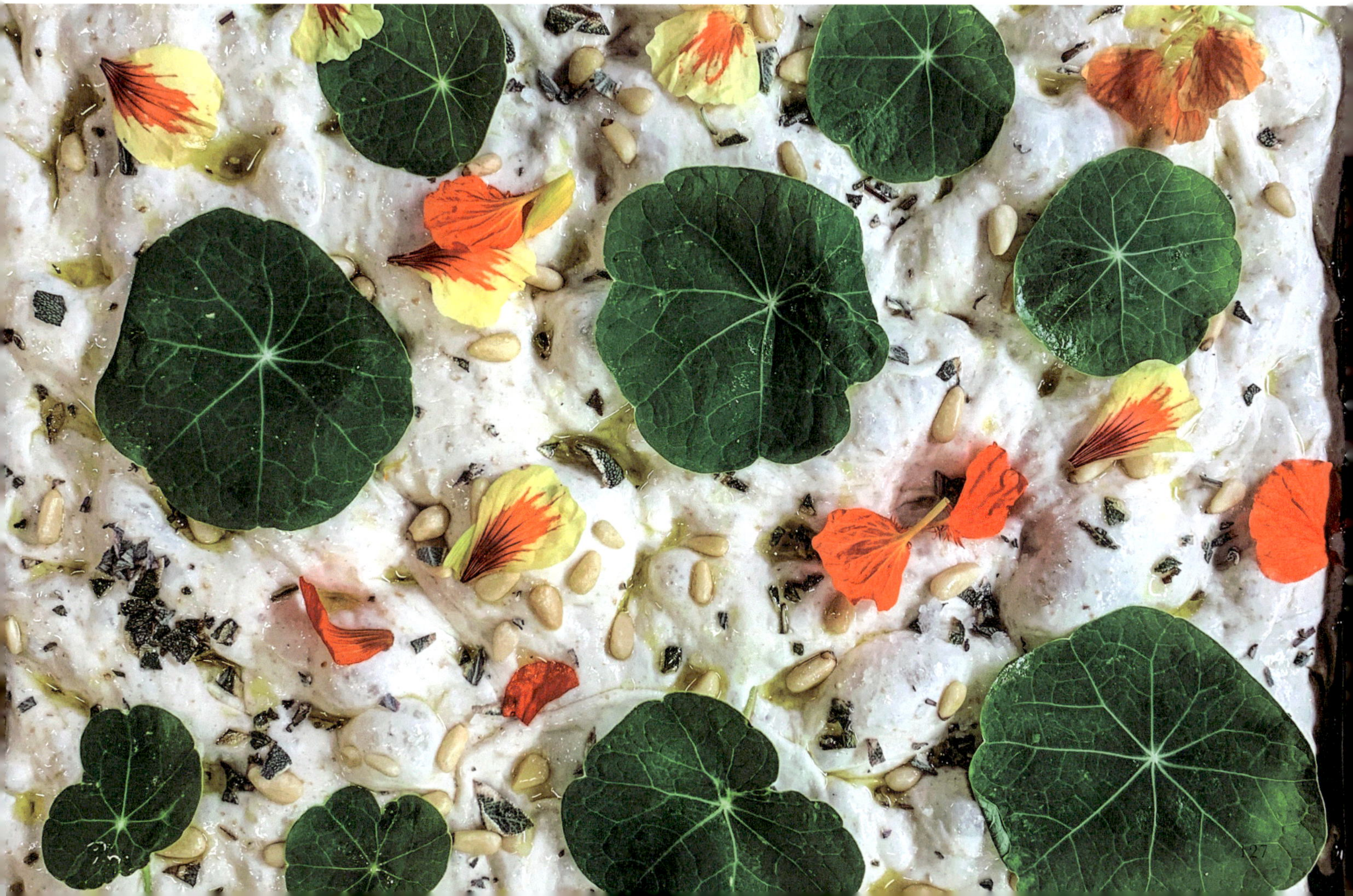